PORTRAITS OF
AMERICAN PRESIDENTS
VOLUME III

THE EISENHOWER PRESIDENCY

ELEVEN INTIMATE
PERSPECTIVES OF
DWIGHT D. EISENHOWER

EDITED BY

KENNETH W. THOMPSON

UNIVERSITY
PRESS OF
AMERICA

LANHAM • NEW YORK • LONDON

Copyright © 1984 by

University Press of America,™ Inc.

4720 Boston Way
Lanham, MD 20706

3 Henrietta Street
London WC2E 8LU England

Library of Congress Cataloging in Publication Data

Main entry under title:

The Eisenhower presidency.

(Portraits of American presidents ; v. 3)
1. Eisenhower, Dwight D. (Dwight David), 1890-1969—
Addresses, essays, lectures. 2. United States—Politics
and government—1953-1961—Addresses, essays, lectures.
I. Thompson, Kenneth W., 1921-   . II. Series.
E176.1.P83   1982   vol. 3   973'.09'92 s   84-7368
[E836]   [973.921'092'4]
ISBN 0-8191-3985-8 (alk. paper)
ISBN 0-8191-3986-6 (pbk. : alk. paper)

Co-published by arrangement with
The White Burkett Miller Center of Public Affairs,
University of Virginia

Dedicated

to

all

those who lead

without unnecessarily raising their voices

and

who guard against both arrogance and weakness

TABLE OF CONTENTS

III. EISENHOWER AS POLITICAL LEADER

IV. EISENHOWER AND THE BUDGET

V. EISENHOWER'S MORAL AND POLITICAL VALUES

FOREWORD
General John S. D. Eisenhower

Along with other close associates of the late President Dwight D. Eisenhower, I would like to express my intense satisfaction that the White Burkett Miller Center of Public Affairs, University of Virginia, is publishing a volume on the Eisenhower presidency. A distinguished group of former cabinet and staff members, each of whom is able to supply his own individual perspective, have agreed to contribute.

The Eisenhower administration has sometimes been described as the most misunderstood in recent history. I concur in that evaluation. In particular, it has been disturbing to realize that so many, even intelligent, well-read people, still casually assume that President Eisenhower, one of the most dynamic and purposeful of men, tended to be dilatory in attitude and vague in his objectives. One may not always agree with his policies or actions, but it is a grave mistake to assume that they were not very consciously his own. The essays which follow on these pages should do much to dispel that misapprehension.

There is no purpose, at this late date, in attempting to set the record straight simply for its own sake. Dwight Eisenhower has long been gone from among us, and the hobby of evaluating presidents, unless such evaluation affords either insight or inspiration, is no more significant an activity than watching pro football on television. But I believe that a renewed appreciation of the Eisenhower presidency can afford both insight regarding his methods and objectives and inspiration in the realization that a public servant need not, even in modern times, be arrogant, self-serving, or weak.

PREFACE

A pattern has emerged in the course of organizing Miller Center Forums which has led to the present volume. We have discovered that the leading authorities on particular presidents have helped the Center to draw others with common background to the University of Virginia. By "word of mouth advertising," they have encouraged their friends to come to Faulkner House. Their help has been of inestimable value to a fledgling public affairs center. It has enabled us to further presidential studies through the contributions of distinguished visitors to the understanding of contemporary presidents.

Partly by accident and partly by design, then, we have discovered our guests were turning the spotlight on certain American presidents. They were viewing particular administrations from different perspectives and vantage points. The product is a portrait, not a photograph; it helps us see the character and spirit of a leader, not the more or less important details a photograph tends to convey. It tells us what was central to his life and works, not what was peripheral. The photograph reveals what can be seen with the naked eye. The portrait shows one thing the photograph cannot reveal: the human essence of the person portrayed.

With this volume, we continue a series of publications, *Portraits of American Presidents.* We are grateful to the University Press of America for making this series available to a wide audience. We hope the next volumes will deal with the presidencies of John F. Kennedy and Lyndon B. Johnson and subsequent volumes with other presidents. In the Introduction, the editor traces the history of the Center's interest in the presidency of Dwight D. Eisenhower.

INTRODUCTION

The year 1983 marked the 30th anniversary of the beginning of the Eisenhower administration. On October 14, 1990, the country will celebrate the centennial of Eisenhower's birth. Some of his closest associates have formed an Institute for the study of urgent problems with which he grappled. As its contribution, the Miller Center invited during the course of 1982—83 eleven of his most intimate associates and family members to come to Charlottesville and discuss the Eisenhower presidency. Among the participants were: Governor Sherman Adams, Herbert Brownell, Dr. Milton S. Eisenhower, William B. Ewald, Arthur Larson, and Bradley H. Patterson. Of this group of eleven, seven found it possible to make the trip to the University of Virginia. The editor visited the other four in their homes and offices and conducted the interviews found in the volume. We acknowledge with profound gratitude thanks especially to Dr. Milton Eisenhower and Bryce Harlow who graciously met with the editor, Professor Richard Melanson and Clyde Lutz in Baltimore and Washington. We are also most grateful to General John S.D. Eisenhower, former Ambassador to Belgium, who kindly visited Charlottesville shortly before the volume was to go to press and wrote the foreword.

It is always difficult to organize a book that deals with a man and his works. However with President Eisenhower, it seemed appropriate to divide our discussion into five parts: Eisenhower the Man; The Eisenhower White House; Eisenhower as Political Leader; Eisenhower and

the Budget; and Eisenhower's Moral and Political Values. The reasons
for this division included the particular interests of the contributors as
well as the logic of approaching our subject in this way.

To begin the volume, the choice of the first intimate to speak about
the President was the simplest decision we had to make. From child-
hood, Milton and Dwight D. Eisenhower were so close that the life of
the one became a natural complement to that of the other. Dr. Eisenhower's "Portrait of a Brother" reflects the intimacy of their relationship and the common interests and values they shared. Dr. Eisenhower
has had a distinguished career in his own right as educator (president
of three great universities) and public servant. William Ewald is one of
the Eisenhower biographers, a former speech writer for the President
who joined General John Eisenhower in assisting in the preparation of
the *Memoirs*. Arthur Larson has had a distinguished career as a Law
School Dean, speech writer for the President, high official in the
Labor Department and a renowned authority on international law.
Larson is particularly well-equipped to write on Eisenhower's World
View.

There follow three extraordinarily clear and comprehensive essays
on the Eisenhower White House. General Andrew Goodpaster was
head of the staff secretariat but his influence rested even more on his
association with Eisenhower in SHAPE and SHAFE. Relatively young
at the time, General Goodpaster went on in NATO and Vietnam to
become one of America's foremost military leaders formed in the
mold of General Eisenhower himself. Karl Harr, who is President of
the American Aerospace Industry, describes the National Security
policymaking process and the role of the Operations Coordinating
Board. Bradley H. Patterson, now senior research scholar at the
Brookings Institute, has written a careful and penetrating analysis
enriched with a host of concrete details on the Eisenhower White
House.

In recent months, historian and political scientists, and notably Professor Fred Greenstein of Princeton University, have placed increased
emphasis on Eisenhower's skills as a political leader. While confirming
certain aspects of this view of Eisenhower, the contributors to the second section of the volume help to place this view in a broader context.
Bryce Harlow is among the foremost living witnesses of Eisenhower's
political talents. Surprisingly, he chooses to see the diversity of talents
and skills which for him made Eisenhower the "compleat" President.
As speech writer and political advisor with long experience in
Washington, Harlow was uniquely positioned for his evaluation.
Governor Sherman Adams as chief of staff was more responsible for

the inner workings of the White House than any other member of the Eisenhower staff. He graciously assisted in the preparation of the volume as did his remarkably able secretary, Mrs. Watson. No two people have been more generous in sharing their thoughts and in bringing a text to fruition.

Maurice Stans, who was Deputy Postmaster General and the Director of the Budget, discusses the Eisenhower budget.

Arthur S. Flemming has been called the conscience of the Eisenhower administration. Distinguished educator and university president, his review of Eisenhower's stands on certain fundamental social issues helps to underscore the moral and political values of the President. While disagreeing with Flemming on particular questions, the President was willing to hear him out and abide by his responses and those of others in Cabinet meetings.

The breadth and outreach of the eleven perspectives should enable American citizens concerned with the Eisenhower presidency to gain a more comprehensive perspective of the man and his presidency.

I.
EISENHOWER
THE MAN

PORTRAIT OF A BROTHER
Milton S. Eisenhower

MR. THOMPSON: It's a pleasure to visit with you, Dr. Eisenhower. We haven't gotten into foreign policy as much as we would like in other interviews. Most of the people, including Bryce Harlow, have talked about domestic politics and domestic political leadership, and we've talked with the contributors about the hidden hand revisionist thesis.

MR. EISENHOWER: Let me say that John Eisenhower is the expert on military affairs, he and Andy Goodpaster. I thought I knew a good deal about World War II until I read John's latest book called *The Allies* and every page is new information to me. So there is a lot I didn't know about.

MR. THOMPSON: One of the things we wanted to ask you about was how you felt about this revisionist point of view, which may not be revisionist to you at all.

MR. EISENHOWER: Not revisionist to me at all. Let me point out that my brother and I, even when I was a youngster, for some strange reason had an affinity. Starting in 1933 we began working together. He was assistant to MacArthur and I was a coordinator of the U.S.

Department of Agriculture programs and already working for the President of the United States. I had worked a little for President Calvin Coolidge and Herbert Hoover but massively for President Roosevelt. When I came to Washington, Ike was called *"Milton's brother."* No fooling, because by that time I was pretty well known. I had become the administrative troubleshooter for the President, both domestic and in some other places. Then, when I became his principal confidant, his ambassador and a lot of other things, it was just natural. Needless to say, later and even now I am *"Ike's brother!"*

I think there is one thing I would like to say to you. Your correspondence didn't indicate whether you were interested or not and I've never made a great point of it. I was a different kind of confidant from a Colonel House or a Harry Hopkins. Colonel House fawned all over President Wilson who developed a messianic complex in which he could do no wrong. House, who was a pretty intelligent fellow, nonetheless in order to maintain his relations with Wilson agreed with him and just fawned on him. This doesn't do a President any good whatsoever.

I don't know whether you know the story, you probably do, but it is very interesting. Mrs. Wilson, the second Mrs. Wilson, induced the President to make House the deputy head of the American delegation for the peace conference in Paris. When President Wilson was there he wouldn't accept a change of a comma. There was no sense of compromise in the man. Well, politics in both international and domestic affairs is the art of creative compromise by getting your way. Wilson wouldn't change anything. In his absence, House made minor changes, not changing the sense and the direction of things or policies, but just grammatical changes—commas and semicolons and all this. Wilson got so mad he never spoke to the man again. Mutual confidence was over, broken up. And of course, then Wilson wouldn't compromise on anything. That is why the Senate would not approve his 14 points, including the League of Nations.

Harry Hopkins did things that had a great effect upon me as to why I behaved differently. Harry Hopkins would get an idea and go directly to the President and pursuade him to take action. For example, he pursuaded the President that Secretary of Agriculture Claude Wickard who had inherited the office from Henry Wallace was unable to run the massive department which was now spending around twelve billion or more per year on the economic aspects of agriculture. The United States had become the war food producer. It had to be stepped up. So without consulting the secretary of agriculture, Harry Hopkins induced the President to divide the department in two parts—the one part into research and education, the other part into the action programs to get maximum food and distribution. This was typical of everything Harry Hopkins did. He was a very intelligent man. He did some great work in London and in the Soviet Union.

When my brother became President we didn't change our ways. It was natural for us to continue to work together. I made up my mind that I would never *urge* the President to take any action. I did not feel that that was my function. After all I didn't have access day after day to the same information and visitors and research that he had. But on the other hand we had a relationship which he could depend upon. I knew the right questions to ask and he knew that I had no selfish interests. I was the one person in the world who wasn't subservient to him or wanted something from him. And further, the questions I asked were simply designed to help him think through his own problems. Any trouble that came to my attention I worked through the relevant officers. I never took an issue to the President unless I first had the approval of the Cabinet officers responsible for that liaison.

You see, in any human organization—and we're failing in this today—if you want your policies carried out you had better have the top people who are going to carry it out working with you in the formation of the policy. They will understand it better. They will feel they have made a contribution to it and with loyalty they will carry it out. We're forgetting this in international affairs today. You know, we unilaterally make a declaration that there can't be any use made of American technological materials in building a pipeline from the Soviet Union to France and other countries. Well, of course most Americans believe the pipeline is good. But after unilaterally deciding against it, President Reagan went to our allies to ask for their cooperation. We didn't get it. Remember, in the Yom Kippur War we were the only nation supporting Israel. Our allies wouldn't even let us land in Britain or Germany or any place else to refuel, so we had to pile more and more fuel and less and less war material in the plane. And those examples are just two of what's been going on since 1961.

MR. THOMPSON: Do you think that President Eisenhower's wartime experience and his whole life of working with leaders of other countries is something which we are not going to have again in our time simply because that wartime leadership is unlikely to recur?

MR. EISENHOWER: I think it is unlikely to occur in the same way. I would hope that the end result is not impossible to achieve again. President Eisenhower knew personally every leader in the free world. He had been the only man who had supported de Gaulle. Winston

Churchill and Franklin Roosevelt would have nothing to do with the man and de Gaulle never forgot it. And notice, no intransigence ever started on de Gaulle's part while Eisenhower was in the White House. But as soon as he was out, de Gaulle recognized North Vietnam and eventually kicked NATO out of France where we left billions of dollars in airports and all the rest. Incidentally, and unrelated to what I have been saying, one of my proudest moments was when I had the President of the United States and the prime minister of Britain in the same commencement exercises at Johns Hopkins during my presidency. The students made a plaque and put it on the steps of the auditorium and people always walk around the plaque.

This personal association with Europe's leaders suited his temperament. Cooperation in forming partnerships was the rule for eight years. Now, I must confess that one can adhere too slavishly to a good policy. Any policy in the world may require a deviation once in a great while. I personally had to modify my policy once, with serious consequences.

I had been making studies as an ambassador about U.S.-Latin American policies in Panama. It was perfectly clear to me that serious trouble was in the offing. I prepared a nine point program. Let me say it was mainly to help them with housing. They would provide the labor and local costs and we would provide the funds from the Export/Import Bank to pay for imports. The plan also proposed getting Panamanians into higher paying positions rather than holding the lower service positions, all Americans having the higher ones. If Panamanians weren't trained, we would train them. The plan was comprehensive but these items are sufficiently basic to remain alive.

Well, Dulles agreed one hundred percent with the plan so I was all right with the State Department. Then I went to see the secretary of war who was directly in charge of the Panama Canal policies and he would have none of my plan. A year later, I'll have you know, he called me on the phone and said, "Would you rush over to see me?" I ran over and he said, "We're going to be in trouble in Panama and I think we need to take action." And believe it or not that man sat there and said, "I think we ought to do the following." And if I had pulled out my quotes of one year before they would have been identical. So I said to him, "Under the circumstances, I'm staying at the White House as usual this weekend. Would you like me to brief the President?" And he said, "I wish you would."

My brother hit the ceiling and called a meeting for early Monday morning. But before he could begin action the trouble broke out, very serious trouble as you know. Well, now we couldn't do anything because if we took action right away the world would get the idea, and particularly Latin America would get the idea, that the way to get things out of Uncle Sam was to insult him and make trouble. All of this is more than I meant to say but I wanted you to understand the nature of the confidential relationship I had with my brother.

MR. THOMPSON: I mean nothing disrespectful by the question but it pops into one's mind. Was there ever any sibling rivalry or jealousy that caused the slightest problem between the two of you? One of the jokes that two of our guests have told that you've undoubtedly heard many times, I'm sure, is that the man who went to the phone for the Columbia Board of Trustees to invite your brother to be Columbia's president called the wrong Eisenhower.

MR. EISENHOWER: That's just nonsense. It is true that there was a Remington family, a very rich family, one of whom was on the board of trustees of Columbia and one of whom was president of the American University in Beirut, or at least had supported that university greatly. One of the brothers, I can't recall his name, did come to see me in Kansas to ask whether I would be interested in going to Columbia. But Tom Watson, who was chairman of the board, and the rest of the board were unanimously in favor of General Eisenhower and let me say that they were right in being that way because they were having a tough time of things. The financial situation was bad. They needed something new and something vigorous and, while Eisenhower had never been an educator as such, he knew a good deal about it, a lot more than people thought. Actually he was a pretty good president at Columbia. He established new departments such as one to study the Soviet Union and Slavic cultures. He established a wonderful symposium which is still underway, the American Assembly, originally financed by Averell Harriman. He put University finances in order, all during a short time, for he didn't get to be President very long. He was called by Truman and made head of NATO. He was the one man at that time, by historic accident, who knew the leaders of Europe well enough to sell the transnational package and get it put into action. He succeeded.

MR. THOMPSON: Greenstein puts much weight on the idea of the hidden hand, that President Eisenhower was very sensitive to the politics in each and every situation but he wanted to carry out policy behind the scenes rather than appearing to be an activist.

MR. EISENHOWER: Let me say, first of all, that I think Greenstein has done more hard research, more dependable research and probably deserves more credit than any other single person in changing the view of Eisenhower one hundred and eighty degrees. But that doesn't mean I think he's right in everything. No doubt when Eisenhower left office, the prevailing thought was that he'd been chairman of the board, rather than an effective President. Things were kind of taking care of themselves, it was said, and others made decisions; he had a pretty good time playing golf. Well, now all is turned around, because Greenstein and others discovered that he was very wise politically. He made all the fateful decisions. He was the one President in history who ever set up a mechanism to see that presidential decisions were faithfully implemented and carried out. The coordinating committee he established was comprised of the deputies and undersecretaries plus an adequate staff.

So the hidden hand is prominent in Greenstein's presidency book. He keeps justifying himself too much. He was a Democrat and anti-Eisenhower during the Eisenhower administration. He makes me think of James Reston; I've know Reston for years. I was in Washington recently—three months ago (during one of the periods when I wasn't sick) and Reston phoned me. We've been good friends for many years. We talked by phone. He is only one of the two persons in the world I ever let call me "Milt." He said, "Milt, I called you to say hello and also to tell you how happy I am you're doing what you're doing to set up a private foundation to work on the problem of crime." Then he said, "I want to tell you something. In my whole long career I am only ashamed of one thing and I wish I could undo it." He said, "I misunderstood and misrepresented your brother's administration. I now know about it and I just wanted you to know I'm terribly sorry I didn't wake up sooner."

All the way through his writings, Greenstein, by repetition, stresses one fact, "Look, I was one of those who thought he was no good and now I know a lot different. Therefore, let me convert you." But you asked me a specific question about what he had said.

MR. THOMPSON: Yes. That Eisenhower made all of the political decisions but he deliberately confused people as to whether he was actually doing it. Is there truth in that?

MR. EISENHOWER: A little of it but not as much as Greenstein says. First of all, Eisenhower was a very honest man, which is untypical of Presidents. I worked for eight of them. The effect on the vote is always so important. As a matter of fact in Washington today the reason we don't solve our problems is because everybody is voting for what will get him reelected rather than for what is right. He was never that way. If an essential policy or decision happened to have a bad political effect, too damn bad. But he really had enough confidence in the American people that he believed that they would accept the truth and then act wisely.

He was always building up the other fellow. He did this during the war and it was perfectly natural for him to do it in the presidency. He wanted people to be responsible and to grow and develop. He never said, "I have told the secretary of agriculture to do so and so." Never. He might say, "I have approved the secretary's recommendation." I repeat: he was always helping the other fellow. I'll never forget the U2 incident. He was the one person who months before thought we had gained all the information we could and that it was now too great a risk to run. But everybody else, the War Department, the State Department, the CIA thought otherwise and he said, "Well all right—a little longer." If a break came, an advance press release was always read. The President had never seen it. They put it out and said the U2 had strayed off course by a mistake. And then when the truth came out it looked like the President of the United States was lying and he never made any effort to correct it. I remonstrated at the time, but he said, "What would you have me do? Name a culprit and then fire him?"

He was capable of beautiful English prose and he also wrote beautifully. I think that John and my brother and I all inherited a little bit of ability in this regard. Often Hagerty would tell him some of the questions that would come up in the news conference and say, "You may want to say you don't wish to discuss it at present." Then Ike would say, "Oh, leave it to me, Jim, I'll confuse them." He would go in and he would be doing two things. One, he would not reveal more than the security situation would permit. Second, he didn't want to make a dishonest answer. Now that's quite a chore. So he would start and stop in the middle of a sentence and realize that he wasn't going to get it right so he would back up and start over again. So you couldn't follow his syntax or anything else. A lot of the press thought he didn't know any better. That was a show. But note, he established firm relationships with the Democratic congressional leadership. He had a Democratic Congress for six of eight years. He had more luck with the Democrats than he did with the Republicans. In the first two years the trouble was that the Republicans had been opponents for twenty years and they didn't realize that you behave a little differently when the party controls the executive office. So they continued to oppose the President just by definition. In eight years he only had two vetoes overridden and they were pork barrel bills. The relationships with Congress were certainly not what they are like now.

I don't think there was as much planned action as Greenstein has concluded. I think Greenstein is quite correct in the ultimate decisions he reached as to who was making the decisions and why and all the rest but there was not so much conniving.

MR. THOMPSON: Could you say just a little about his views toward the Soviet Union? He gets a great deal of credit for normalizing the domestic scene and yet it's seemed to many of us that he was trying to do that even more in the foreign policy field with the idea he had about the exchange of ordinary citizens, people to people, the idea of meeting Khrushchev at the summit and so many other things he tried to do. He didn't go into any of those relationships with any illusions about Soviet ambitions, I'm sure, but still he thought that in the kind of world we live you did have to do a certain amount of business with them, it seems.

MR. EISENHOWER: I could talk about this one a long while. Let me go back to the campaign in 1952. His next to the last speech was in Boston. We took a plane from Boston to New York where he was to make the final speech via radio for an audience brought together by the *New York Herald Tribune*. It was to be largely on economic affairs. I had worked with others as well as with General Eisenhower in doing drafts and he always redrafted them about eight times. However, during the campaign he didn't have time to do that. He said, "Milton, I want you to write a paragraph in here someplace saying that I want to develop active two-way trade with the Soviet Union to our mutual benefit." I said, "Well, I'll do it if you say so but let me say that as you know very well it's a complicated subject and here we are just the night before the election. Why do you want to introduce a new subject which you are not going to be able to spell out anyway?" He said, "Now you are trying to make a politician out of me." Well, we got Senator Duff and a lot of others and they all came up and talked to Eisenhower and he said, "Ah, all right, I give up."

From the first he worked very hard to overcome, to reduce the intensity of the cold war. He wanted good relations with the Soviet Union. He realized that these two powers were going to be competitive in the world scene but he thought we could learn to work together. He was happy when Khrushchev visited this country; he put everything at his disposal, including television. On TV, Khrushchev screamed that he wanted to visit Disneyland and wasn't permitted to do so. Well, we all knew that we wanted him to visit Disneyland but his own secret service people in advance planning vetoed it. There were no security arrangements so at the last minute we couldn't take him down there.

And I'm not sure he didn't know it but it was a chance for him to show off.

I'm convinced—I can't prove this but I'm convinced—that if Eisenhower had made the return visit that he would have been acclaimed everywhere. In 1959, I was assistant head of the American delegation that went to Russia ostensibly to open the American exposition as they had had an exposition in New York. I was Khrushchev's guest wherever we went. We stayed in his dachas. One afternoon he came out to his dacha and put me in his racing boat with 50,000 people on the shores of the Moscow river; he, the driver of the boat, and me. Mr. Nixon was someplace else. He'd pull up at the shore and he would make a speech against the United States about the Captive Nations Resolution that had been passed just before we made the trip over there. He said to the people, "Do you all feel like you are captives?" "No, hooray!" And then he introduced me and they would be very cordial.

By the way, that afternoon we sat down to lunch under a canopy outside of his dacha. A plastic canopy. We sat down at three and got up at 9:30 at night. No drunkenness. Not too much drinking on anybody's part. The conversation never ceased. Khrushchev convinced me that he was earnest when he said that atomic power meant mutual annihilation if ever used and that we therefore had to learn to work together.

So I would say to you that Eisenhower did everything he reasonably could to develop better relations. He was sincere about it. He did succeed in reducing the intensity of the cold war which was later enhanced for other reasons by Kennedy.

MR. THOMPSON: The related issue, of course, is the industrial-military complex. We've heard so much in the last few years about how far behind we are and how we need to build up before we can even have any discussion. President Eisenhower certainly never underplayed the importance of defense. But on the other hand, in that one phrase he pointed to some of the dangers in the industrial-military complex.

MR. EISENHOWER: Not only did he see the danger but also he was satisfied that at the time he left the White House there was no disparity in the strength of the Soviet Union and the United States. Kennedy had tried to make the "missile gap" an issue in the campaign. But MacNamara three months later as secretary of defense said, "There is no gap." I think he was entirely right and by the way more people have tried to take credit for having helped write that speech about the industrial-military complex. I can assure you that that was about as one hundred percent Eisenhower as you can get.

It makes me think—I've got to tell you a funny story. The Links Club in New York is made up of authors and writers and so on. They had tried time and again to get him to make a speech. They were all friends of his. So when his two terms were over at the White House, he felt obliged to go. He made a speech on making speeches. He said there is always the person who comes to you and says, "Mr. President, all you have to do is just stand up and say how happy you are to be there and just greet the people." He said, "Now by this, they expect you to give a thorough analysis of our relations with Europe, the Communist powers, Latin America, and a little bit about the world economic situation and then answer questions." He said, "The one that always makes me see a little red is when he comes to you and says, 'Mr. President, if you'll come we'll do a draft and all you have to do is just tone it up to put it in your own language.'" He said, "This is like a red flag to me." It's true he would rewrite some speeches over a dozen times. Even after he approved a speech and had it mimeographed for the press, the press had to bring their copies and listen to the speech because it was always different from the original. In this speech to the Links Club he said, "I once accepted one of those and when I finished a man came up to say, 'Mr. President, I want to thank you for keeping a few words of the original draft in because I wrote it.'" "Oh," the President said to him. "What part was that?" He said, "Ladies and Gentlemen."

MR. THOMPSON: I have a speech story, too. One time when he was at Columbia he came down to the Rockefeller Foundation. I was vice president and worked with Dean Rusk. Dean Rusk was the host. When then General Eisenhower finished, a senior scientist whom you must have known from the early days, Warren Weaver, said, "If General Eisenhower told us to walk to the window on the fifty-seventh floor and jump out, eighty or ninety percent of us would have done it."

MR. EISENHOWER: I want to say he came the closest—if you'll forgive me for this—to being the ideal President of the ones I knew. I started with Wilson, on a nodding basis at least. But I worked for eight of them and found I admired much about Roosevelt. I disagreed terrifically with his economic policies and he loved it. He kidded the life out of me. He would make a statement and then look at me out of the corner of his eyes and see what I'd say in return. But he was a great man. He was the best communicator I have ever known in the White House.

And may I say that this is where we are suffering today. The problems we face now are so complex that they are beyond the comprehension of most citizens. This does not prevent them from having views because most of them belong to one or more pressure groups and we have 2,500 such groups with power. They have representatives in Washington. Therefore, the mass judgment that Jefferson saw would be valid so long as there was an ever rising level of education and understanding just doesn't exist today. Now the Congress and the President—unless they're stupid like Reagan—get to know more than their constituents do, but they suffer the horrible disease of yearning to achieve electoral immortality—to stay in politics as a career. It consumes elected officials. I can offer the example of one of the dearest friends I have and whom I've admired very much. I was trying to get him to take at least a reasonable approach on gun control, a problem on which I am radical—I wanted to confiscate sixty million civilian handguns. And he said, "No, I don't dare bring it up. Because if they agree with everything else I stand for, on that one issue alone they will vote against me." By the time you consider all the things that will cause uninformed voters to turn against you, the modern politician feels he must deal in generalities, not in specific things, such as how to reduce inflation or crime. We are not making any progress. We are not solving our problems.

The President is so proud of bringing down inflation. Well, anybody can bring down inflation by creating a recession with twelve million unemployed and interest rates at twenty percent. If you are willing to have twelve and a half million people suffer—be cold and hungry and starving—sure! Now they think we are having a recovery. If there hadn't been a single appropriation from the government or any control whatsoever, we would have recovered under the "boom and bust" historic system. Well, that's what we're doing. And we're not going very far because the automobile industry and the steel industries which so permeate our total economy, are not going to respond long enough. They can't.

MR. MELANSON: It's become a truism that since the Vietnam War we have not had a domestic foreign policy consensus and that we can no longer agree upon the purposes American power should be put to internationally. People seem to think that we had a consensus in the 1950s. My question is did President Eisenhower consciously attempt to curry support and create a domestic consensus that he could then use as a base for his foreign policy or did he assume that that consensus was already there and he didn't really have to worry about it.

MR. EISENHOWER: I think I'll have to say that in my judgment he helped create a consensus. You may remember that when he came home long, long before he had any idea of ever running for President—and by the way he was very sincere in that letter to the editor in New Hampshire that he never would be a candidate—he went up and down this land speaking all the time. He spoke feelingly before a joint session of Congress as a five-star general that the free world could exist only if we developed transnational cooperation and made sure it was dependable. This extended throughout his war years and subsequent years. It was very natural for him when he became President to keep on working cooperatively for a consensus. That was an exceedingly sincere and constant effort.

Once or twice our allies, without consulting him, made serious moves, as in the Egyptian/Suez problem. Israel, France, England acted in concert. The President expressed strong disapproval and was prepared to go to the United Nations on it. But he hadn't been consulted and it was a violation of all we had agreed to in the Charter of United Nations. I think you are right.

It was a great disappointment to him that the partnership, which had worked so beautifully, failed in this instance. I guess they knew he would not agree so they didn't want to consult him.

MR. THOMPSON: We are terribly grateful. Thank you, Dr. Eisenhower.

A BIOGRAPHER'S PERSPECTIVE
William Ewald

NARRATOR: I'd like to welcome you to another session in our series of portraits on the Eisenhower presidency. We are especially pleased that someone whom many have mentioned as the author of the best overall biography of Dwight D. Eisenhower could be with us today, William Ewald. Mr. Ewald started in the academic field but then either escaped it or transcended it, depending upon your viewpoint. He was a member of the English faculty at Harvard University. He met several of you at Oxford.

We used to talk in the Rockefeller Foundation about the possibility of scholars being participant-observers, but after three or four false starts we gave up the idea and said that if you were a participant you couldn't any longer be a detached and objective observer. Mr. Ewald is the exception that proves the rule. In contrast with some others who have written on Eisenhower, he was there and actually served as a speechwriter. He was tutored, as his book so cogently explains, by men like Bryce Harlow in "the hard knocks school of politics." He also was assistant to the secretary of the interior Fred Seaton. With John Eisenhower, he assisted President Eisenhower in the writing of

"Mandate for Change" and "Waging Peace," the two-volume memoirs of the Eisenhower administration. He now is associated with IBM. He has come here all the way from Connecticut, and we are terribly grateful that he has been willing to do this.

MR. EWALD: Thank you very much. It is a real pleasure and a real honor to be here. First of all, let me tell you I am not a Virginian, but did the next best thing. I married a Virginian.

I thought what I'd do is speak rather briefly because I think I detect an audience that likes to ask questions; and I hope so because I find that the most fun. It's like opening presents on Christmas morning—you never know what is going to be inside the package. But, I can't help thinking that when I was at Harvard one of the great professors then in the English Department, Professor Douglas Bush, who died very recently, always talked about the problem Milton faced in writing *Paradise Lost*. The poet has a hero who was not very interesting, and he had a villain who was very fabulously interesting, Satan. And Satan always comes out to be, in many interpretations, the more fascinating figure, whereas to Milton the real hero was God, if you want, or Jesus Christ, depending on whether it's *Paradise Lost* or *Paradise Regained*. In a way you feel somewhat the same way about Eisenhower.

I remember one Sunday morning, when we were in Washington—our children were very small—one of them toddled over to the television and turned it on. His older brother, who was then about four, looked at him and said, "Charles, don't turn on the television set on Sunday morning. On Sunday morning there is nothing on there but God." And that is about the way it is with Eisenhower. He was a good President, but who wants to read about him and who finds it interesting? Because really, you look for drama and you find much more drama in Bob Donovan's great two-volume series on the Truman presidency. Bob said he thought Eisenhower was the more successful President, but he said Truman was a lot more fun to write about because something was always popping and happening.

I'm sure that is true because when you look for drama you don't find, say, drama in the streets in Washington with smoke curling up over the city, or you don't find drama on the battlefields because there really weren't any battlefields. We didn't have American soldiers overseas fighting and dying as you had in preceding and succeeding administrations. And you didn't have really any drama in the stores, where you can find that the price is changing on products day by day or month by month from heavy inflation. Eisenhower had a record of

1.4% annual increase in inflation, and he had no wars, and really no riots to speak of.

So, I've always taken the position that the real drama with the Eisenhower administration was in the Oval Office, in the mind and heart of the man who sat there in the Oval Office and who engineered all this, engineered us through those eight years, and got us through it pretty safely and pretty well. The comment is sometimes made, "Well, anybody could have done it." You know the old saying: Eisenhower proved we didn't need a President.

But, if you remember back, and run through those years in 1953, you had a hot war in Korea; in 1954, a hot war in Vietnam which we could have got into but didn't; in 1955, the Communists shelled Quemoy and Matsu—we could have got into a war with that; in 1956, in Hungary, Soviet tanks rolled through the streets of Budapest, and there was the uprising in Poland; and to top it all off the British, French and Israelis invaded Egypt. At that moment Eisenhower really did think we were confronting the possibility of World War III, but the crisis came and went. In 1957, the Russians put up Sputnik and everybody went beserk over that. In 1958, Eisenhower sent American troops into Lebanon, a relatively big force went in there and quieted things down. In 1959, Khrushchev threatened to end Allied rights in West Berlin and we came up to the edge of World War III once again. Then the last year, which should have been a quiet year for an old man going out of the presidency, what did you have? You had the U2 crisis, you had the Summit Conference shot down, you had the crisis in Laos, you had the crisis in the Congo and Khrushchev coming to the UN banging his shoe on the table. So, given these circumstances which the man in the Oval Office had to deal with, I will not say that the decade presented itself as a decade that anybody could have sat through kind of fat, dumb and happy, and managed.

I'd just like to run through briefly the kinds of analyses of this presidency that have occurred. I found, having written the book, that the one interpretation of the Eisenhower presidency that I come up against most often is the silliest one of all and the most persistent, and that is that Eisenhower was a do-nothing President, a know-nothing President, that he played golf all the time and had a nice grin. If he had a tough problem he would push it off on Richard Nixon or Sherman Adams or somebody else and he floated above it all, like Tom Landry, in a way, without really calling the signals. That myth started even before Eisenhower became President. It got started in the 1952 campaign and it went on through the Eisenhower presidency. And it has persisted more or less to this day in one form or another, although

I think now when you talk to people on the streets they say, "Oh yes! You know, I used to think he played golf all the time but now I think he is a bit better." So we've gone from point A to point B.

In the middle of the Eisenhower presidency the people around the President, not the President himself, but people around him, saw this image forming and they said, "You know, this isn't really right. We ought to do something about the image." So what they did was to let a very fine liberal, democratic, knowledgeable Washington reporter named Robert Donovan of the *New York Herald Tribune* into the White House. They had a fellow down there who got his instructions from Sherman Adams and really gave the keys to the family jewels—a lot of them, not all of them by any means—to Donovan and let him into the records. In other words, they let him into the minutes of the Cabinet meeting. They let him into the minutes of the weekly legislative leaders meetings. They let him into the records of certain Eisenhower correspondence. It was very selective, but on the other hand, he was seeing more while a man was President than anybody had ever seen before. And Donovan wrote a book called *Eisenhower: The Inside Story,* which came out in 1956, and showed a lot of the behind the scenes. It was a very well done book, especially considering the access that he had and considering the amount of time he had.

When Eisenhower personally found out what had happened he blew his stack. He didn't know about it. Sherman Adams had done it and Eisenhower was furious. He said, "What are you doing, letting one reporter in while there are all these other fellows out there trying to make a living writing history?" He really singed Sherman Adams over that. And Adams remembers that, too, to this very day.

The Donovan book did something to correct the image but the image still persisted. And if I had to single out two men who typified the point of view and really crystalized this whole anti-Eisenhower, Eisenhower-the-passive-President point of view, I would say it was Arthur M. Schlesinger, Senior and Junior, both of whom invented this cyclical theory of the presidency, which is, as most of you know, in a simplified fashion, that you have good guys and bad guys in the White House.

You have the activists. These are the people who go out and stretch the presidency to the limit. They go over the heads of Congress, the people, and when necessary they bend the Constitution and they make the office of the President as big as it possibly can be made. The Schlesingers really felt that this is what the President was supposed to do. Other people are supposed to hold him back, but the good Presidents are the activists. They are Abraham Lincoln, quite obviously,

Andrew Jackson, quite obviously, and Franklin D. Roosevelt in our century. The great heroes.

On the other side you have the dopes. They are do-nothings, the people who come in when the activists have got the whole country exhausted and then give it eight years of rest. You have Calvin Coolidge, or you have Warren G. Harding, or you have a Herbert Hoover. And sure enough, whom have we got now? Dwight Eisenhower. He fits the mold. So you have this theory that most people listened to, and they said, "Yes, the good guys are the activists, and the bad guys are the passive ones."

This hurt Eisenhower. And it hurt Eisenhower particularly in his second term, I think, because it was then that he found himself confronted with an event which I've described in the book, the Russian orbiting of Sputnik. It made people think, well, the Russians are getting ahead of us; they are getting ahead of us in space; they are getting ahead of us in defense; they are on the move; they are going to overtake us economically. And what do you have in the White House? You've got a lame duck Republican. He can't run again. You've got a man who really believes in the kind of a balanced approach to things whereby you are not riding off on a white horse every ten minutes to try to save the country. You've got, really, a kind of old fuddy-duddy, stick-in-the-mud. And this was Eisenhower in his second term. He suffered under the shadow of the Russian Sputnik that whole time. So if you put Sputnik over here and Arthur M. Schlesinger right next to it, you have a rather good idea of what preceded the 1960 election.

After the Nixon/Kennedy election Kennedy, stepped out into history, into the mold, almost as though he was stepping into a landscape painting through the frame and was going to be an activist President. He signed up Arthur Schlesinger. Arthur worked for him, in the campaign, in the White House, and he was going to get America moving again. So who were his heroes? Well, we could go back to the Schlesinger analysis. They were Franklin Roosevelt, they were Andrew Jackson, they were Woodrow Wilson and Teddy Roosevelt. People like that who were strong.

Dwight Eisenhower was a sitting duck, in a way, in his second term for this because what did Eisenhower stand for in his second term? He stood for, of all things, a balanced budget. People thought, we don't need that. The Russians are coming. We want a strong defense. We will spend three billion, or five billion or ten billion or whatever it takes. Eisenhower knew the defense budget. He would go over it item by item, line by line. He knew what was in it. He knew where the fat was. He knew where the people were trying to load extras onto the defense budget, things you didn't need. And he had no use for it. He said what he was in favor of, in the second term, was military sufficiency. In 1957 the administration had a policy on nuclear arms: all we needed. We didn't need to have ten times as much as the Russians. All we needed to have was a guaranteed second strike that would assure that if they hit us first we would assure their obliteration with a second strike. That is all we needed. You could pile ten billion dollars on top of that, but Ike fought that move. Now the other people who opposed that said, we can't stand still. We are going to spend that ten billion dollars and look as though we are moving ahead of the Russians.

I would say the same thing was true in domestic policy. Ike really did try to hold the line and he was genuinely worried about inflation. Most people weren't in those days—because we didn't have any inflation records, they were very, very low. He worried when it got up over 2%. And all that hurt. It hurt him. It hurt his image. It certainly hurt Nixon, and I think it had a great deal to do with the Nixon loss to Kennedy in 1960.

Now coming into the sixties, you have a number of books that are written about Eisenhower. First a spate of books written by people who were associated with him. Sherman Adams wrote his book after he left the White House in some kind of disgrace in 1958. Ezra Taft Benson wrote a book, Lewis Strauss wrote a book. These are Cabinet officers unburdening themselves of their own recollections. But, they aren't very good books, most of them. They are rather stodgy, and they are very controlled and very self-serving. They are useful because they do reveal where the man stood and so on. Adams' book does have real merit. But basically, they are books still written under a shadow because all these people were still public figures and they had to watch every word. So they had to be very careful. If you look under each sentence in Sherman Adams' book, lift up the rock, there is a lot there that he knows and will tell you about today, but it didn't get into the book for one reason or another.

Emmett Hughes' book came out while we were in Gettysburg in 1963. I was working with the President and his son, John Eisenhower, doing the two volumes of the memoirs and Emmett's book came out right in the middle of that whole process. I will never forget this. I've described it in great detail in the book—exactly what happened when word of Emmett Hughes' book was brought to Gettysburg by his publisher, who was also our publisher, and you can imagine the consternation that caused. Now Emmett's book—and a lot of people will disagree with this—is really one of the best books on Eisenhower ever done. I would say Arthur Larson's book is another. The great merit of

Emmett Hughes' book is that if you take all of Emmett Hughes out of it, take Emmett's personality out of it, take Emmett's philosophy out of it, Emmett's analysis of international events out of it, and leave Emmett's portrait of Dwight Eisenhower in camera talking to him underneath and behind the scenes, it is fascinating. Emmett was a fine journalist and he did really a very brilliant job of bringing out the true Eisenhower in his office, the intimate moments. But, you do have to read it, believe me, with some care. But that book was regarded almost as an act of treason by most Eisenhower loyalists. Emmett Hughes' name was absolutely mud.

Eisenhower's own books on the presidency are, I think, very, very solid. They were worked over with great care. They were filled with information. I'm very proud of them, I'm proud of my own part in them. On the other hand, a sitting President does not have, in a sense, the credibility that somebody coming in from the outside has. In Gettysburg, we had the cream of the crop of Eisenhower's presidential records. They were carted up from the White House office and kept in the custody of his personal secretary, Ann Whitman, and they are now known in the Eisenhower library as the Whitman files. Ann kept these documents, believe me, right with her. She would send off all the chaff and stuff across the street to somebody else to be filed away, and they would file it away in great bales. But, the good stuff she had. She squirreled it away and we took it to Gettysburg. Those documents are really the source documents for *Mandate for Change,* and *Waging Peace.* We read them and reread them and combed through them and talked about them. They appeared; they eventuated in the Eisenhower memoirs.

On the other hand nobody came out and said, "Well, now we really see the inside of Eisenhower." These books really have a built-in problem, I think, that is true of almost any presidential memoir, whether it is Harry Truman's or Dwight Eisenhower's or Lyndon Johnson's or Jimmy Carter's, or whatever, which has the President talking about himself. He has to be self-serving, he has to be defensive, he has to make his case. He feels he has been President, he's not going to be President again, he is an ex-President. This is his last chance at history and he's going to unload on it. If you accept those constraints you will see the merits of the book, and I think Presidents should write their memoirs. But, you also see the limitations or the problems that the books have had.

Scholars recently have been admitted to the Eisenhower library to see the Whitman papers. A lot of people are reading them. Fred Greenstein spent a lot of time reading through them, Blanche Cook has read through them. The Eisenhower library is full of scholars reading them. Their eyes are popping. They say, "Look at this document, this isn't the Eisenhower we knew." And we can say, "Well, look, Mac, back in *Mandate for Change* on page 262 there is the document, if you will read it," but it's in the wrong context. It's in the context where it has Dwight Eisenhower's imprimatur, and it does not have the ring of the scholar pulling out a file for the first time and reading it and saying, "I thought one thing and now when I read this original document, I think something else." So, the new wave of scholars who are coming into the field and into the documentation for the first time, from the outside, is having a very salutary effect, and there is nobody that can do this better than those people.

In 1967, *Esquire* magazine published a little article which has had enormous reverbrations. It was written by a man named Murray Kempton, who is a liberal New York and White House reporter. He came up with a reinterpretation of Dwight Eisenhower that really set a lot of people on their ear. He said, "Look, you've got Eisenhower all wrong. You think he was stupid, he was out playing golf all the time, didn't care anything about what he was doing. But really Eisenhower was the sneakiest, most cunning, most devious, most Machiavellian, and in some respects most treacherous, meanest President we've ever had." And he has a wonderful image. Kempton said Ike was like a great big tortoise. "Eisenhower was under the shell and he was so smart, all the rest of us were sitting up on top of the tortoise and we never knew the cunning underneath the shell. If he had a tough job to do, what would he do? He would send out Richard Nixon to walk through the mine fields or he would send out Sherman Adams to take it on because he would find somebody to do his dirty work for him. He was a real first class sneak. There is no other word for it."

This theme of the Eisenhower presidency is another interpretation that does have to be reckoned with and that continues in later years. I would say it came up most vigorously and most seriously in 1975 when the Select Committee on Intelligence of the United States Senate under the chairmanship of Senator Frank Church, Democrat, Idaho went into the mystique of the CIA. This was in the wake of Watergate: "Boy, it's a great year, 1975. Nixon is just out of the presidency, and we're going to nail a lot of these people." They found out the CIA had, indeed, been up to an awful lot of mischief in this period and they found that the mischief was scattered on both sides of the political aisle. They found Bobby Kennedy engaged in plots to do in Castro, and they found of course that Nixon was guilty.

On Eisenhower they came upon this curious set of events that occurred in 1960 when there was, indeed, in the CIA a project afoot to
assassinate a Communist political leader in Africa named Patrice
Lumumba, and they traced these CIA documents. They went out to
Abilene. They crawled all over the files out there and they really did a
job on this episode, I believe, in order to be evenhanded about it
politically. But, they said, "You know we cannot believe it, but the
evidence leads us to the conclusion that Eisenhower must have known,
or must have ordered, or condoned the assassination of Lumumba."
So they nailed him with the assassination of Patrice Lumumba.

I've got a chapter on that episode in the book, and to make a long
story short I don't believe a word of it. I have gone through all the
evidence of the Church committee. I began questioning eyewitnesses,
whom the Church committee did not question. And as far as I can tell
there is no credible evidence that can really establish the link between
Dwight Eisenhower and that ridiculous assassination plot, which was a
farce if you read it. I mean, they send a Dr. Strangelove down there
with a suitcase filled with hypodermic needles and a lot of poison and
rubber gloves. He shows up down there and fools around for three
weeks and the poison goes bad. The shelf life expires. He goes back
home. They never did kill Lumumba. Somebody did, but *they* didn't.
But they tried. There is no question about it. From Allen Dulles on
down in the CIA, no question about it. There was an order given: Get
Lumumba. But it fizzled. My contention is that if you look at all the
evidence, step by step, record by record, document by document, talk
to everybody you can possibly find until any new evidence sur-
faces—and I do not believe it will surface because I think the Church
committee, believe me, would have found it—you cannot establish
Eisenhower as an assassin.

So that brings us almost up to date. So I guess the question is, with
all these writings on Eisenhower why add my book? I guess I have the
simple answer which most scholars have when they write a book. That
is that all the other books were wrong. Of course that is an overstate-
ment, and what I will say about all the other theories is: I would not
reject any single one of them completely. I think each one of them, including Murray Kempton, has something to add. And I would say of
the other parts of the portrait, that each one of them has a snatch at
the truth. He *did* play golf! He loved golf. He played bridge, he loved
bridge. He was a man with a grin, he liked people. But, he also was a
very cagey President. So with all those different parts to the puzzle,
maybe I ought to stop here and let you ask some questions.

NARRATOR: And don't hesitate to ask the hard ones because those of you who have read the book know that it is not a book without criticism. At the end of several of the chapters Mr. Ewald says, "On this point I think Eisenhower probably was wrong. For instance, the Wisconsin speech in which the text that Sulzberger and others had wanted to be included defending General Marshall was removed." So, don't hold back in your heartfelt concerns and questions.

MR. EWALD: Oh, no, I really welcome that.

QUESTION: I'd like to ask a procedural question. How did President Eisenhower gain information about current issues? What was the vehicle for his learning and forming opinions of things that were going on around him?

MR. EWALD: Well, it would depend on the issue. Eisenhower frequently made a point of saying that he didn't read the newspapers, especially that he didn't read columnists. He told one guy, "If I catch you reading Drew Pearson I'll fire you because you don't have enough to do," or something like that. But I'll tell you he read the newspapers. He got up early. He was an early riser. He would have arrived having read the *New York Times* and the *Washington Post,* the *Baltimore Sun* and whatever. He read the papers. He read them just as much as anybody.

Eisenhower was a man who was a superb organizer. He was a man who could organize an organization whether it was a squad, army, set of invading armies or the executive branch of the government. When he was President, he really felt he was the President of the entire American population and he had to respond to every kind of sensitivity within that population. This is one thing about civil rights. People say, well, why didn't he just go in when Earl Warren said we are going to desegregate the schools? Eisenhower said, yes, that's right, it has been too long. But Eisenhower felt he had people living south of the Mason-Dixon line, he had people north of the Mason-Dixon, and he really had to hold them together. This was always his concern: How do you hold this crowd of people together, whatever the size of the crowd, and get them rolling forward toward some kind of a worthwhile goal out there.

Now, on organization, Eisenhower appointed people whom he trusted. He put them into positions of authority. He let them make decisions and run their departments. If he had a question he would call them in and he would ask them a sharp question. He would get briefings from them on how they were doing and so on. But he did not feel that it was up to him, say, to inform himself, power dam by power dam, on what was going on in the Bureau of Reclamation, what was going on in the Corps of Army Engineers, or what was going on in the Department of Agriculture. He didn't put a microscope on each one and make up his own mind and have endless factual information. He tried to shovel an awful lot of detail out there onto the shoulders of people whom he really did trust.

I'll give you as good an example as I can think of. In the last year of his administration his attorney general, William Rogers, came to him and said, "Mr. President, I've got some news for you." He said, "We found that the heads of the major electrical manufacturing corporations in the United States have been engaged in probably the greatest anti-trust price fixing conspiracy in the history of the United States and we're all set to prosecute. Now I'll tell you, a lot of these people have been coming to your parties. I mean people like the head of General Electric and the head of Westinghouse." These were business movers and shakers and blue ribbon sorts, the kind of people Eisenhower liked to talk to. He liked to have them around him, and he was friendly with them and got along well with them. If they weren't his closest intimate friends, they were still people he knew. They were honorable people. And here comes the attorney general in and says that these guys were crooks: "We are going to prosecute them, and if we convict them they are going to jail." So, Eisenhower sits there for a minute. Now he could have done a lot of things, he could have said, "Okay, now look, you bring me all the evidence and I'll read through it myself and I'll let you know in a week what I think." Instead he said to Rogers, "Have you got the facts to prove it? The evidence to prove the crime?" Rogers said, "Yes." He said, "Can you make this evidence stand up in court?" He said, "Yes." Eisenhower hesitated a moment and he said, "Well, it's a sad thing. Go ahead and indict them."

That, I think, is a good example of how he worked and the kind of factual trust that he would repose in an attorney general—and now you can say, well, he was a dumb, do-nothing President because he didn't insist on going down into each case fact by fact. Jimmy Carter would have done that, I suspect. Richard Nixon would have done that, I suspect. Richard Nixon might have put 600 people on it: *you* see what you think, and *you* see what you think, and don't tell this guy that you are working on it; and we'll both work against the Justice Department, and then *I'll* come up with my own view. Eisenhower didn't even spend five minutes on this case. Justice went out and they sent them to jail.

Now, having said that about certain areas of the government, I will say that on other areas Eisenhower really felt he had to spend his time in detail, be knowledgeable up to the minute, as thoroughly informed as any man in government on especially one area of government. That was national security. That was State, the CIA, and it was Defense. He spent his time on these things. He had Foster Dulles come into his office, and they talked by phone, and Foster Dulles would send him memoranda, and he would have the assistant secretaries in, and he would have the under secretary in and he would burrow into these things in great detail.

On the subject of the Bricker Amendment, for example, which was a conservative constitutional amendment which limited the President's treaty making powers, Eisenhower personally worked through that thing word by word. He would write substitute amendments himself. He worked with the lawyers, he brought them in with great detail on certain things. That was a top drawer constitutional, presidential, national security issue, and by golly he was going to know all about it. And he knew everything that anybody could tell him from State and from Justice on down, from Dulles and from Brownell, and from the people who worked for them.

I mentioned the defense budget. He would go through that line by line: What do the marines need with an aircraft carrier? He could see these phony items. He wrote to friends and said, "You know, someday there is going to be somebody sitting here in this office who can't look at that defense budget and separate the phony things from the valid things, and I just feel sorry for him because he is going to be at the mercy of the military-industrial complex," the idea which he came out with there at the end. So, he went over this with a fine tooth comb in great detail. Some areas, like the Department of the Interior, he left to Fred Seaton. Fred Seaton ran it. Fred Seaton did what he wanted to do over there. He would report in to the President from time to time, and he would get in touch with the White House staff. But, believe me, Dwight Eisenhower felt it's in good hands, it's down the line from our cardinal responsibilities and therefore I'm not going to spend my time on this. He knew how to divide up his time.

Now I don't know whether this is what you are thinking of. I would say, certainly, that he had briefing information, say, from the CIA. He would have a daily briefing on what is happening around the world. It came in from the CIA through his White House Chief of Staff, General Andrew Goodpaster. Goodpaster would come in and brief him, sometimes Allen Dulles would come in with Goodpaster and they would have briefings every day, what's happening, step by step. He kept informed, and believe me, if something happened in the middle of the night they would call him up in the middle of the night and tell him.

Goodpaster is one of the brightest people he had. He was later superintendent of West Point and Supreme Allied Commander in Europe, a brilliant man, Princeton Ph.D. in international relations, and a man who sat there in the shadows, low profile, nobody ever heard of Andy Goodpaster in the White House. Sometimes I would ask about these people. I sometimes said, "You know in this day when the national security advisor becomes either a political threat or a political liability or political symbol, how many of you can name Eisenhower's chief national security advisors?"

QUESTION: (From an retired Air Force General) On the defense budget, Eisenhower was exactly right. Johnson was duped and Reagan is being duped about the military-industrial complex today. They don't see what's doing on. I worked with General Goodpaster all my career and I worked for Frank Nash and he was knowledgeable on every one of these points you mention. The point that this country keeps missing is the fact that President Eisenhower knew the military inside and out. He wouldn't let us get away with a damn thing. These other guys got into Vietnam, they got into the Bay of Pigs, they got into all these things.

MR. EWALD: I will say one thing now once you've said this because I think the key word about Eisenhower, if you think about it in so many contexts, is the word "balance." Eisenhower was a middle of the roader. I think Eisenhower would have agreed with an awful lot of that, the necessity for maintaining balance. A lot of people say Eisenhower was right about that. Bob Donovan, for example, thinks Eisenhower is the father of detente. He really wanted peace in the world. He wanted to get some kind of a *modus vivendi* with the Russians. He though it was ridiculous, the piling up of all these armaments. He tried and didn't succeed. We haven't succeeded yet. But he started the process, he started it from a standing start, in 1953, in his first major foreign policy address.

But once you've said all that, then you have to look at the other side of the balance and look at what a technological decade the fifties were, at the things he brought out of the closet: the IRBM, the ICBM, the U2, the first American space satellite, the X15, circumnavigation of the globe by an atomic submarine, one thing after another coming out, year by year. You go through the whole sixties and seventies, and they don't produce much. He brought the scientists in, had scientific advising. George Kistiakowsky was his second scientific adviser and he wrote a book about his experience with Eisenhower; he much admired him. His predecessor, Jim Killian, has also written a book on the President. Eisenhower brought in the President's Scientific Advisory Committee, and believe you me he brought them into the Oval Office, and he had them talk to him, and he listened to them, to their presentations. He had all kinds of technical presentations from these guys. So, he understood the hazards of nuclear testing of one sort or another, or where are we going with this weapon or with that weapon. On that kind of thing he really went flat out to get the best kind of professional, academic, scientific and technological advice that he could get, and he spent many, many hours on it. He did not shovel that group off to the National Science Foundation or to some other agency and say, "Let them smoke their pipes over there, and we will call them in from time to time." They were part and parcel; they spent a lot of time over there. A man like George Kistiakowsky could come in and butt heads with a man like John McCone, who was head of the Atomic Energy Commission. McCone didn't particularly like that, but this is what Eisenhower liked, that contention between knowledgeable advisers representing different points of view. So, I would say that he had a tremendous technological decade. He had a tremendous thrust for peace. He was suspicious of the military-industrial complex at the same time he got us on a military-industrial footing that has stood us in good stead for many, many years.

QUESTION: I was a member of the faculty at Columbia during the whole time that Eisenhower was President. We had a saying around Columbia that whatever qualifications Eisenhower had or did not have to be President of the United States, he was much better fitted to be President of the United States than to be president of Columbia. But, he had sense enough not to interfere with anything academic.

Anyway, I gained an impression of Eisenhower. One thing that I've never had any doubt about was that Eisenhower was a good man, and the father image was very appropriate for Eisenhower. He greatly admired Washington, and there can be no doubt that he had a proper sense of a relation between civil and military authority. And I wish to goodness that we had him sitting up there in the Oval Office right now dealing with the problems of defense and national security rather than the man who is there. He couldn't be fooled.

MR. EWALD: I think somebody once said that James Madison was a man who absolutely could have been anything in the United States he wanted to be and succeeded brilliantly at it, except as President of the United States. And then they said about Abraham Lincoln that he wouldn't have succeeded at anything *except* being President of the United States—and I agree.

I've heard this about Eisenhower at Columbia, and I know he was restless at Columbia. I can't help thinking about university presidencies and the story they tell about Woodrow Wilson. They asked him about his political experience, and he said, "Look, I never learned anything about politics after I left Princeton." Eisenhower, I think, was always restless at Columbia, and they were not his greatest years. The question was why he went to Columbia and I think he felt he had gone to the end of the line in the military. He always abhored and resented the idea that he would go into anything commerical, even a board of directors.

I remember within about an hour after he left the presidency a very close personal friend of his said, "Okay, Mr. President, you are out of the presidency. How about doing an ad for Studebaker?" You could just see the cold fury—it was a friendly letter but boy did it burn. And the idea that he would take this national reputation, which in a sense had been conferred on him through all his public service, and turn it into anything commercial really felt alien to him.

I think he looked at the position of Robert E. Lee and admired him almost as much as he admired George Washington. Those two really were great heroes of his. He saw Robert E. Lee going down to become a president of a college and he thought, well, this is something that I can do, in the footsteps of a man like Robert E. Lee. So he went to Columbia. But as you say, he felt restless there. It was not the greatest period in his life but I must say I think he really had an abiding respect for Columbia University, for its faculty, for what they were doing, and he also had a great respect for people who came out of the academic world who had exceptional talents. I've got a whole chapter about people with advanced degrees in order to prove that there were some around the White House.

QUESTION: I know that you do not excuse it, but I wonder if you would give us your own explanation for Eisenhower's failure—and you may do it in the book—to stand up for George Marshall, that famous Wisconsin address. That was a very uncharacteristic type of thing for him to do and I wondered what sort of explanation you could offer. There isn't an excuse for everything but there is an explanation.

MR. EWALD: I assume everybody knows the episode we are talking about because I really think you have to take this one apart, step by step. Let me say at the outset, it was a mistake, it was a terrible mistake.

Eisenhower regretted it. He was told it was a mistake; and people who were loyal to him, around him, knew it was a mistake. It went with him all through the rest of his life. He had to carry that with him, and it was one thing he was very defensive about, very uptight about when we wrote about it in *Mandate for Change* and *Waging Peace*.

Eisenhower was going into Wisconsin in the 1952 campaign in the month of October. He had told the political leaders in the state of Wisconsin he did not want to come in after the Republican primary in which Joe McCarthy would have been renominated for another term as senator. If he came in after the primary McCarthy would be a nominated candidate, and he, as the presidential nominee, would have to endorse him. He didn't want any part of that. He said, "I'll go in earlier before McCarthy is renominated; then I can't endorse anybody." There was a foul-up. The people scheduled him into Wisconsin after the primary against his will. He didn't want to go but he got scheduled in. Wisconsin had twelve electoral votes. He needed them. They thought, you know, it's going to be a tight race and we've got to go into Wisconsin. It was big Taft country—Taft had opposed Eisenhower— and it was an important state, a major state. So he went in.

Now, as he was getting ready to go into Wisconsin, Arthur Sulzberger of the *New York Times* sent him a paragraph, or they had a discussion, but at any rate they cooked up this idea that it would be just a great idea to get up in Milwaukee on the climactic night of the appearance in Wisconsin and hit Joe McCarthy right between the eyes, criticizing McCarthy for having, in effect, called General Marshall a traitor. And this paragraph was honed and polished, believe you me, by all kinds of liberal speechwriters, and it was in there. It was in there the day before Eisenhower went into Wisconsin. The night before they were going into Wisconsin, McCarthy flew to meet Eisenhower. He was going to ride on the train. He wanted a meeting with Eisenhower and Eisenhower called him into his hotel room. This was in Peoria, Illinois, and in the course of the next half hour Eisenhower gave him the worst kind of blistering tongue-lashing. One man who sat outside the room listening to this had never heard Eisenhower skin a man alive as violently as he skinned McCarthy, just the two of them in the room alone with one man listening outside. So McCarthy crawls out of the room and gets back on the train. They are riding the next morning into the state of Wisconsin, whistle-stopping at little places along the way with this Milwaukee speech scheduled for that night ready to come out. Various politicians honed in on the speech. They looked at it and said, "Great speech, General; but the Marshall paragraph, it's out of place. In the first place, several weeks ago out in Denver in a press conference you made absolutely clear what you thought of people who called Marshall a traitor.'' Eisenhower had gone on record and was very, very emphatic about it and there was no secret. ''So you made your position clear. What do you want to do now? You want to come into Wisconsin, which is a swing state, it could go either way. You've got a senatorial candidate sitting there on the stage. We are trying to hold the party together. The Taft floor manager came from Wisconsin. He even walked out of the campaign. We are trying to get the Taft people back so they'll swallow their pride and vote for you. And we're trying to carry this state for you, General. Now what are you going to do? You're going to hit your senatorial candidate right there in Milwaukee a second time, because you already hit him out in Denver and everybody knows where you stand. Please take that out of there.''

This went on all day and they bickered and believe me the forces lined up. So what did you have? You had on the one side the chairman of the National Committee. He was in favor of taking it out. Also, alongside of him you had the Republican prospective majority leader in the senate, William Knowland, who was riding the train. He favored taking the thing out. Who else? You had the Governor of Wisconsin, Walter Kohler, who had fought, bled, and died to get Eisenhower the nomination, against members of his own family. It really had been an awful battle and Walter said, ''I think you ought to take it out, to save Wisconsin.'' You had then General Wilton Persons, who had been General Marshall's legislative liaison chief during the whole war, a brilliant southern Alabama conservative, a genius in manipulating agreement on the Hill, and an Eisenhower stalwart, and Jerry Persons said, ''I personally told McCarthy what I think of his attacks on Marshall. I bitterly resent them.'' Marshall, to Jerry Persons, was a god, just as to Eisenhower. And he comes to Eisenhower and says, ''Take that paragraph out.'' So you've got all of these people on one side.

On the other side, back in New York, you have Arthur Sulzberger. You have Emmett Hughes, back in New York; he wasn't even there. You've got Harold Stassen, who probably wanted it in. He wasn't there. You've got C.D. Jackson, another liberal, very strong anti-McCarthyite. He wasn't there. Who was there? Two men. Bobby Cutler and Gabe Hauge. Gabriel Hauge later became chairman of Manufacturer's Hanover Trust in New York, but at that time he was an editorial writer for *Business Week* magazine with no clout at all. So that's your lineup around Eisenhower. And who's got the key vote? Sherman Adams. And Sherman Adams hated McCarthy's guts. He was absolutely loyal to Eisenhower and so he listens to these people, all of them, and he bites the bullet and he goes to see Eisenhower, with Persons, and Eisenhower sees them coming and he says, "What do you want me to do? Do you want me to take that paragraph out of there?" And they say, "Yes," and he said, "Okay, take it out." And it went out.

It was a mistake. You can take a paragraph out of the speech, except for one fact. And the one fact is that, meanwhile, back in the back cars with the press you've got campaign staff people talking to the *New York Times.* The *New York Times* people see Eisenhower and McCarthy get up at this little whistle-stop at the beginning, and they are both now on the train. So this guy, Bill Lawrence of the *New York Times,* a very, very avid, aggressive and wonderful reporter, very liberal and knowledgeable says, "Okay, Ike's endorsing McCarthy." But, Fred Seaton says, "Wait a minute don't print that. Just wait until tonight." Fred thinks the speech is done, it's set, it's in concrete. Eisenhower has gone through it, and nothing can stop it.

Lawrence had learned about that paragraph in the speech, so he knows about it. He didn't get it from Arthur Sulzberger, his boss at the *New York Times.* He didn't know beans about what the upper level of the *New York Times* had sent to the candidate. He was a working reporter. He got it from Seaton. He knew about the draft. Once he knew about the draft, it was public domain. So Bill Lawrence of the *New York Times* sits there, and he waits, and the paragraph gets taken out. They stencil it and hand a copy to Bill Lawrence. He looks at it and says, "Where is the Marshall paragraph?" And that's page one.

That's exactly what happened, with one additional addendum. There was that meeting at the Peoria Hotel between Eisenhower and McCarthy, all by themselves with one lone listener outside, the lone listener didn't talk to anybody as far as I know—with one exception, years later—until he talked to me and told me what happened. But of the other two participants in that meeting, Eisenhower and McCarthy, one of them never did say what had happened. The other guy, Joe McCarthy, went out and guess whom he talked to? Bill Lawrence of the *New York Times.* He said, "I got him to take that out last night in Peoria." The s.o.b. told Lawrence that. Excuse the language, but it really becomes awful at this point. That's exactly what happended. So, you get the story in the *New York Times:* McCarthy personally persuades Eisenhower to take that paragraph out. And there it goes.

I'll tell you one more thing about Joe McCarthy's talking to Bill Lawrence. Later on Bill Lawrence found there was a subcabinet officer, Harold Talbott, secretary of the air force, who was engaged in some chicanery, and he exposed him. His source was Joe McCarthy. Joe liked to talk to reporters. He got along well with them as drinking buddies and so on.

The other thing was that at the moment when they took that paragraph out—I asked Sherman Adams about this explicitly and I'm quite sure Eisenhower agreed—they did not know that the paragraph had gone public. In other words, they didn't know that they were now erasing a piece of the record that had already got out there and was going to come back to haunt them. They thought they were editing a draft, and believe me when you edit a draft you can put anything in there you want and you can take anything out you want and nobody needs to know or should know. I favor privacy in that respect. But this was unfortunate, and it was a terrible mistake. People ask me to this day about it.

QUESTION: With respect to Dulles as Eisenhower's secretary of state, what kind of input did he have?

MR. EWALD: Well, Eisenhower was not a vain man. He once told Emmett Hughes, "There is only one man in the United States really who knows more about foreign policy than Foster Dulles does, and that's me." He really felt that. Then there is another quote that Foster Dulles used to give. Foster Dulles would come to see Eisenhower and say, "You know we're the greatest team in the world. After all, you've been around, you've talked to all kinds of world leaders, you have been on the world stage and have been a world figure and you know everybody. And since 1905, I've been studying international relations. I've been really deeply and seriously and assiduously studying, and I think we're just the greatest team in the world." John Eisenhower sat back and listened to Foster Dulles' description of their teamwork and said, "Well, you could set it down this way. With your contacts and my brains we can't miss."

Now, Eisenhower and Dulles were like two peas in a pod. They started off at sword points. Dulles was not the easiest man to get to know. He was prickly, and he was concerned about his relationships with the President, and about having other advisors in there. All of that kind of stuff. A very, very jealous kind of man. They started off and worked through these problems. Eisenhower liked to listen to a variety of advisors, but as time went on, I think you really find these are two men who sat down and worked through these things together. They talked them out. He leaned on Foster Dulles. Foster Dulles was the secretary of state, there was no question about it. There was none of this quarreling with the national security advisor. The national security advisor, Bobby Cutler, never raised his head. He was no intrusion on the Eisenhower/Dulles relationship—and neither was Goodpaster, neither was Gordon Gray, and neither were any of these other people who served in that national security role in the White House. Dulles was number one in foreign policy and Eisenhower looked to him. He gave him the responsibility and Dulles knew he had it. If Dulles had ever felt he didn't have it, he would have quit. Eisenhower said he knew he would have quit. He was a big man, big enough to walk out of the office over a policy difference, or over the fact that he was not being accorded the responsibilities and the powers that were his in the office. So they worked minute by minute by phone, by memorandum, in person, worked through meetings day by day, the two of them, very, very closely and in very great detail on these international problems.

I never felt Foster Dulles was the power behind the throne, pulling the wool over Eisenhower's eyes. I do not believe that. I also believe that Eisenhower at times would defer to Dulles. He would argue with Dulles and Dulles would say, "No, it's going to be this way." Eisenhower would say, "I want it that way," and they would come to a fork in the road and Dulles would get his way. Not every time, but sometimes. Sometimes at those forks in the road I felt Eisenhower was right and Dulles was wrong. Eisenhower went the wrong way in leaning on his principal advisor. But that's the way he operated and I think the two men saw eye to eye and I do not see a dime's worth of difference. They say Dulles was trying to get us into Vietnam and Eisenhower was the man of peace trying to get us out. That's nonsense, it's really baloney if you read the records of the meetings and the conversation. It didn't happen like that.

QUESTION: You do say in the book, on the Suez Crisis, that Eisenhower was more concerned about the aftermath and about the Russians getting into Suez, about the consequences after the condemnation of the British and the French; and even that Eisenhower would have been willing to have the meeting with Eden and the French foreign minister. But, Dulles vetoed it, and he called back and told Eden not to come.

MR. EWALD: Yes. That's a key example. Eisenhower had talked to Anthony Eden a minute after Eden stopped the forward motion of their troops, and there was a truce. Eden and Mollet of France said, "We'll fly over tonight." You know, it's just like a family spat. You've got troops landing in there and the world's going to war and Anthony's calling up his old friend Ike and said, "We'll fly over this evening and polish this all up and get it all worked out." Eisenhower said, "Fine." He was ready to meet with Eden. Dulles was at Walter Reed having an operation and everyone went out to see Dulles and Dulles said, "No, it's the wrong timing." So Eisenhower had to get back on the phone to Eden, and it was not an easy thing to do, to say, "Cancel your plane reservation. You are not coming."

Now I will say the first thing Eisenhower wanted to do was to patch things up. It took him several months because, obviously, Eden went down the tube after Suez. Harold MacMillan, another great crony of Ike's, came in as prime minister and in March of 1957, about four months later, Eisenhower met with MacMillan at Bermuda to put the whole alliance back together again. This is a key example of where Dulles overruled Eisenhower on timing and Eisenhower deferred to it.

Another example was the student foreign exchange program. Eisenhower was so sick and tired of all this fiddling around with diplomatic negotiations and maneuvering and exchanging documents and proposals for ending testing and all that kind of thing. He said, "I'm so sick of dealing with old men set in their ways. What we really need is an enormous student exchange. With Russia, about twenty years ago, they had about twenty/twenty over there, twenty here." Eisenhower said, "I'm not talking about twenty. I'm talking about 5,000, 10,000, 15,000. Bring them over in huge numbers. Americans going to the Soviet Union. Russian students coming to the United States. Open the doors. Let them come in, and over time it will do a lot of good." The first person he checks this out with is J. Edgar Hoover. He gets J. Edgar Hoover on board. J. Edgar Hoover says, "It's a great idea. They aren't going to cause any trouble. We can take care of any of the malefactors," and he wasn't worried about it.

Then Eisenhower goes to Foster Dulles. Foster Dulles writhes and squirms and sends it around the State Department; it goes through bureau after bureau and comes back: "No, we can't do this because in the first place where are we going to put all these students, how are we going to give them all visas?" It was all passport stamping Mickey Mouse little objections, one thing after another. "We don't have 10,000 Americans who speak Russian, what are we going to do sending them over?" Eisenhower said, "Forget all that, just do it." And he got up to the place where he was going to make a major address. Arthur Larson really was getting ready to explode the speech and right behind him he had Milton Eisenhower who was gungho for the project, and right behind him he had another speechwriter, Kevin McCann who really thought the idea up in the first place. All three of them were just roaring down the way, and Eisenhower himself had stars in his eyes and said it was a great idea. Meanwhile, the State Department cut it to pieces. It breaks your heart, but in the end he bit his tongue. He leaned on and trusted his organization. He trusted the people he had delegated power to. He would take their advice over his own. He was not headstrong.

Goodpaster tells a perfect example. He said Ike came out of some meeting, on something he had done, and he was just furious, red-faced. He said, "You know, I get the best advisors I can get. I get the most brilliant people I can assemble. I listen to their advice and I even take their advice. But goddammit, I don't have to like it!" This was typical.

QUESTION: In all of these incidents I can see bubbling from the top the Eisenhower personality. I would be interested to find out why, and by what procedure, he took the almost unprecedented step of taking presidential responsibility for the U2 mission?

MR. EWALD: In the first place he didn't at the beginning, but things got out of control. The minute you lose a plane, one of these so called "weather planes," you put out a cover story. So they put out the cover story; we're up there looking at the clouds or doing something scientific. This kind of got out of hand. They didn't know. You see Eisenhower thought all along that he had been told by Allen Dulles that no American pilot would ever be taken alive. They won't capture the pilot, they won't capture the equipment, they won't have any evidence. Therefore if you lose a plane you can tell the cover story. It was kind of a knee-jerk thing. And then the State Department had put out another story. But basically what happened was that Khrushchev had Francis Gary Powers in the flesh, and he had his baggage along with him. He had parts of the plane. All this had come crashing down in the Soviet Union. In a way, Allen Dulles had not really told the President what would happen.

They were caught red-handed and at that point Eisenhower had to make up his mind what to say. He was advised, "Just tell them, Ike, you didn't have anything to do with this. Tell them it was done by the CIA or the military." He objected to doing that for two reasons. In the first place, it wasn't true, and it was far from being true. There was not a single flight of the U2 that was ever made that was not personally designed in the Oval Office with a map laid out on the desk by Eisenhower himself, tracing the route, and giving the times when he would permit the flight to take place. He would tell the CIA, "Okay, I'll give you a week. You are going to make this flight within this next week and you can do that. After a week you have no more permission. You come back here and get another permission for another flight." And that's the way they worked. They worked for four years that way. The

Russians knew about the first flight, incidentally. They saw it, but they couldn't do anything about it, they couldn't shoot it down. So, Ike personally was in it very deep. He ran the thing himself personally in the Oval Office.

Secondly, if he had said he didn't know about it there are two things underneath, and this is the secondary thing. Underneath, he bridled at the idea that Sherman Adams was running the government, Foster Dulles was running the government, other people were doing things, or that he wasn't and he resented that. And I think that contributed a little something. The big thing was that he did not want to tell the Soviet Union the United States military is out of control, that they are doing things as wild as this without the President's knowledge and without his approval. You are going to have a summit meeting with a figurehead who doesn't even know about these flights. So, he was caught red-handed. He admitted it. He stepped up to it. He wasn't apologizing either. He said, "We needed to know what they had so we knew that we didn't have to spend three or six or eight or ten billion dollars more in defense, or that we didn't have to go slam-bang out for a twenty billion dollar air raid shelter program. We didn't need it because we knew they didn't have the things that they claimed that they had and we knew it by taking these little pictures." And he had no apologies whatsoever in this world for having made those flights.

What was terribly unfortunate was the timing of this thing. In retrospect he probably shouldn't have had the flight on the eve of the summit conference. Sure, they'd flown for four years and hadn't had one shot down, and all of a sudden there it was. So that's why I think he did it. He stepped right up to it and I think in the end it was the honest thing.

NARRATOR: There is at least one difference between Bill Ewald and General Eisenhower. Maybe there are many, but in the book you point out that Eisenhower truly enjoyed himself most with men who had been great successes, tycoons in industry or government, that he judged people a little by the results of their life efforts. He wasn't quite as much at home with intellectuals. I think what we've listened to this morning proves that Bill Ewald is the opposite. The one unfortunate dimension of all this, the book and what we've heard this morning, is that if he couldn't stay at Harvard we really wish that he might have come to Virginia because he certainly has all the marks of a great teacher. We're most grateful.

EISENHOWER'S
WORLD VIEW
Arthur Larson

NARRATOR: We are very happy to welcome you to another of our Forums on the Eisenhower presidency. We have, as you know, published a little profile of the Roosevelt presidency based on discussions within this room with intimates of Franklin Delano Roosevelt. We're undertaking to do the same thing with the Eisenhower presidency. Last week Karl Harr discussed national security policymaking in the Eisenhower administration. Sherman Adams and Milton Eisenhower have both committed themselves to be part of this profile. As Mr. Larson said a moment ago, it would be a coup if Sherman Adams will come out of retirement for this discussion.

We are especially pleased that an old friend and fellow South Dakotan, Arthur Larson, can be with us today. His parents and my parents lived within six blocks of one another in Sioux Falls, South Dakota so we have common roots of which neither of us are in any way ashamed.

MR. LARSON: It's better to be from there than there.

NARRATOR: It seems to me what makes the Eisenhower profile project timely is that there are a number of leads that appear in books that have been published. As you know, Fred Greenstein did a fair amount of his research on *The Hidden Hand Presidency* at the Miller Center, although his permanent position is at Princeton. Arthur Larson, in addition to publishing a book which Mr. Eisenhower used to like to quote and have at his bedside at Walter Reed, *A Republican Looks At His Party,* also published a little later in 1968 *Eisenhower: The President Nobody Knew,* which in many ways foreshadows and lays bare some of the same things that are said in the later Greenstein book. But it also, as the Greenstein book does not, deals with policy as Mr. Larson viewed it in the Eisenhower administration. I've looked in the last couple of days at a third book, Emmett Hughes' *Ordeal of Power,* which is also a contribution.

But from them all, one gets intimations of what becomes in the last few years a major thesis, namely that there was a political purpose and political skill at the heart of the Eisenhower administration that sometimes is underestimated and that Eisenhower himself was far more conscious and active in the achievement of these purposes and far more discreet in the choice of those to help him execute these ends. Both Mr. Larson and Mr. Hughes in their books talk about their role as speechwriters and the extent to which key issues were formulated and developed in that capacity without reference necessarily to some of the people like Mr. Dulles and Mr. Humphrey who were out front in Cabinet positions.

In any event it seems to us it is especially timely to explore the question of Eisenhower's World View. Arthur Larson is well known in the legal field. He began his great work on workmen's compensation, which now has reached the proportions of a major ten-volume treatise, when he was at the Cornell Law School. He was dean of the University of Pittsburgh Law School. He was called to Washington soon thereafter. He was under secretary in the Labor Department in Washington but quite early was tapped by Mr. Eisenhower, for example, to write Eisenhower's acceptance speech for delivery at the Cow Palace and a long succession of speeches thereafter. I think he saw the workings of the White House from inside. He left Washington in 1968 and became a distinguished international law scholar at Duke University but has continued his life-long interest in the workers' compensation area where he is undoubtedly one of the world's, if not *the* world's, foremost authorities in this area. It's a great pleasure to have him as one of our early visitors to discuss with you the Eisenhower presidency.

MR. LARSON: I agree emphatically that your timing on choosing Eisenhower as your third subject was nothing short of inspired. It's not only because this is an anniversary of sorts—it hardly seems possible that it's thirty years since Eisenhower took over—but this change in the attitude of scholars, particularly historians and political scientists and other academics, toward Eisenhower has reached such proportions that it is now routinely called "revisionism" by historians. Nobody is enjoying it more than I am.

When I was in the White House, in the Eisenhower Cabinet, I was troubled by the fact that my natural associates, the people I felt most at home with, the academics and scholars, almost uniformly felt contempt for Eisenhower if not something worse. I kept arguing with them, and I kept saying, "Look, you can't judge a President in the abstract. Just wait awhile and see what successive Presidents can make out of this troubled world. Let's talk about it three or four Presidents from now and then see how well Eisenhower did." Well, that's exactly what has happened. Several presidencies have gone by and we are now witnessing a flood of books, not just the ones that Ken mentioned but a whole succession of them. Every book that has come out on Eisenhower has been favorable. There is the Greenstein book. There's William Ewald's book, a beautiful book—one of the best. There's a book by Robert Divine called *Eisenhower in the Cold War*. There's a book by Kaufman called *Trade or Aid: Eisenhower's Economics* and a big book by Herbert Parmet, the historian; a book by James Killian, the scientist; a book by Steve Neil; and they're generally favorable. Not entirely so, of course.

There is a very interesting article by a historian, Stephen Ambrose, in the *New Republic* in 1981. He said in this article that just after the Eisenhower administration a poll had been taken of a hundred and some historians, and in rating Eisenhower among all the Presidents of history, they put him practically at the bottom of the list. Today, said Stephen Ambrose, if the same poll were taken he was confident that they would rate Eisenhower easily in the first ten and probably in the first five. That is remarkable revisionism. In fact it has been so abrupt and vigorous a swing of the pendulum that inevitably the pendulum is going to be arrested and swing the other way. Stephen Ambrose in his *New Republic* article has adumbrated this. Indeed, the article says in a footnote that he is preparing a definitive biography of Eisenhower. I haven't seen it yet but toward the end of a long and otherwise complimentary piece in the *New Republic* he says, "Well, I think maybe revisionism has gone far enough," which is a sort of warning perhaps that when his book comes out he may try to apply a few correctives and so we will have a revision of the revisionism. But in any event the place of Eisenhower in history is going to be entirely different and unrecognizeably more favorable than it at one time appeared to be.

In trying to identify what made Eisenhower different, if not better but we'll just say for the moment different, one didn't have to look very far. Eisenhower was the only President of what by any definition could be called the modern era who did not reach that eminence by the route of practical politics. Every one of the others, Roosevelt, Truman, Nixon, Johnson, Kennedy, Ford, Carter, and now Reagan all were practical politicians. A very great part of the Eisenhower record can be explained to a considerable extent on this ground.

Eisenhower could be said to be a man who made his decisions on the basis of principle rather than politics. It's perfectly true, as Ken has mentioned, that it's being increasingly brought out that he was not politically naive. He was politically shrewd and as the events demonstrated, his political judgment was far better than that of the practical politicians around him. But when I say he was not a politician I mean that he wasn't motivated by political considerations. Every other President that we've had, at least until Reagan, and I'll come to that a little later, I would class as a person who was motivated by politics, but not Eisenhower.

Principles may be a little bit too pretentious a word for what I have in mind. But I noticed very early in my association with Eisenhower how often he said, "I always," or "I never," and then he would dredge down into some general principle of life or rule of life and come up with his decision. And this applied to major decisions as well as trivial ones. He did like the word "principles." He used it very frequently. I remember when we were preparing the acceptance speech that Ken mentioned, he started right out by saying, "You must live by principles; principles, not expediency." For the most part it served him in good stead; once in a while it tripped him up. I have to temper this characterization a little bit, because if I said he was a man of principle it obviously wouldn't explain a lot of the things he decided and did. He was also a pragmatist, as every President has to be sooner or later. But I would distinguish him from the others by saying he was a principled pragmatist and they were political pragmatists.

Let me give you two examples of how he made decisions by principle: one monumental, one trivial. The big one had to do with the decision not to become involved in Vietnam in 1954 before the fall of Dien Bien Phu.

I was unusually fortunate to have a ringside seat for this entire story. I had come to the Labor Department in early March of 1954, just when the Dien Bien Phu crisis was heating up. James P. Mitchell, the secretary of labor, who next to Eisenhower was the most magnificent public servant I have ever known, had a spell of bad health about that time and, as under secretary I became acting secretary and had to attend Cabinet meetings. I found myself sitting at a table something like this, a little larger, and there was the President and there was the secretary of state and there I was and there was Nixon and the secretary of the treasury. For several weeks in a row I watched before my very eyes, as a real novice at this business, the decision of peace or war made right on the spot. As a beginner you can imagine how that impressed me. The meetings were much longer than the usual Cabinet meetings. The discussions would go around the table. They would always start with the military analysis. Down there were the Joint Chiefs of Staff, and we would get an assessment by General Ridgway and General Persons and Admiral Radford and others of how the French generals were doing. It is impossible to reproduce here even in these permissive times the language that was used about the idiocy, the unspeakable clumsiness, and stupidity of the French generals in getting themselves boxed in in Dien Bien Phu. I could just see the French generals getting flunked out of West Point and Annapolis.

Then the talk would go around the table—practically no one spoke up for intervention. Then as often happens in discussions of this kind all of a sudden there would be dead silence. Nobody had anything more to say and everybody would turn and look at the President. He would say, "Not this week, thank God" and walk out. That went on for three weeks and the issues were extremely complicated. An enormous amount was at stake.

Later on I was at my first stag dinner and I found myself standing in the corner with the President and a Catholic priest, just the three of us, after dinner. The priest said to Eisenhower, "Tell me, why did you decide not to intervene in Indochina?" The President said, "Nobody asked us." Three words summed it all up—"Nobody asked us." I thought, was it as simple as that? And I got to thinking, well, he's right. Nobody asked us. So if we had gone in, as I regret to say later happened, but if we had gone in unilaterally we would have contributed to the slaughter of thousands because *we* wanted to, not because somebody asked us. Nobody of any faction among the Indochinese asked us, and that was what counted with Eisenhower.

The French hadn't really asked us. That takes a little explanation but they really hadn't, in any acceptable way. They would have welcomed our troops and our help, but on one condition—they had to be under French command. Well, can you imagine, after listening to this discussion of this supernatural idiocy of these generals, that we would put our boys under the command of such imbeciles? Certainly not, that was absolutely out of the question. And they stuck to that until almost a day before Dien Bien Phu fell and then they came off of it but by then it was too late. By that time it didn't make any difference, principally because the other condition never came close to being fulfilled. Eisenhower said, "The request has got to reflect the wishes of the population," and of course the French couldn't have cared less about that. An absolute condition was that the end result of the war had to be independence for the Indochinese and the French never came close to that. There were other conditions as well but those were the main ones. So in a way it was not a very difficult decision for Eisenhower. He summed it all up by saying, "Nobody asked us."

A minor example: Eisenhower disliked comparatives and he was death on superlatives. Never would use them. The reason was General MacArthur. I have to toss in a little aside here about General MacArthur because when we were working during the 1956 campaign I was writing about half his speeches and Emmett Hughes was writing the other half. He was getting the reputation of being inarticulate and not being able to put together a coherent sentence. He was sort of chuckling over that because by contrast people would say, "Look at the ringing oratory and the beautiful phraseology of General MacArthur, for example." Eisenhower said to me, "Do you know who wrote General MacArthur's speeches? I did." So he had some idea of the MacArthur style. MacArthur always wanted to say, "Never before in history has an operation of such magnitude," or "General so and so is the greatest field commander in history," or "General so and so is the greatest strategist in history. . . ." Well, quite apart from this being alien to Eisenhower's nature, this overblown exaggerated style, it being impossible to prove the proposition that was being stated, he had a practical reason. He said, "If you say that General so and so is the greatest field commander of all time you make one general happy and a thousand angry who take themselves to be within the comparison." In the little minor items of style, as well as major earthshaking decisions, he always had some kind of principle like that to draw on.

I've said that Eisenhower was completely nonpolitical in the sense that in the scale of motivations for a decision, political advantage, the effect on votes and so forth, was not only very low on the list, it was absolutely non-existent. If you wanted to get thrown out of the Oval Room, all you had to say is, "Look, Mr. President, this is going to cost you votes in West Virginia." Well, you wouldn't get past "West"—you'd be out. He was reminiscing one afternoon about Senator Taft. He said "You know, Taft was more liberal than me on domestic issues, like federal education aid and so forth." That was the example he was bringing out. He said, "Taft wanted to have federal education aid to all states whether they needed it or not." Eisenhower said to Taft, "Well, why should we take five dollars in taxes and then nick off 40 cents for bureaucrat salaries and give $4.60 right back to the same state, like New York." Taft said, "You have to do it to get votes." Eisenhower said, "In that case, the hell with it."

I remember I was preparing a speech during the 1956 campaign when I had to learn this. I had the idea that when you went to a particular constituency and there was a congressman standing for Congress at the time and he was sitting right there in the bunting-draped platform, you out of courtesy said something nice about the congressman. Nothing could be a more standard order of procedure in political speeches. So, thinking that this was expected of me, I wrote a little paragraph ahead of the speech about Congressman So and So. He got out the blue pencil and said, "What in hell is that doing in there?" I said, "There's the congressional election on there." He said (these are out of my little notebook), "Frankly I don't care too much about the congressional elections." I learned very, very quickly.

I should really have gotten a feeling for this when I had my first interview with James P. Mitchell. I hardly knew who James P. Mitchell was and I was up in the Cathedral of Learning in Pittsburgh minding my own business, trying to be a dean, when I got this mysterious call to come to see Secretary Mitchell. It appeared that this one job of under secretary was open. This was early 1954, and so all the political appointments had been long since filled, all of the good ones. An under secretaryship is considered quite a plum, and practically every congressman and senator had his own candidate for it, so this had to be handled rather carefully. He called me in and we talked for about twenty minutes. Finally he said, "How would you like to be under secretary?" I said, "I'd love it." We shook hands and I had headed for the door and got partly out the door when he said, "Oh, by the way"—and he turned kind of green—"are you a Republican?" And I assured him I was securely registered in Cayuga Heights as a Republican and he looked relieved. But it had never occurred to him to ask in advance. That was characteristic not just of the President but it permeated the administration. As a matter of fact he disliked professionalism in politics. This is not very generally known but he favored a constitutional amendment limiting senators to two terms and congressmen to three or four. He liked this idea of a government in which lay persons came and went instead of having somebody dug in for a life-long job as a politician.

Now having said that, of course, then we come around to the other side of the coin, which is that nonpolitics is sometimes very good politics. I think this is why so many people, starting with Murray Kempton in his famous article in *Esquire* which was an adumbration of all this, and then Fred Greenstein and others have pointed out the sort of higher level of political judgment that he seemed to have. Actually in some ways, if you weren't blinded by the fact that you were a dedicated partisan politician, it was pretty simple. The Republican party, during the entire time we are talking about, represented sixteen percent of registered voters. Now how are you going to win the White House if, with sixteen percent of people registered for your party, you go out and make the theme of your campaign a wholesale attack on all Democrats? It was very clear to Eisenhower you couldn't possibly do that. One of the first things he said in connection with the acceptance speech, "I will not attack Democrats as such, I will not say that the Republicans have a monopoly on peace as an issue. . ." and so on. In retrospect it seems fairly clear, the only way you could win was to win over what he would call "discerning Democrats and independents." That's his phrase right out of the acceptance speech.

There is of course the criticism, and this is perhaps one of the principal things that Nixon held against him, that while winning two more or less landslide elections he never was able to transfer this support to the Republican party as such. He never rebuilt the Republican party into a majority party as, say, Roosevelt had done to the Democratic party. I don't want to spend too much time on that but I really don't think that was primarily Eisenhower's fault. I don't say that this was a top priority of his but he had led the party to two very substantial victories as a result of identifying the Republican party with what we called modern Republicanism, a number of moderately liberal stands on most domestic issues. But the trouble was that as fast as Eisenhower would go out and say, "This is where I stand, this is Republicanism," Senators Goldwater and Mundt and Bridges and others would come along and say, "No, that isn't Republicanism, this chap is a freak." What's the public supposed to believe if the Republicans themselves keep saying that isn't Republicanism? I think the fault lies more with the right wing Republicans for repudiating what was handed to them on a golden platter.

Having set the stage with this contrast of political pragmatism and principled pragmatism, I'd like to try out this idea of principled pragmatism on what is unquestionably the most pressing issue of the time and perhaps has been ever since Eisenhower, and that is the issue of military power particularly in relation to a balanced budget. The word "power" is a very fashionable word, even now. It was even more so some years ago. Power, power, power was all you heard. Richard

Neustadt and others stressed that what you had to know is how to use power, and implied sometimes that perhaps Eisenhower didn't. Well, it kind of reminded me of a little incident. I was watching one of my grandchildren playing with some construction blocks one day. He had built a rather ominous, menacing-looking thing which I couldn't quite identify. I looked down to him and said, "What's that?" He said, "That's a power." I said, "Why is it a power?" He said, "Because it goes pow!" I got to thinking that is a perfect definition of power according to a very large part of the people who have been making policy in the meantime.

Eisenhower's concept of power was extremely sophisticated and very complicated and made up of a lot of ingredients, of which raw military power was certainly only one. His definiton of power was simple: Power is the ability to produce a desired result. And judged by that definition he did pretty well. He closed out one stubborn war and, in the same stormy world that gave us Korea, Vietnam, and all the rest, no other war broke out. Not a drop of blood was shed.

I've tried to disentangle this complicated concept of power as he used it. I'm just going to catalog quite quickly, I hope, some of the ingredients. He had a model which more than one person has reproduced and it went like this. He said never use force in international affairs. Never! Never use force in today's world in international affairs. But if you do, use it overwhelmingly. That obviously has got two pieces to it. First, never use force. Why did he feel so strongly about that? It's obvious he had presided over the greatest war and greatest victory in history. He had had all of these military toys at his fingertips to play with. He did not need any more playing with military toys, thank you, he had had enough of that. Along came a succession of civilian Presidents, and I honestly got the impression sometimes that they just couldn't stand the idea of having the greatest military machine in the history of civilization and then getting pushed around by a little half-country in Southeast Asia. But he had been through all that. And as a result also I am convinced that he placed a much higher value on the component of loss of human life than anybody else because he had lived through that, too, on the largest scale. It didn't come as easy for him as somebody else who might say, "Well, we'll throw in so many thousand troops here or there," knowing that many of them are going to get killed. That would have been extremely hard for him to do and he never did it.

The second component was, if you use force use it unanswerably. He reached for force only once or twice in his presidency and it was of course only a demonstration. Not a shot was fired. The most remarkable exhibition was the landing on the beaches of Beirut. Back in those days Beirut was the paradise of the universe. When I visited it in 1958 there were these green hills, this azure sea, the beautiful beaches, not to mention the most magnificent shops in the world, the American University flourishing, and so on. They had achieved for the first time in history what seemed to be the perfect balance of power for a multiethnic community. They had proportional representation in their parliament, Moslems and Christians. As for the administrative setup, the president was always a Christian, the prime minister was always a Moslem and so on down the line. It was all working beautifully. Chamoun was president, Sami Sul was prime minister. I met with them both in 1958, and both were very proud that they had achieved this balance. It's heartbreaking to see what has happened since.

Something like this almost happened in the Eisenhower administration. It was during the time of Nasser. Egyptian troops and others were filtering over the mountains. It was getting worse and worse until this government was really in peril. A telegram came in from Chamoun and Sami Sul and the Cabinet asking for immediate military assistance because otherwise their government was going to go under. I watched this with my own eyes happen. A telegram one day, the next morning Eisenhower called in the National Security Council, Joint Chiefs of Staff, joint leadership of Congress, right down the line. By 4:30 in the afternoon, sixteen thousand troops were on the move, including contingents from Okinawa, and an Honest John rocket battalion with nuclear capability from Turkey, ships, and planes. They came up to the beach in an overwhelming force and that was it. There was no more trouble. The invaders disappeared.

We had some very interesting arguments during that time that rather foreshadowed the future, especially with General Maxwell Taylor, who kept arguing that we ought to send our troops up into Beirut and back into the mountains and really drive these fellows out. Eisenhower said absolutely not. He said, "They stay on the beach so they can get away just as fast as they can if anything goes wrong." And he said, "If, with all that support, Camille Chamoun and Sami Sul don't survive, then maybe they don't deserve to." But it worked. He wasn't going to get bogged down in street corner fighting or any of that sort of thing à la Vietnam. As soon as it was possible to do so he turned the whole operation over to the United Nations as he had promised to do from the beginning.

Contrast this with what happened in Vietnam. In Vietnam, in the hands of people who didn't have this kind of experience and this kind of motto, there were less troops put into Vietnam in the first three years of our military involvement than there were put on the beach of Lebanon in this one lightning stroke within a week. They put in a thousand troops, we put in two thousand; so they put in two thousand, five hundred and we put in three thousand. This is why we got defeated by a half country, a tiny underdeveloped half country, because we did it on their terms. They couldn't have put in an overwhelming force. We could, and didn't do it from the beginning. It is what you might call the vaccination principle—if you just keep putting in small enough injections, it's not only tolerated, it actually makes you more healthy. That is what happened in Vietnam by contrast with the Eisenhower principle: use force overwhelmingly.

There are many other large and small illustrations of Eisenhower's personal application of this principle. The way he closed out Korea, for example. At the time I first revealed this I thought it was alright to do so after ten years and it is now general knowledge. He told me one afternoon that what really closed out Korea, which had been stubbornly failing to go away, was that he passed word through a third country that if they didn't settle up we would drop the atomic bomb. Now, nobody will ever know whether he would have done it or not. Bluff or no bluff it worked, and the Korean war was closed out shortly after. To take another little illustration: Eisenhower used to like to walk around Morningside Heights when he was president of Columbia, and even back in those days it was a bit of a risk. When he took his stroll he carried a .38 revolver. He was licensed to carry it and he knew how to use it and if some punks had come up and attempted to mug him he would have used force overwhelmingly.

Little Rock. Here he was finally challenged to a showdown. What did he do? He sent down to North Carolina and airlifted an overwhelming force of the Army. And that was it. It was all over in a moment.

A second principle which I can identify is what you might call the conservation of power. You don't use it everywhere. He dropped a curious remark once during the very critical period of August 1956. It was critical in two respects. Stassen was trying to dump Nixon, and Nasser was about to nationalize the Suez Canal. I walked into his office just as Stassen came out from his historic interview. Eisenhower was pacing around and he said, "Art, have you ever been Nasserized and Stassenized at the same time?" Well, the Nasserized part of it was that Nasser was really throwing his weight around and it turned out he did indeed nationalize the canal. Eisenhower gave me a little sermon on what he called "the tyranny of the weak." He then really pulled me up in my seat by saying, "I guess we'll just have to put up with it." When I contrast that with President Kennedy's inauguration address:

Anytime, anywhere, anybody asks for us we will be there to defend freedom, etc. . . . Lyndon Johnson said exactly the same thing. Whenever freedom is endangered anywhere in the world we will be there. And of course you know what it has gotten us into, starting with Vietnam. This doesn't mean that you are going to be indifferent to all these things. Quite the contrary. Every conceivable kind of action should be considered, diplomatic, economic, UN, regional organizations, CIA, anything, but not open military action.

Another principle involved was sheer economics. I don't know how many times he's pointed this out to me. The toughest thing he had to put over every year was foreign aid. It was never popular. It never got more than forty percent in the popular polls. He believed passionately we had to have more. One argument was pure economics. He said it costs $424 a year to hire a Greek soldier and $3,500 to hire an American. It was as simple as that.

Closely related to that is retaining the choice of weapons. Late in the Eisenhower administration Max Taylor wrote a naughty book called *The Uncertain Trumpet,* which reflected a profound difference in military strategy. Taylor and a number of other people believed that we should have a military preparation for every kind of war, including brushfire wars, and counter-insurgency. Counter-insurgency was very fashionable in those days. Eisenhower said, "No. If we prepare for these wars we'll wind up fighting them. And since I'm not going to fight this kind of war I'm not going to prepare for it. Then I won't be able to fight them." This was the big showdown with Max Taylor. Max Taylor of course left and came back with Kennedy. His policies took over and we decided to fight brushfire wars and we got Vietnam.

World opinion is a source of power. This sounds perhaps like something that might be in a speech but not be very real. It was very real. I could give you many illustrations of it, but here is just one. A curious thing happened when the original vote took place on sending United Nations forces into the Congo. Russia was bitterly opposed to this, but voted for it six times. Later it refused to pay for it. Why did they vote for it? Because if they hadn't they would have alienated the whole Third World overnight and they didn't want to do that. World opinion.

Another factor: a country's moral posture is a source of power. He believed this thoroughly. We must maintain our posture, which I regret to say that we have not, as the friend of independence, the friend of the underdogs. Somehow we had been getting into the position of always being on the side of the establishments, the country club sets in Latin America and so on.

I remember once I was sitting there by his side and Dulles called and Eisenhower hung up and he said, "Goddamn it, we've got to lose either Tunisia or France. Bourguiba is the best friend we've got. I've just given the French an ultimatum, I'm really fed up with the goddamn French." And a little later he said, "I wish for once we would get on the side of independence in advance." That's really where his heart was. He had big arguments with Churchill about this. The condition about intervening in Indochina that I mentioned at the beginning is a perfect illustration of that.

Let me come to my main point, for present purposes, to tie in with what's going on now, because it is so intensely relevant to what's going on in the Reagan administration. Eisenhower believed very strongly that a strong military defense required a sound economy. Therefore, if expanding the military budget would threaten a sound economy he refused to expand the military budget. He was under intense pressure from all sides including, of course, Kennedy and many others, some in his own party, saying as we hear so much now that he's putting the budget ahead of our national security. But a weak economy was a weak defense. He stuck to his guns, he listened to all the talk of a bomber gap first, later of a missile gap. As it turns out, as everybody knows now, there wasn't any missile gap and there wasn't any bomber gap. He inherited a $50 billion defense budget. He immediately cut it to $40 billion and it stayed at $40 billion throughout his administration. I read in the *Washington Post* this morning that, if the Reagan military budget goes through, it will reach $386 billion in 1988—that's ten times the Eisenhower military budget.

He had some advantages, of course. He knew the Pentagon budget better than anybody in the Pentagon. He knew where everything was. He knew the Russian setup better than anybody. I remember once a senator explaining, "How the hell can I argue with Eisenhower about military matters?" And he used that advantage. In 1956 he wrote a letter to his friend Hazlitt, I'll give you the full quote because it is so portentous: "Some day there is going to be a man sitting in my present chair who has not been raised in the military services and who will have little understanding of where slashes in their estimates can be made with little or no damage. If that should happen while we still have the state of tension that now exists in this world I shudder to think what could happen to this country." Very prophetic. A $100 billion deficit.

That's $30 billion more than our budget was in the last year of the Eisenhower administration. Of course there are some things wrong with that comparison but it's close enough.

In conclusion I'd like to bring Reagan into this. Where does he fit in with this pattern? Not quite like the other politicians and not certainly like Eisenhower. I know the Reaganites would like to say that Reagan is the heir, the resurrection of Eisenhower. With all this popularity that Eisenhower is enjoying he'd like to get on the band wagon. But what's the difference? The difference is that Reagan is an ideologist, which is quite different from being a man of principle. An ideologist is somebody that has a ready-made set of ideas, a complete set handed to him by somebody else which he accepts as a total package. The man of principle is somebody who has individually within himself worked out from experience, from training, from morals some basic rules of life that he can adapt if necessary to new situations. I suppose the most troublesome thing about being an ideologist is that they are perfectly capable of holding in their mind at the same thing two utterly opposed and inconsistent ideas and it doesn't seem to bother them. Now I don't want anybody to misunderstand me by bringing in the example of Communism because nobody is going to accuse Reagan of that—yet, anyway. Mr. Welch of the Birch Society accused Eisenhower of being a Communist and they may get around to Reagan yet. But so far I don't want any such implication as that. But it illustrates the present point. A Communist is a person who believes, first, that the state should own everything, all the instruments of production, and run everything, and, second, that the state will wither away. They're quite content with the two ideas side by side. Reagan is quite content to say that we absolutely must have a balanced budget to have a strong economy, at the same time we absolutely must expand the military even if it shatters the budget. They just sit there side by side. Eisenhower put the two together. If the military budget threatened the balance of the budget the military budget had to give, at least up to a point, until he got a reasonable balance. That's the difference.

Because ideology is all self-contained and more or less secondhand, when something goes wrong and the ideology doesn't work out the way it's supposed to, the ideologist doesn't know what to do. Both your political pragmatist and your principled pragmatist will roll with the punch. They'll think of something and they will maintain their leadership. The ideologist has leadership snatched away from him because he doesn't know what to do next. Witness the jobs bill. In the first place the bill has been forced upon Reagan. He said a year or so ago he'd absolutely veto it. And he has embraced it now as his own, which doesn't deceive anybody. But beyond that there is phase II that Congressman Michelle was talking about this morning which goes way beyond this and is being sponsored by a lot of Republicans as well as Democrats. In other words, Congress has now taken the lead in this entire jobs picture.

To sum up, if Reagan's presidency is a matter of comparative performance, then the longer Reagan goes on the better the comparison will look, and we may not have a revision of the revisionism after all.

QUESTION: Mr. Larson, I wholeheartedly agree with your general view of the thrust of the revisionary trends that are going on among historians and political scientists. There is one area, one major area in the Eisenhower administration that, it seems to me, has not been subject to that revision. I ask it as a sympathetic question that perhaps with your law background and your intimate knowledge of what went on, you may want to give us your understanding of Eisenhower's views on his Supreme Court appointments, particularly the often reported comment that after having appointed Earl Warren he felt it was one of the major mistakes that he made during his administration. I'm simply reflecting what is often reported. What is your view on that kind of controversy and do you have any insight on his view on this topic?

MR. LARSON: Yes, as a matter of fact. Actually this is a case where one wisecrack tossed off has outweighed all the other facts that are available and that are now beginning to come out. I don't have them all at my fingertips, but they are in this succession of books, quite a bit in Herbert Parmet's book, in William Ewald's book, and in the *New Republic* article. Actually Eisenhower all along had a very high opinion of Warren. I remember one time when he was being asked about people who would be the most suitable candidates for President. Rather early, this was. Warren was one of the first three that he mentioned. I think that basic admiration remained throughout. He apparently did toss off this one crack about "This is the worst mistake I've made" or something like that. But he got over that and retained on the whole a very favorable attitude toward Warren so far as I know.

I was the first one, I believe, in my book to come right out and say that Eisenhower simply did not agree with Brown against the Board of Education. This is one of the bombshells the book contained. Eisenhower was still alive at the time and he was very ill. Some of the people around him didn't like it very much, but I felt I had to put in the rough with the smooth. I had been called in right after Little Rock because the President was about to meet with several governors including Luther Hodges and several others about what to do next in the civil rights picture. So just the two of us were sitting there discussing Brown against the Board of Education and he rather shook me up by saying, "Frankly, I don't agree with it." Now, nobody knew of this. The public never knew this certainly. So like a good lawyer I began to explain to him the legal rationale. He said, "I know all that, I've studied that." And he did, he knew it through and through. He just didn't agree with it. But that didn't mean he wasn't going to enforce it, as of course he did vigorously in Little Rock. But what he would not do was go out and crusade for it. This is what he has been criticized for. The reason he didn't crusade for it was not just the issue itself, on which he would have been hypocritical if he did, but that he didn't believe the President should go around crusading for any good causes that weren't assigned to him by the Constitution as part of his duties.

Here again was something that set him off completely from other Presidents. His concept of the presidency was that its inherent constitutional powers were so awesome that the President himself had to go out of his way to limit his own power rather than try to expand it. He has, if he wants to use it, so many extracurricular ways to parlay this position to get powers that are not assigned him by the Constitution that a person who was tempted to grab power has all kinds of opportunities, as we know, and some of them have done it. So he deliberately limited himself. He didn't think it was his job to go out and carry a banner for some cause, whether it was civil rights or anything else. Well, I argued with him about that but that was what he believed. I had to respect him. In other words very frequently it wasn't because he didn't believe in a particular cause that he didn't assume this role. He just didn't believe it was what the President was supposed to be doing.

QUESTION: I hope that you might be helpful at least to some of us in trying to understand better another area of Mr. Eisenhower's presidency. The revisionist writings do point out certain things, his amazing popularity which of course we all knew, but beyond that a certain amount of political skill which we didn't know, the fact that he worked hard, that he paid attention to details, that he went to many meetings. I've read those Hazlitt letters in the library. They are absolutely magnificent and your quotation there was simply marvelous and they're simply loaded with them, showing a man who has a good grasp of things, who was intensively moderate and sensible in all of his attitudes. Now of course these are the reasons why I think the recent research on Mr. Eisenhower has permitted him to go rather high in the polls.

But that leaves unanswered for me the question of policy because one thing that these writings did not do is to deal very much with policy and yet it's the policy that among us lives. That is what one inherits, that's what one leaves to successive administrations. For example, look at the Roosevelt administration—he has all these skills, too, but it is sometimes difficult to find much relationship to those skills and his popularity and his foreign policies. Mr. Eisenhower inherited a body of foreign policy all rather well in place from Mr. Truman. They were filtered through eight years of his leadership and at the end you have policies that others inherit, and among them non-recognition of China, pursuit of liberation in Eastern Europe, a tremendous commitment to Vietnam, no preparations made either for getting out or for fighting there, and so on. These are the inheritances. What I would like for you to do is to explain this problem here that I say exists between a good leader, a man who knows, and yet a group of policies that either are non-changing or leading either to meaningless results or tragic results. How can a historian such as myself, who's concerned with this form of history deal with this particular problem?

MR. LARSON: You almost have to take it on a case by case basis. Let's take relations with the Communist world in general first, which at the beginning of the administration were absolutely at swords points. Right after the war there was a brief honeymoon, if you want to call it that, a brief lull. It didn't last very long. About three years and the cold war was on. And it was in full force when Eisenhower came in. I think it is historically correct to say that he had modified it a great deal, had softened it a great deal—if you look at what was actually done as distinguished from some of the things, let's say, that John Foster Dulles might have said. Several people have pointed out that John Foster Dulles performed a useful function for him because he could take the hard line at times. I've seen this enacted before my eyes many times. Of the two Eisenhower was much more anxious to get along with the Russians, and by the time his tenure was over we were indeed much closer to the Russians than before, in all sorts of ways. And if we weren't, most of the resistance was coming from their side, for example in the Open Skies program, the Atoms for Peace program. All these things were wide open invitations to Russia to come off it and get on with it through mutual cooperation through United Nations and they just slapped it down as fast as he offered these things.

I can give you a little illustration, for example, of this sort of thing in action and the way Dulles figured it. We were trying to think of something concrete in relation to relations with the Soviet Union, and right off the bat Eisenhower, sitting at the desk in the Oval Office said, "Let's invite 5,000 Russian students in." This was about 1956 or 1957. I thought that was a wonderful idea. Of course at that time we had almost no exchange back and forth of any kind, commerce or tourism or anything else, between the two countries. Anybody that could even get into the Soviet Union and out again was good for at least two books in those days. Five thousand—and I think we were going to put it in one of the speeches, maybe the acceptance speech, I've forgotten which one, but then Dulles got hold of it and was horrified and thought it was a ridiculous idea and started raising every conceivable kind of objection. You might say, why didn't Eisenhower do it anyway? The answer to that is he didn't like to disagree with his secretary of state unless he absolutely had to. And he told me this. He said, "I don't like to disagree with him unless it is absolutely crucial." He disagreed with him when it was necessary five or six very important times, as is now of course coming out in Fred Greenstein's book and other places. I really think, given the magnitude of the job of improving relations with the Russians, he made quite a bit of progress.

As to the business of the build-up in Southeast Asia I absolutely reject the idea that what went on under the Eisenhower administration was the lineal ancestor of what Kennedy and Johnson did. I cannot see that at all. I've gone into this. I wrote a book called *Vietnam and Beyond* and I was one of the first people to write on the subject of Vietnam, as early as 1962. I was with the delegation that went to the White House representing the American Association for the United Nations along with Ben Cohen and a couple of others. In 1962, mind you—this was not a very popular thing to do. I had editorials in the *Saturday Review* and all this. The idea that 300 advisers, which is about what we had budgeted for but we never reached, was somehow the lineal ancestor of 500,000 armed men just doesn't make sense. From all the reasons I have indicated earlier there never would have been a time when Eisenhower would have undertaken a venture like that. I visited him regularly down at the Palm Desert. I know what he thought every step of the way. He never would have done it.

Another illustration of this sort of thing is the attempt to say that Eisenhower really started the Bay of Pigs invasion. I can't imagine anything more out of character than for Eisenhower to have launched the Bay of Pigs invasion. After what I've said about using force overwhelmingly, here is this miserable little group of people with no air cover, no cover of any kind. There were pictures of them in the *Post* and the *Times* training in the swamps of Georgia. Everybody knew about it. They go and make this miscalculated landing—and that's an Eisenhower operation? Certainly not. What happened during the Eisenhower administration was that some preliminary planning had been done. I shudder to tell you some of the things for which there are preliminary plans in the Pentagon involving some of our dearest friends abroad. There are plans for everything. The fact that some plans have been started doesn't mean a thing, so there is no conceivable causal relation there.

I absolutely reject the idea that the period of relative tranquility of Eisenhower was deceptive because it only stored up trouble for the future. Everybody who comes in, not excepting the Eisenhower administration, every administration blames its troubles at the beginning on what it inherited. We're having, of course, a rather protracted example of that with Reagan. How much longer the recession continues to be laid at the door of previous administrations I don't know, but so far it still is. I think I can speak with some confidence on this because I had a certain amount of inside view even after Eisenhower. I was quite close to Kennedy. I talked with him one week before he was shot. I was foreign affairs consultant to Johnson, believe it or not, and was involved in a towering argument with him about Vietnam when it became apparent he was beginning to build up to increase the forces. I was never asked back. The thing about the Vietnam war that I can say with the fullest of confidence, having been right there during very much of it, is that it could have been stopped at any time, by one man saying one word, NO. Kennedy could have said it, Johnson could have said it. I can't tell you how World War I could have been prevented after reading Barbara Tuchman's *Guns of August*. I can't tell you how World War II could have been avoided. I can't even really with much confidence say how Korea could have been avoided although I suspect maybe it could have. I *know* how Vietnam could have been avoided—by one man saying no. They didn't want to say it and that's why it happened, not because they inherited something from Eisenhower.

QUESTION: I'm wondering if Mr. Larson would like to comment on the formation of SEATO. What was President Eisenhower's position on that?

MR. LARSON: SEATO was formed right after the breakdown of the French-Colonial period in Southeast Asia, the Dien Bien Phu fiasco and so forth. To try to forestall anything like that for the future, SEATO was formed, and was a good idea at the time. It never really worked very well because some of the parties to it simply did not live up to its terms. But the general principle involved was that everybody would consult with everybody else and everybody would come to the aid of everybody else. The parties simply didn't live up to it. That of course became apparent during Vietnam. I suppose all the parties to SEATO should have joined in if they meant what they said in the SEATO treaty. Actually, if you examine the exact language of the treaty it isn't quite that cut and dried. It doesn't absolutely commit people. It commits them to consult and that's about all. It was basically a fairly weak treaty. In other words it wasn't like NATO. Many people think SEATO and NATO, because they sound alike, were similar treaties. NATO is an honest-to-God defense alliance; SEATO wasn't.

QUESTION: If I may do a follow-up on the question about the Court, do you think there was, if you took all the elements in President Eisenhower's selection of Supreme Court Justices, a legal philosophy that he would have desired reflected on the Court? There are a lot of arguments that Nixon wanted law and order and so he selected his Justices accordingly.

MR. LARSON: I don't think so. That would have been alien to his character and it doesn't reflect itself in the kind of people he selected. If I'm not mistaken he selected William Brennan. I'm almost positive of that and Brennan, whom I've known for many years, of course is now the most liberal survivor on the Court. And then of course, Warren. No, I don't think he could have had any preconceived idea of producing a certain kind of Court with a certain kind of result, which some subsequent Presidents have.

QUESTION: I believe he also appointed Whittaker and you do have an odd mixture of people there. Just as a follow-up, what did he think about in relation to Supreme Court appointments? When a vacancy occurred what did his mind run on to in thinking about prospects?

MR. LARSON: I honestly don't know because I was never involved. There must not have been a Supreme Court appointment under discussion at any time when I was involved because I don't remember it coming up. I guess I'm grateful to you for remembering that he appointed Whittaker—I guess. I once debated Justice Whittaker somewhere in Kansas and so I have a rather personal feeling about him which I probably shouldn't express. But let's just put it this way, I don't think the appointment of Whittaker indicates much one way or the other.

QUESTION: Anymore than the other two, I suppose, is that right?

MR. LARSON: I think that's right. In the case of Bill Brennan, there wasn't any question about it. Bill has always been a liberal judge. When he was in New Jersey, and I knew him then, I happened to know him better than usual because of workmen's compensation. It was one of his specialties and still is. I don't think Eisenhower could have been under any illusions about the fact that he had a reputation as a liberal judge. He appointed him anyway. I think maybe because he consciously wanted a balanced Court. Why he appointed Whittaker, I have no idea.

NARRATOR: I think I speak for all of you in thanking Professor Larson for this clear, forceful, and candid treatment of the Eisenhower presidency. It adds to his book and it adds to the literature on the Eisenhower presidency represented in other books. It doesn't answer all the questions and it doesn't come down on the side of all the partisans who have their own view of what exactly Eisenhower stood for in every area but it does try to set some principles in general, propositions to help us know more about this important presidency. We thank you very much.

II.
THE
EISENHOWER
WHITE HOUSE

ORGANIZING THE
WHITE HOUSE
Andrew Goodpaster

THOMPSON: We are very grateful to you General Goodpaster. You are not only a respected figure in the whole discipline of political science and international relations but have been kind enough to associate yourself with the Miller Center and for that we are terribly grateful. My colleague, Richard Melanson and I are pleased to visit you.

We have, as you know, as part of the Eisenhower portrait we are trying to paint, met with a number of people who were close to the President. In every case we have asked them certain questions and perhaps we could begin by asking about your association with the President, when it began, how he drew you into the Eisenhower administration and what some of your initial impressions were of that administration, of your role in it and your relationship to him.

GENERAL GOODPASTER: My association with President Eisenhower went back to the time when he came back to be Chief of Staff of the Army. I was serving in the Operations Division of the War Department general staff. I had come back in the last months of the war and

continued in that post for several years. The first real working association I had with him was in the Spring of 1947 when he asked General
Norstad, the head of the Operations Division to detail an officer to
him to set up an organization that he was interested in creating that
would do advanced study, looking to the longer range future of the
army. He wanted some keen-minded young officers and Norstad
asked me to set this up.

I worked then with General Eisenhower, proposed a couple of
people to him and stayed with the group myself for a few weeks in getting it started and making sure that it was oriented and organized to do
the job that he had in mind. My next association with him was at
SHAPE (Supreme Headquarters Allied Powers Europe) in Paris. I was
sent as one of the initial staff officers there and then when he came over
I served in the capacity of a special assistant to General Gruenther, who
was the chief of staff. I had numerous contacts with General Eisenhower during the organizational period of SHAPE and of the Allied
Command in Europe. But my particular association was to serve as his
representative in a session of several months downtown in Paris conducted by the first of the NATO groups called The Three Wise Men.
This was Monnet, Harriman and Gaitskell initially, later Plowden
from Great Britain. Their job was to try to come up with a force program that would meet the security needs in Europe and at the same
time be within the political-economic capabilities of the member nations. Of course Eisenhower followed that very, very closely. I served as
his representative and had an opportunity to do a great deal of work
with him.

The last task I had with him came just before he came back, leaving
the command and leaving the army, to begin his run for the presidency.
On the American side, the American military wanted to set up some
kind of a unified American command in Europe to pull together our
American forces. These were under him in his allied capacity but some
kind of a U.S. control headquarters also was needed. I worked with
General Eisenhower to develop a suitable headquarters plan and statement of the functions, the authority and the responsibilities of the
commander in his American capacity. We did not finish that work
before he left. Instead, it was completed under General Ridgway, who
did very much what Eisenhower had recommended.

My next contact with him came when he was President, in the summer of 1953. His Assistant for National Security Affairs and the
Secretary of State together set up for him a study group called the
"Solarium Study Group." That was the code name of the group,
which was to study three alternative basic foreign policy or security

policy directions for the United States. Eisenhower himself went over the list of those who should participate and put some names on it, of which mine was one. I was called back from SHAPE to participate in this. It was about a five-week study effort here in Washington. We presented the results of this to Eisenhower and the whole National Security Council and all of the related people in government at the conclusion of our work.

I might just say a word about the final report of the three groups—one group advancing the so-called role-back theory, one group advancing what amounted to the containment theory (that group, I might say, was headed by George Kennan for obvious reasons), and a third group pursuing what might be called a "Spheres of Interest," "Spheres of Influence" or "Drawing a Line" type of policy. On hearing these final reports Eisenhower immediately jumped up himself and said, "Now I would like to summarize and evaluate what we've heard." He did this, speaking extemporaneously for forty-five minutes or so after the several-hour presentation that had been made, coming down finally on a policy which was essentially the containment policy. George Kennan in talking with me in later years about this used the phrase that "in doing so Eisenhower showed his intellectual ascendancy over every man in the room." Coming from George Kennan that is quite a statement.

I then went back to SHAPE, leaving in the middle of the following year, 1954, to become District Engineer in San Francisco, returning to the Army Corps of Engineers. At that point General Paul Carroll, Eisenhower's Staff Secretary in the White House, died very suddenly of a heart attack and the President asked that I come into the White House to take that job. So I then took the job as Staff Secretary, with a collateral duty as what was called Defense Liaison Officer, which was closely concerned with the day to day security operations of the government. I'll come back to that later.

I might tell a little of how the Staff Secretary job was created. Eisenhower, of course, was accustomed to a well organized headquarters, including a Secretary of the General Staff in large headquarters who was responsible to see that decisions were recorded, that actions pursuant to the commander's decisions were initiated, that reports came back in on time, that the paperwork was all handled properly. Well, that didn't automatically happen in the White House, and Eisenhower, on one occasion when the paper had been lost or action had not been taken, said with some asperity, "I don't think I should have to be my own Sergeant Major around here. I want to have this kind of thing handled properly." Apparently the same thing happened again within a week or two and talking to his principal staff he said, "I said just a week or so ago I was not going to be my own Sergeant Major and I'm not. I'm going to have a Staff Secretary and Carroll, you are it." That was the job and that was my duty—to serve in that capacity.

I mentioned earlier the job of staff assistant for the handling of the day to day security operations. That could involve, for example, memoranda that came from the State Department, instructions that went back from Eisenhower to the State Department, the same with the Defense Department, the same with CIA. One of the duties that Carroll had and that I then took over was to give the President the morning intelligence briefing using material that had come from CIA, the Defense Department and the State Department early each morning. Really, that was the way he started the day.

THOMPSON: Was there ever any suggestion that the NSC adviser should do the briefing?

GENERAL GOODPASTER: Not while I was there. Now I come to the question of the relation that we had between myself and the NSC adviser. That could have been a difficult relation but it always worked out in most harmonious fashion. Also, in much the way he had looked to Carroll, the President liked to discuss with me a bit about telling the U.S. story in the world—how we could let the people and the governments of the world know what the United States really stands for and how the United States is prepared to work with them cooperatively. That brought both of us, Carroll and later myself, in touch with what had been the Psychological Strategy Board and later became the Operations Coordination Board. They were the formal organization for doing that but the President liked to toss these ideas back and forth more informally. He liked to have a chance to talk things out and he did that with Carroll, and to some degree with me, on quite a number of issues of that kind over the years.

So that was another function that I came to perform—rather an informal function, but one which involved his bringing up things that were on his mind, concerns that he had, directions in which he would like to move in the international sphere, with the idea of then reducing them to some specific tasking of the NSC or the State Department or the Defense Department, the CIA, the AEC, the whole range.

THOMPSON: This turning to you to talk about important subjects must have evolved and grown out of the SHAPE experience to some extent.

GENERAL GOODPASTER: Yes, he would on occasion refer to what we had done over there. Views of relations with our allies or how to deal with allies were a matter to which he had given great thought, in which he had had a great deal of experience. He liked to discuss that in a very broad way, particularly when he had concerns of some sort on his mind. And he always welcomed anything that I would raise, suggesting to him that there was something that he ought to be thinking about. It was a part of his method of operating to have talks like that with a great many people. He developed his ideas a great deal through that kind of conversation.

You asked also about my impressions of how he operated. I saw that he had—I'm now speaking of the White House years—quite a strong sense of the mandate that he felt he had been put into office to carry out—a mandate concerning putting the United States economy on a sound basis; a mandate concerning establishing the United States' position in the world as that of a willing friend and supporter for countries that were trying to develop self-government and sustain themselves in the world, and so on. He came into office with a rather well adjusted set of policies that in fact defined certain principles by which he operated. That was a term that he often used—that we should follow the principle of doing thus and such: the principle for example, of building strength in these countries so that they could defend themselves; the principle of maintaining a sound economy because that was the base from which we were able to do the other things that we were doing; the principle of supporting our free institutions, which give freedom of choice in so many fields to the American people.

Another impression that I had was that he had a very great ability to lead groups in the examination of complex issues—issues that were complex and often of a very fundamental nature. He had a keen sense of getting to the most central and most basic considerations, but at the same time placing them in the context of broad policy. For example, in holding down the budget he had very clear and very strong ideas, but was quite ready to consider what the impact of that would be on various of the programs that seemed to him to be essential. I should also mention the principle which he often emphazied of organizing our defense establishment for the long pull rather than having stops and starts and fluctuations, which he regarded (and quite correctly) as very, very wasteful. He was extremely effective in drawing out the views of people in meetings such as Cabinet meetings, NSC meetings and so on, and in the *ad hoc* meetings in his office where specific issues were very often considered and decided—very good at drawing out the views of these people and then showing them other aspects that had to be taken into account, hearing the views of the whole group and beginning to elicit and draw out a common position through persuasion, through analysis and consideration of the substantive content of the issue. He did that, I would say, with the feeling that this was in some sense a crusade to do the things that he had been elected to do. He had a strong sense of the need to work with Congress, having had before him the example of the difficulties President Truman had had with the Congress as the Korean War was prolonged. He needed to work not only with the Congress as a whole, but also in particular with his own party representatives in the Congress—who he often said had been in opposition so long that they didn't know any other way to act. He devoted a great deal of effort to that. Then of course after the 1954 election the control of the—I think—the whole Congress passed to the other party. Then he had an even more demanding task to work effectively with the Congress, and he devoted great attention to that.

He concerned himself with an agenda of foreign problems that needed to be cleared up and cleaned up—Trieste, Iran, the situation of Austria, to name but a few. Of course before I joined him he had been very deeply concerned with bringing the Korean War to an end. That task had been essentially completed by the time I got back to join him.

Also, he had an agenda of domestic problems in which the actions of Senator McCarthy certainly had to be very close to the top of the list. The impact of that altercation on the country he regarded as very serious. And all of this had to be done as he went about trying to reestablish, in the term that he used, "budgetary and financial discipline" within the government.

THOMPSON: One of your colleagues mentioned there were two things the President never discussed with this colleague and one of them was McCarthy. Did he ever talk with you about McCarthy?

GENERAL GOODPASTER: He had some conversation with me, particularly I think when McCarthy attacked General Paul Zwicker, because both Eisenhower and I knew Zwicker. Eisenhower had a very high regard for Zwicker, who had commanded a regiment, an infantry regiment, of the Second US division on the northern shoulder of the Bulge during the Battle of the Bulge. Eisenhower felt that we owed a great deal to the valor and to the effectiveness of that division and to Zwicker and his regiment in particular. So McCarthy could hardly have chosen a worse target. I recall Eisenhower making the point that it was simply unconscionable for somebody in McCarthy's position to attack a man like Zwicker.

THOMPSON: He didn't talk about General Marshall or the Wisconsin speech?

GENERAL GOODPASTER: He never talked directly about that although I had a sense, particularly in later years, that he was very regretful of the damage that had been done to his relationship with General Marshall. He sought out ways of showing respect for General Marshall and honoring him, including having General Marshall come to Blair House for an award very late in General Marshall's life, but never spoke directly about it. I did, however, sense this feeling of regret over the impact of that incident.

One further comment. Initially, one had a great sense of initiative and new thrusts, movement in new directions, in the administration. A natural cycle then occurred, wherein the administration set about to define its positions in these new areas pursuant to these new initiatives that were introduced after they came in. As those policies and positions were established in the NSC and on the domestic side, there was less initiative and more operating within the framework of these policies, which had been put in place and into effect. A consequence of that was that as his second term drew to an end initiative then began to be exercised by people from the outside who were attacking his administration for one reason or another—charging, for example, that he was doing too little for defense in allowing a "bomber gap" or a "missile gap" to develop. Of course it was later demonstrated that neither of those was happening, and that he had intelligence sources that gave him a very good appreciation at the time of just what the strength on the other side was. But you did see then this shift from initiative to the defining of policies, to the carrying out of the policies with attacks being made from the outside.

And finally, I would say that one of the impressions I had of his work was his effort to establish a US international policy and posture along the lines I previously described—to present the United States in the world in terms of what we were doing in a positive way to encourage, to assist, to help many countries that were either assuring their continued freedom and self-development or in the case of the new countries, assisting them to develop their governmental and economic institutions. Along with that he worked to improve our relations with the Soviet Union, to take away some of the highly militaristic tone of confrontation that had existed, to take away much of the harshness of the exchange that had existed. Some progress was made in that. For example, as a result of his Atoms for Peace speech we were able to get the agreement of the Soviet Union, not immediately but after a while, to join in pooling some fissile material in the hands of an international agency, the International Atomic Energy Agency.

Again we had the meeting in Geneva in 1955 which eased some of the confrontation. In the meantime, through diplomacy we had been able to achieve the Austrian Treaty, to bring an end to the state of war with Austria, in which the Russians joined. Then they and we and the French and British all removed our forces from Austria. It was not an easy road but it was a road on which we were making progress. The Khrushchev visit was hopeful, I think, in overcoming what had been in effect an ultimatum against the United States having to do with the status of West Berlin. All that came to an unfortunate end in the alter-cation over the shooting down of the U2. We then had a kind of tone of confrontation with the Soviet Union that lasted through the re-mainder of the Eisenhower presidency.

I could mention also the progressive drift of Cuba into a stance more and more hostile to that of the United States. Initially, it was far from clear just what Castro was and where he would stand. Efforts were made to try to work out a reasonable relationship, but there was deterioration there. Similarly, there was deterioration in southeast Asia where by the end of his administration, although the South Viet-nam government had been established and great progress had been made in unifying South Vietnam, the North Vietnamese were on the move in Laos and were beginning the process of infiltration into South Vietnam. It was thus a mixed picture, but running throughout his ad-ministration was this desire on his part to assure that we were present-ing America to the world in a manner that would give attention to what we were doing in a positive way to assist and support countries around the world.

MELANSON: Historians more recently have noted that the fifties were times that American foreign policy was blessed with a firm domestic consensus about the purposes of American foreign policy. Was President Eisenhower aware of that and did he try to exploit that in any kind of positive way in terms of his own policies?

GENERAL GOODPASTER: He was quite aware of the rapport that he had with the American people and the support he had from them. We often talked about that, and the fact that he and I had grown up about three hundred miles apart, although with some twenty-five years difference in time. This was something that we talked about and we also admitted to each other on occasion that we thought, coming from the Midwest as we had, that we were pretty close to understanding the thinking of the American people. I would have to say, with all due reservation, that I'm still inclined to think we did.

Now he knew that he had that kind of support. Of course it went to a great many things. It went to his own contribution as a war leader—a very successful one. They liked what they saw in him, and I'm sure he knew that he could draw upon that. He worked at it also with the Congress—building that kind of support. One principle that he followed was that he would never undertake a military action such as Korea without having the Congress with him. There was to be no failure to consult the Congress. As a matter of fact he went quite far in the other direction, almost insisting that they come down and meet with him when a situation such as Lebanon or many others came up. So instead of having a situation where congessional leaders felt that they weren't being consulted, oftentimes it was very clear that they wished instead that they were not being put on the spot. But he was sort of a master at that.

Yes, there was a consensus and it came from a good many sources. I think the people had confidence in what he was doing.

MELANSON: Did he feel that his opportunities were limited at the same time and that perhaps he couldn't get too far out ahead of what that consensus was particularly in terms of Soviet relations?

GENERAL GOODPASTER: No, I don't think that he ever felt that he was restrained from going as far as he wanted to go by public support. There was an interesting tension, I'll say, between Eisenhower's desire to project this positive sense of America to the world and a more cautious, more careful and reserved approach at the diplomatic level which of course was operated by Secretary Dulles. But the President recognized that in this diplomacy that Secretary Dulles was conducting, much of it had to be directed to containment, to letting the free nations of the world know that they had support and could have some assurance that they were not going to be overwhelmed or dominated by the Soviet Union. He supported very strongly the diplomacy that Secretary Dulles was conducting. Nevertheless, at the same time he felt that we should through our contacts with the Russians undertake to ease—to reduce the causes of tension and reduce the tensions themselves through exchange of views and making it clear that we harbored no offensive military designs against them. I think once he had decided against the rollback policy (and that decision I think really was finalized at the time of the Solarium exercise) then he was prepared to see the Soviet Union continue without threat from us so long as they did not threaten us and our allies. He had to put all those things together—the relations with allies who were threatened or felt they were threatened and with other countries who felt that they were under pressure from the Soviet Union, some of which was indirect or subversive pressure, but beyond this, dealing with the Soviet Union and then dealing in a more constructive (and to him more hopeful) way directly with these other nations to assist them to build up their own strength and their own security, for the well-being of their people. I think that's about the way it came out in his mind. And he felt that he had the support of the American people in doing that.

Now you run into budgetary constraints. One of the things that vexed him a great deal was that to do this in the foreign field, economic aid was one of the great instruments, the very valuable instruments. There was great resistance by many in the Congress to the foreign aid program, as such terms as a "give away program" and so on were used, whereas he saw it as the means of building the kind of a world in which the United States along with the other countries could be prosperous and secure. He was very vehement on this and had to put a great deal of effort into getting those bills through the Congress every year—not only through the Congress but through each successive committee of the Congress.

THOMPSON: May I ask one last footnote type question on this topic. Did it ever matter to him where the major support for an idea came from? For example, on the Summit idea or going to the Summit, Senator George and Senator Russell were expounding this view. So was Winston Churchill and so were a number of others. On the cultural exchange program for bringing a million Russians to the United States, at least the literature we've read, seems to suggest this came from people like Emmett Hughes and others who were terribly excited when the President took hold of the idea. But there were not as many powerful political figures who held that view—for example, Dulles was against it. Did that matter to him?

GENERAL GOODPASTER: He didn't mind that an idea would come from somebody else. As a matter of fact he often encouraged that, and used the expression to me one time—quoting, he said, General Marshall, who in turn was quoting somebody else—that you'd be amazed how much you can accomplish if somebody else can get the credit for it. He was more interested in getting these things accomplished. As a matter of fact, on occasion he would deliberately use that method.

One example that comes to my mind is the Atoms for Peace proposal, the idea of pooling some fissile material and then working toward a cutoff of any increase in the nuclear weapons that either side had. He had the feeling that by making this proposal, doing it in a non-provocative, non-confrontational way with the Soviet Union, then even if they weren't disposed to do it initially the pressures on them would be such that they would finally come to do it. Indeed it worked out that way. I would say that he was quite ready to see the idea or the momentum build from some other direction so long as it was working toward the objectives that he himself thought was right.

THOMPSON: The second topic we were interested in exploring has been a much discussed topic in some of the revisionist literature on the style of his leadership and the hidden hand idea. I don't know if you have any thoughts about that.

GENERAL GOODPASTER: Well, I could say a little about it. I've already mentioned how persuasive he was with his peers and his senior subordinates. He had, I guess the term is charisma. No one could meet with him without really being lifted, without coming out just bubbling with enthusiasm. You may remember the story that when he was ill, when President Nixon came to office, President Nixon asked each of his Cabinet officers and senior appointees to go out and see President Eisenhower and cheer him up. And his comment was that they all came back with the same response, "We didn't cheer him up, he cheered us up." That was true throughout his administration.

Now people have jumped from that to a feeling that this was just geniality and that he was thought somehow just to deal with problems in an easy and a genial way. Nothing could be further from the truth. In his office he was very intent. He was all business. He gave very keen concentration to matters before him. I recall that I would carry in each morning a group of papers to be worked on or things to take up with him. I would set them up in a certain order and I'd begin to present them and he would begin to discuss them, to challenge them, to want to argue about them, to raise questions about them. There was a very intense give and take, all done in a very dignified and cordial way but very, very serious. Very, very intent. I think that the dedication he had to the serious consideration of the problems at hand and the sense that he was trying to base it on some considerable depth of principle came across to his associates, and that combined with his inherent magnetism gave them a sense of confidence. It was reassuring to them. It gave them a sense of real involvement, which brought him and what he was trying to do quite a lot of support.

He was very confident of the basic soundness of what he was doing. He was willing to examine or to review, but he had no doubt that working for a balanced budget was in the interest of the United States. He had no doubt that a very low rate of inflation was in our interest in order to maintain the soundness of our economy and the prosperity of our people. When inflation looked as though it was going to reach 4% one year he was vehement on the view that this was just plain intolerable. As a matter of fact an inflation rate of 2% he said was grounds for real concern throughout the whole administration.

The same thing applied with regard to our security position in the world. He was quite confident about that security position. He knew that we require effort to sustain it but he worked from a base of confidence and he exuded a confidence that other people absorbed. That had been true during the war. Many people had commented that his associates had picked up that sense of confidence and that it had solidified the action of his headquarters, as contrasted with times when people became shaky or unsure. Of course he had the resources behind him. He knew it and he knew how to employ them. I mentioned earlier that he was confident of the basic popular support which was always there.

On the question of the sources of his strength, that public support was a great part of it. In addition, he was a master executive. He knew what it was to be a superb executive and he knew that he knew it. So again he had great confidence in his powers of organizing, of delegating, of assuring that the people to whom these things were delegated did indeed work to carry out policies—policies that were set in broad guidelines, and were set after thorough deliberation and with his approval.

He had confidence in his powers of reasoning and powers of logic. Oftentimes he would question something, saying, "That's just not logical." He would trace the line of logic through the problem, doing so, for example, where someone began to get off base (as he would term it) instead of following the central line of policy, or where someone would begin to pursue some parochial or other interest that had not been given policy approval.

I mentioned that he worked from a set of principles. These were very high, often very broad principles. "What's right for America?" was a question he would frequently ask. He would talk about a "decent relationship" between countries, even countries that were in opposition to each other. He had a great sense of what all of us as public servants owed to the people of the United States and was very harsh and strong in condemnation of any impropriety. Early in his administration, it was reported to me, he called his White House staff together and said, "If anybody comes asking for special favors or special consideration on the ground of their association with me, even my relatives, I want you to throw them out of your office." That kind of principle I think was part of the base from which he operated.

An interesting thing was his ability to use these principles instrumentally. He could call them into play in certain arguments around the Cabinet table for example. He could be rather selective at that and would choose the particular ones that would advance the cause that he truly wanted to support. He had a philosophy of limited government and was fond of quoting from Lincoln that the government should do only those things that the people cannot do or cannot do so well for themselves. And he had as well a belief that there were many social situations that simply would not be solved by, as he termed it, "throwing money at them," but must be solved through a process of education, through a process of leadership that would change attitudes between the races for example. He thought that problems of this kind would take a long time to overcome and to eradicate because, as he said, you were talking about changing the attitudes of whole generations.

He had a quick mind and a very strong and vigorous personality. When he was ready to take a position on an issue there was no doubt left in anybody's mind that the decison had been made. But he could do that without being overbearing. As a matter of fact he often referred to the desk pounders, declaring that he didn't believe that was true leadership.

The other side of this, I know from your question, is what were the weaknesses. I think the question will always be asked, "would more aggressive action have been appropriate?" For example, in dealing with the problems of race or poverty he felt that you must really work at that from below rather than try to impose solutions from the top—that it could not come simply by edict or fiat from the leader. When it came to race he felt that assuring the vote for the black population would over a period of time be the most important thing to improve their situation. In the meantime, he of course was opposed to discrimination and to inferior treatment for the blacks. He certainly was opposed to any breach of the law which worked against the blacks—as Governor Faubus of Arkansas learned late in Eisenhower's administration.

Now about this hidden hand let me say that I myself have a little uneasiness with the term. I think it may somewhat overstate and overdramatize the tendency he had always to work to multiple objectives.

He would be looking, as he would put it, at how you can kill two birds
or many birds with one stone. Some of his objectives he would be
reluctant to show. I think on occasion he deliberately kept some of
them concealed, especially some of the things of a longer term that he
had in mind. Also, as to his methods, I have already mentioned his
tendency often to use indirect methods—to take actions so that
somebody else (maybe unknowingly) would be making a proposal that
he really wanted to see made. Or he might work at setting up a situation where the natural pressures, for example, on the Soviet Union in
response to his proposal to pool fissile material and to cut off weapons
development, together with their sense of where their best interests lay,
would lead them to take this action rather than his trying to push it on
them in some heavy-handed or more direct way. Whether that is hidden-
hand I'll leave to other interpreters but it is true oftentimes that he
wanted to see things done, that he was looking at a problem in a longer
term sense and that rather than overtly pushing and trumpeting his
own participation in it he would rather encourage it to come from
below. In many cases he wanted to see action from the countries
themselves as he felt that their security and their security arrangements
should be matters for their determination rather than our trying to
force a particular plan of action on them.

THOMPSON: Then there is the question of how he used his Cabinet
and how he dealt with individual Cabinet members and what your part
was in the relationship with the Cabinet.

GENERAL GOODPASTER: I would regard or describe the Cabinet
as a forum for discussion and deliberation and for the building of consensus through this discussion and deliberation. Now the same was
true for the NSC, and for the Legislative Leaders Conference. Each
week he would have a conference with the congressional leaders, normally those of his own party. They would discuss current business, actions that he was proposing to pursue, positions that he was proposing
to take in order to deal with certain legislative proposals that were current in the Congress or soon would be. Also, we would have a kind of
deliberative session in the morning before his press conferences each
week. That was the kind of approach that he liked to follow. The items
on the Cabinet agenda were suggested by the Cabinet Secretary Max
Rabb and his assistant Brad Patterson and in the case of the Cabinet
approved normally by Sherman Adams and then by the President. In
the case of the NSC his NSC special assistant brought the agenda in
for his approval. I attended the Cabinet meeting as an observer or to
answer any questions if asked, but I did not participate. The same was

true in the NSC. I did participate fully in the pre-press conference meeting and I attended the Legislative Leaders through most of his administration as an observer.

THOMPSON: Did you see the agenda items? Someone remarked that Eisenhower, as far as they knew, never rejected any of the agenda items that Rabb and others prepared.

GENERAL GOODPASTER: I can't speak to that. I doubt that he would reject them. He might ask for something else to be done or set them back to a later time for further development of the issue. I think this was part of the duty to keep consideration active of what matters should be coming before the Cabinet and be talked out with the idea of looking at all angles. Contrary to the idea of some that Eisenhower did not like to hear opposing points of view, he actually tried to draw those out and then develop the area of common interest, frequently setting them in a broader context to see if agreement couldn't be reached on some more fundamental basis. That was the technique that he used. Doing that then defined the policy or the position that the administration would adhere to.

THOMPSON: One of the reasons we've wondered about the Cabinet relationship was that the Eisenhower administration seems to have come closer to Cabinet government than almost any administration one can think of and yet there are many as you know who say Cabinet government is impossible. It simply doesn't work. Successive presidents have tried and then abandoned it.

GENERAL GOODPASTER: Well, he did use the Cabinet as a forum for deliberation—and the NSC as well and certainly the Legislative Leaders conference. In addition he would have the ad hoc meetings in his office on specific items for decision. Many Cabinet officers, of course, if their business didn't have broad implications, would prefer to handle it directly with the President. But where matters had broad implication and where issues were involved such as the state of the economy and what this said about taxes, about fiscal policy, and about the monetary situation, those would be brought before the Cabinet. Perhaps a policy of budgetary stringency would be agreed upon there. Cabinet officers being what they are, when they went back home if they had something that they needed in their particular department, were still willing to push against it. They would now be doing it, however, against the background of knowing that the Director of the Bureau of the Budget (who had also participated in the Cabinet meeting) would have the backing of the President in trying to impose budgetary stringency on them.

THOMPSON: There seems to be less spillover of the kind of comment one sometimes hears about administration, regarding the relationship of Cabinet members and White House staff and that leads to the question of how the President organized the White House, what he thought about his key White House aides. In every discussion of a President that we've had so far we seem to get varying lists of closest advisers but I wonder if the other side of Cabinet government is the role of the White House and close advisers and who make up that list. I wondered what you thought of that?

GENERAL GOODPASTER: On the question of advisers, Eisenhower has a very large number. They extended over a quite wide range, and he used them in a variety of ways. There were some people with whom he wanted to talk the basic determining policy issues, even the principles that should guide us. With others he would want to talk about "how do we go about doing this? What are the methods? Are these specific methods proper?" These were very much two way discussions with him. It was not that he was simply sitting there receiving the advice of somebody who was pumping it out. Very quickly it became not just a dialogue but almost a wrestling match of challenging and testing ideas. "Have you thought of so and so?" "Well, what are you going to do about so and so?" Some aspect that may have been left out. He of course had the advantage, because he was the President who had to look at these things in their totality. He used that advantage to challenge people who were taking a narrower and sometimes parochial view. Then you had different sets of people depending on the general area involved. In foreign and security matters for example his prime adviser was certainly the Secretary of State, particularly while Foster Dulles was alive. Next, probably came his Special Assistant for Security Affairs—Bobby Cutler, later Dillon Anderson, later Gordon Gray. Next I suppose would be myself. Then came his adviser for the psychological activity that I mentioned—C.D. Jackson, then Nelson Rockefeller at a later time. And he would expect either Pete Carroll or later me also to be prepared to discuss issues of that kind with him. Then you had the Secretary of Defense and the Chairman of the Joint Chiefs who would participate, the Secretary in both Cabinet and NSC, and the Chairman in the NSC deliberations. The Director of Central Intelligence, Allen Dulles, was certainly a key adviser in the NSC. Allen Dulles did not attend Cabinet meetings. He would occasionally meet with the President either with me present or with the National Security Adviser present. Then after the President set Governor Stassen up as his special assistant for disarmament, Governor Stassen would come in and meet with him as an adviser.

He had a very close personal regard for Lewis Strauss who was head of the AEC and the president's Special Assistant for Atomic Affairs. That is all in the foreign and international area.

On the domestic side, certainly Governor Adams would be the prime, top adviser but General Persons who was the head of legislative liaison, deeply experienced in that field, was also a keen adviser. Jim Hagerty was very important because the President had this great sense of communication with the American people, and Hagerty was very able in that field as his press secretary.

With Vice President Nixon, Eisenhower liked to talk out broad issues of public attitude, and important social issues. It isn't well known, I think, that Vice President Nixon would generally be found among those taking the—I almost hesitate to use the term—the more liberal attitude in terms of human affairs and social programs, always very conscious of public opinion and of that human side of things.

Again, Ann Whitman, his secretary. He relied on her heavily for secretarial assistance, but also in maintaining relationships with influential individuals whose opinions he respected and wanted to hear.

Gabriel Hauge was a key economic adviser, in addition to the head of the Council of Economic Advisers. Gabe would deal with the more difficult, sticky issues, oftentimes having to do with tariffs and exemptions and things of that kind. On some aspects of domestic matters, including the domestic aspects of foreign matters, he would talk to me and I would have some role in that.

Bryce Harlow had a very important role with the President. The President made great use of his speech writers and Bryce was a superb speech writer in addition to being a very key man in legislative liaison with the Congress.

Then the President of course consulted with the head of the Republican party, Len Hall as chairman of the Republican National Committee and with Arthur Larson.

With regard to his role as the leader of the American people I suppose he talked to Hagerty and Adams and myself a great deal about that, and to General Parsons as well.

Then he brought in advice in special areas where he had keen interests, particularly on the scientific side. He had great respect for Jim Killian, later Kistiakowsky as scientific advisors. He had set up scientific panels in the early period of his administration to analyze main areas of great concern, the Technological Capabilities Panel of course being one of the most important.

John von Neumann was a man he very greatly admired and respected, and Edwin Land of Polaroid. He liked to meet with the scientists who had the ability to get to the center of many of these issues.

He had Special Assistants in areas such as international trade, the coordination of water projects and the like. In all of these areas he would have consultation with them in his office or through some of the forums that I've described. Then he had a tremendous range of unofficial advisers or interlocutors or whatever one might call them. I would say his brother Milton was at the head of that list, for he had the highest regard for Milton.

Regarding the White House organization itself, it can be said that it was not a rigid or rigorous organization. Adams was certainly his chief staff assistant on the domestic side and director of the staff. Persons, as I mentioned, was the chief of legislative liaison. Hagerty was responsible for staff assistance on press relations and public relations. Jerry Morgan was Special Counsel to the President. We had a little saying to explain Jerry Morgan's job, that he protected the signature of the President. He looked at every document that would have legal or binding authority such as signing a law or signing an executive order to see that it was legal and constitutional and properly prepared and properly presented. The NSC assistant was Bobby Cutler, then later Dillon Anderson, then later Gordon Gray. Their focus was policy and longer term planning, I would say. And my role as Staff Secretary I guess I've already described, dealing with security operations, that is the day to day affairs.

Let me take just a moment to say how the security adviser and I worked together. That would be a recipe for friction if you did not have a man like Eisenhower to whom and to whose purposes we were all devoted. I think we would have been ashamed of doing anything in our own interest rather than trying to carry out his purposes. So you didn't have these turf battles that have been such an unsavory sight around Washington in later years.

THOMPSON: Did he consciously pick people for this quality?

GENERAL GOODPASTER: Oh, yes, of course. He wouldn't have had people around who couldn't operate that way. And he wouldn't have tolerated it for a moment if he thought the serious business of government was being impeded by this kind of—what he would regard as worse than nonsense. It would be quite improper conduct. Just to give you an example, oftentimes people over at State would call me and say that the Secretary was so tied up, or the Undersecretary, that he wasn't going to be able to come over to bring something to the President. They would send it over to me and ask if I would take it in to the President and explain their thinking "along the following lines." And of course I would. Something might come in to me for action of the President—say from State or from Defense—that seemed to me to have policy implications that had not really been shredded out and I would call Cutler or Gray and ask, "Is this something that you had better have a look at?" If so I would send that over to him rather than taking it in to the President directly. Or Gray or Cutler might have something they would like taken up with the President. If they were free they would do it, but they might have a meeting and ask whether I would take it up for them with the President. We had that kind of easy exchange. There was no vying for, or trying to stake out certain positions of turf. We supported each other so it was almost the opposite of what we have seen on some occasions since then.

THOMPSON: You didn't routinely write an evaluation for the President of the document from State or Defense?

GENERAL GOODPASTER: No. I might, on occasion, put a note recalling to him that this related to something else but in general I took these things in personally and I could talk about it and I might say, "There is an aspect of this that I don't think has been thoroughly taken up. You might want to act on this and start action separately or you might want to ask them about that before you take action on it." It would be up to him. That is the kind of assistance that I would give. I think we had a pretty clear notion—which was reinforced by the President from time to time. I recall hearing him say, "Now wait a minute, boys, that is a policy matter. I'm not going to decide that here. If that needs consideration, bring it before the Cabinet or bring it before the NSC. Then I'll decide." So you did not have competing sources of primary policy. He had a very clear sense of that. And we gradually gained a clearer and clearer sense of it.

I should mention one other area that he established I think during his second administration. That was the position of Assistant for Intergovernmental Affairs, relations with the states, with localities and the like. Governor Howard Pyle first had that job, and then Bob Merriam took it over.

THOMPSON: One of the things that has come up with every President is the question of what his view of the office was and how he evaluated it. That of course has some bearing on the question of the manner in which he viewed his relations with Congress. But there are those who make the comment that President Eisenhower in one sense thought of his greatest accomplishment in life as having commanded our forces in Europe and that he preferred the title General Eisenhower. On the other hand we've had several people who talked about the enormous respect he had for the dignity of his office. I wonder if these are areas you'd discuss within the limited time you have left.

GENERAL GOODPASTER: Oh, yes, I would be happy to talk about it. First of all, relations with the Congress were as I previously indicated. He had a deep sense of the sharing of responsibility as set up in the Constitution which is an inherent part of our governmental system. That meant to him that he had to work with and through the Congress to accomplish the things that he had in mind—budgetary control, for example; in the foreign field working with the other nations of the world; and the AID program. He had to work with the Congress to accomplish that. Then he had to work with the Congress to keep some things from happening such as the Bricker Amendment which he felt would impose restrictions in the foreign field that obviously went beyond what the Constitution provided because it would have to be an amendment. Second, it would be quite harmful to the whole concept of the Presidential direction of foreign policy with consultation with the Congress and subject to the controls that the Congress could exercise particularly through power of the purse and action on treaties. I mentioned he had the deep conviction about the need to consult with the Congress and particularly about the special role of consultation with the members of his own party in the Congress to carry through the program that his Administration, he felt, had been brought into office to do.

But as to the office of the President himself, I think that he saw this as the crucial place in government for the consideration, as he put it, of what's good for America—from the standpoint of what's good for America, insofar as the government was concerned. And then came the responsibility of trying to bring that about, working through the Congress, working directly with the people. I think he felt for example that trying to get people to look at race relations in what he would call a decent way was a part of the role of a President. I think that he felt that the office was crucially important. He did have some disparaging things to say about some of the duties that it imposed on the President. I've mentioned in the past the comment that he made on several occasions that "Anybody that wants this job thereby shows that he's unqualified for it on grounds of lack of judgment." But at the same time he saw that crucial weight that it had to carry in order to serve the American people.

On occasion he would see in addition to trying to lead public opinion, or have a role in forming public opinion, that it would be his task to create public interest in some topic that was of deep importance. In his Atoms For Peace proposal, for example, he felt that some way had to be found to head off what he regarded as a dangerous and even possibly catastrophic arms race. All of that entered into it. Those were duties that fell on the presidency and he was very sensitive to them.

THOMPSON: One other issue that we've not quite touched on is the understanding that you or he might have had on how you executed your relationship with closely related agencies and departments in particular with the NSC. You have touched on that.

GENERAL GOODPASTER: With State, Defense, CIA, AEC, those agencies in particular, my job went somewhat beyond a staff secretary's job to actually being a staff assistant to facilitate the handling of matters with those agencies. That's about the way I did it.

I mentioned giving the intelligence reports to the President each morning, I would also review the diplomatic messages from the summary that was furnished to me each day by the State Department. Later we developed something that we called Staff Notes that could go in to the President which would keep him acquainted with what was happening in the departments and key agencies—important actions taken, important problems that were being addressed in all of the departments of government.

I regarded my role there as assisting him through drawing things to his attention that he might wish to have pursued, taking up matters that had been sent over for his consideration, taking them up with him and giving, in addition to his action, any further guidance that he wanted to convey back to the department concerned. In a way, maybe there was a sense in which the term liaison was appropriate: it was liaison from the President to each of those departments.

THOMPSON: You may not even want to answer this and I don't ask it out of any disrespect but did you have a particular role to play in what we might call covert operations or special projects?

GENERAL GOODPASTER: Covert operations were handled by the Special Assistant for Security Affairs primarily through what was initially called the Fifty-Four Twelve Committee. He considered those with people at the Assistant Secretary level from the interested departments. They considered and reviewed them. Depending on whether he had had general guidance from the President or whether there was some new feature to it, he would take those in to the President. On occasion the President discussed some of those with me but this would be a kind of collateral discussion, not in the primary chain of decision and approval. Now the one exception to that—I think the only major exception to that—was in the U2 operations. On that I was his staff assistant involved in all of it. And as you know that was very, very closely, tightly held. Practically speaking, no one in the White House other than the President and myself and the Special Assistant for Security Affairs knew about that. I served as his staff assistant.

THOMPSON: He did, though, try to organize things in such a way that he could claim deniability. There was a certain chain so that he could always keep himself somewhat removed from the actual policy.

GENERAL GOODPASTER: Yes, in theory, though in practice he had no doubt as to his responsibilities. But that is a kind of minuet that is played in the area of covert operations between governments. They maintain what they call plausible deniability which is something of a fiction in many cases but it's a form that they go through in order, I assume, to avoid these things becoming an actual *casus belli*.

THOMPSON: Before we go to the last question I just wondered if you had any thoughts about one comment that actually a political figure in the administration made and that was that General Eisenhower was the last of the public servants to occupy the presidency and I thought back as he made that comment to a forum you conducted at the Miller Center on that same subject. Even allowing for strengths of character and human qualities, do you think that you both had—do you think that the fact that you were bound together by this code of public service had anything to do with the avoidance of what must have been enormous temptation, particularly, on your side to take advantage of the relationship? Does the public service idea explain the fact that when our other interviewees have talked about General Goodpaster sifting through the material that reached the President that you apparently did it with even-handedness and not with the attempt to push totally or continuously your own ideas?

GENERAL GOODPASTER: I differentiated very, very, carefully between putting my own ideas before the President in these discussions and in any way biasing or twisting or distorting or glossing what came to him. I would feel free to make a comment—and in fact I'd feel bound to make a comment to him when appropriate, indicating it was my own comment. As to how the thing was presented to him I think it would be—well, I would have to say that I would have thought it quite improper, even dishonorable to do other than convey to him what the Secretary of State or the Secretary of Defense or the Chairman of the Joint Chiefs or any other figure of government wanted to convey to him. That would have been a mistake, more than a mistake it would have been a terrible violation of the relationship between us. He was confident that he was getting that, but he also knew that if I thought from his standpoint he had better check on something or that there was another aspect of the thing that needed consideration I would always feel free and feel bound, in fact, to present that to him. I think that was the sense of public service.

One thing; the job quite obviously has carried temptations to use the information that comes there for personal purposes. I just was not involved in that. One of the things that helped my job was that Hagerty was our man who conducted relations with the press and I was free from that except when Hagerty might call me over and ask me to explain something as he did on occasion. But I think that sense that what you're doing is serving the public which has given a mandate to a certain leader, means that your job is to serve the accomplishment of that mandate. That is how I saw it, and that is how Eisenhower saw it. I think that is why we were able to work together effectively and with complete mutual confidence.

THOMPSON: I wonder if you would be willing to give a kind of summing up of your evaluation of the Eisenhower Presidency.

GENERAL GOODPASTER: Well, I could do it in the area in which I worked most closely with him—the area having to do with foreign and international affairs. I think we could say that he cleared up quite well the residue of problems of World War II. I mentioned the Trieste, the Austrian, the Iran situations. He ended the Korean affair. He gave limited support to Vietnam. He maintained a limitation on that. There was no intervention. Part of what he accomplished, I think, can be seen in the things that didn't happen along with some of the things that did happen. He did send our troops into Lebanon very, very briefly, accomplished the stabilization of the situation there and was able to remove them. I think he went a long way in stabilizing our relations with the Soviets. The whole tone was improved. Even after the altercation over the U2 the whole tone was quite different from what it was in the early part of his administration.

I think they saw him as a man who understood the importance of peace, as a man who also understood the importance of maintaining the free institutions of our society and the societies of our friends.

I believe the world was a safer place and that there had been progress, developmental progress in many, many nations of the world in which the United States had a hand during his administration.

The fact that we were able to conduct negotiations which had gone all the way up to the Summit with the Russians, I think, was an accomplishment.

Setting aside the altercation over the U2 and Krushchev's very emotional reaction to that, the Russians and others as well, I think, saw him as a man who would show respect for the people of other countries of the world. Of course he had available to build upon their sense that he had been associated with them in the final victory in what they called the Great Patriotic War.

In the area of defense, the program was organized for the long pull. You may know that he was quite proud of the fact that after Korea there was not this pell-mell demobilization that we had seen after World War II which practically destroyed the cohesion of our armed forces. We had organized for the long pull. He had established the practice of tightly constraining the defense budgets and he had such a strong confidence in his own judgment there that he had no hesitation about laying down the line of how much they could have and no more. He had accomplished some strengthening of the higher direction of the armed forces although I think he was still dissatisfied on that score when he left office—specifically, that there was not the full and effective control and economical relating of programs to policy that he wanted to see.

I think he felt that he had done a lot to stabilize a sound economy and had supported the work ethic and the responsibility ethic among our people rather than reliance on the largesse of government. I think he felt there had been some improvement in race relations especially in giving greater assurance about the vote and greater assurance about education. He kept very much to himself his opinion about the 1954 Supreme Court decision although different people think that they have seen implications of it leak out from him. But there was no doubt of his intention to see us work in the direction of the elimination of adverse discrimination against the blacks. I think he was troubled at the end of his term by some of what he saw developing out in Southeast Asia—the intervention of North Vietnam in Laos and the support by North Vietnam of infiltration and subversion in South Vietnam. And he handed then to his successor an unresolved problem in that area as in the case of Cuba as well.

That's about the way I would wrap it up.

THOMPSON: Others have talked about his being troubled about the military industrial complex. I don't know if there is anything you would want to add to that?

GENERAL GOODPASTER: Just that he had a keen sense of the pressures that were being generated—often very deliberately coming especially from the services in the Defense Department, the individual services, Air Force, Navy, Army—and how they would work with and through the producers of munitions and also through committees in the Congress. These things are now called "iron triangles." In those days the term wasn't used and he omitted from this the Congress, although he had a clear understanding of the role of Congress along with the other two parts of that complex, the military and the industrial part of it. He genuinely wanted to warn the American people. He did not assert that he had all the answers to how to deal with it but he felt that this was something they should be warned about—the military-industrial complex on the one hand and the scientific-technological elite which he also warned against on the other hand. Their roles were inherently so important and so pervasive that in a democratic society it was very necessary for the people to be alert to the scope and nature of that role and then to see, to satisfy themselves that they had means of maintaining proper popular and public control over those combined institutions. The society couldn't operate without those institutions, as large and influential component elements. But it needs to be very alert, as he said, to their implications to make sure that they are kept within the bounds of the purpose of the free institutions of our society.

QUESTION: He never felt insecure, did he, or inferior toward either of these elites?

GENERAL GOODPASTER: No. Not at all. He had great respect for the scientists and enjoyed his sessions with them very much. He had a personal liking for these people and I think he was impressed that those of the finest minds, the ones that he was in touch with, had a clarity of thinking that commended itself to him very strongly—a sense of the relationship of action and purpose. As you know he used them very powerfully to examine some of the technical defense programs that he was not sure were well aligned to the national purpose—and particularly to the strategic doctrine to which he was committed, and to the kinds of relationships between ourselves and the Russians that he was trying to build and create.

THOMPSON: Thank you for contributing immeasurably to our understanding of the Eisenhower presidency.

EISENHOWER'S APPROACH TO NATIONAL SECURITY DECISIONMAKING

Karl G. Harr, Jr.

NARRATOR: Professor Fred Greenstein's book, a good part of which was written here at the Miller Center, suggests the Eisenhower presidency is one which perhaps only now is receiving the full attention and re-examination that it deserves. For instance, Greenstein in his account talks about the five basic characteristics of the Eisenhower presidency with which most interpreters have not dealt. One is the idea of the hidden hand, Eisenhower never publicly showing his position on a great many things but privately doing a lot to achieve his purposes. He talks about the refusal to engage in personal attacks on political opponents, saying that you ought never to drive them into a corner from which they can't retreat; his close attention to the personalities of political actors; and splendid insights on Dulles and on Sherman Adams appear in the Greenstein book. And finally his selective approach to acts of delegation, the seeming enormous delegation of many things to his chief of staff, Sherman Adams, but excluding some other things. Greenstein also mentions his using what is said to be a formal structure of organization, but also using informal contacts with a number of people, including his brother as a source of information.

Karl G. Harr, Jr. is president of the Aerospace Industries Association of America, Inc. and has been so since 1963. He is a graduate of Princeton, holds a law degree from Yale, was a Rhodes scholar and received a D. Phil. at Oxford, was Special Assistant to the Secretary of State for Administration, was staff director to the Secretary of State's Public Committee on Personnel, Deputy Assistant Secretary for Defense for NSC Affairs and Plans, alternate Defense member of the NSC Planning Board, and then from 1958 to 1961 was in combination Special Assistant to the President of the United States, Vice Chairman of the Operations Coordinating Board, and Advisor of the National Security Council Planning Board.

It is not often one can go directly to the papers of the President to get a good description of what someone has done, but President Eisenhower wrote on January 13, 1960, to Mr. Harr concerning his duties:

"Within the frame of your duties as my special assistant, you are requested henceforth to make a special contribution to two major areas of the Operation Coordinating Board's work in addition to continuing to discharge your responsibilities with respect to the normal work of the OCB. The first of these is: in taking the lead and initiating new proposals to the Board for actions within the framework of National Security policies, in response to opportunity and changes in the situation. The second is: in placing particular emphasis on seeing the Board's action implementing National Security policies, contribute fully to the climate of foreign opinion the United States is seeking to achieve in the world."

I could go on and, among other things, mention Harr's activity as Chairman of the Board of The Experiment in International Living and alumni trustee of Princeton. But it is far better that we hear from Mr. Harr on the national security decisonmaking, policymaking processes of the Eisenhower Administration and any other issues he may wish to discuss with us.

MR. HARR: Thank you. I'm going to sort of ease into this because there are so many perspectives one can approach it from. One thing I mentioned to Dr. Thompson is a book, which is out of print now, that Senator Jackson wrote, or at least edited. It is basically a compilation of the testimony of senior people in the Eisenhower and Kennedy administrations as to how they view the workings of the National Security Council. It illustrates well how the procedure is different under the different Presidents. And it's a most useful reference book. As a matter of fact, I borrowed a copy from the Senator's office to refresh my own mind.

I'm going to talk today mostly about the National Security Council machinery—that's where my experience lies—and not very much about the practices or procedures of the non-national security departments or agencies. At any rate it is in that national security area that most of the major Eisenhower innovations were made and most of the new procedures evolved.

Let me begin by two rather random observations, not necessarily related to each other, but I believe relevant to the overall subject. First, I've at least met six of our other Presidents. Also, living in Washington, I get invited to the White House once in a while to the signing of a bill, or to celebrate a successful space event, or to get the arm put on me to raise money, or something. As you get to see them, you get a feel for each President. Just living and working in Washington you also get a feel for how they relate to their staffs. But aside from that I really only know the one President well and so, confessing that bias, I submit that we believed in "our" President and we loved him to a degree that maybe hasn't always been true between other Presidents and their staffs. I'm not saying that we all loved each other, necessarily, or that any two staff members didn't fight from time to time. But the "old man" was always respected and revered by everybody who worked for him. His absolute integrity was so manifest and so pervasive. His appointees had a reunion a couple of months ago on the thirtieth anniversary of his election and the ninetieth anniversary of his birth. We all came doddering out of the woodwork and we all came back mostly because we all held him in such high regard. We said to each other, "Isn't this great? Isn't it amazing how much we all loved that man?" Well, that's true and whether it's relevant or not to today's subject I don't know but I really think it has something to do with how we worked.

I should add to that, you don't find anybody who worked for him, at least I can't think of anybody, who went away and wrote a book that said bad things about Eisenhower, nobody did. They've done that to a lot of other Presidents, as we all know.

Secondly, it's hard in this year 1983 with all the tough news that we've had to live with for the last decade or so on the international front, the last three decades really, to reconstruct in our minds how few our perceived wants and how few and simple our perceived needs were in the international arena after we finished World War II. Basically we unloaded from VJ Day into a philosophy of "Go away, naughty world, and let us enjoy our peace and abundance. We want to get home, we want to get the hell out of here, we want to go to work, we want to enjoy being citizens of the rich and powerful country which has just defeated the evil forces of the world." And to the degree to which that was true, what was foreign policy? In fact, what is the true meaning for us, of the term foreign policy? Before World War II, I find it very hard to pin that term down anyway for our country, particularly—probably it would be easier with respect to the British or others who ran empires down through the years and had calculated concepts of protecting this or that part of the empire or expanding trade or territory. This country seldom had such global view. We never wanted to acquire a piece of property, we really didn't want the rest of the world to do anything but be good boys and not cause us trouble. As close as you could usually get to a foreign policy issue would be where two of our friends or two other nations in the world got into a dispute and wanted our help and we had to decide one way or the other. But in terms of a defined national foreign policy, it's very hard to trace one, up until the cold war, that had any coherence, specificity or any keel. Of course we had a worldwide diplomatic apparatus to deal with our sister nations around the world, but I'm talking about foreign policy. Where did we want to go? We didn't want to go anywhere. We wanted peace, we wanted to be left alone. We wanted to trade, we didn't want to be discriminated against too much in our trading; that was about it.

But World War II woke us up to how simplistic (and puny) our national security apparatus was and had been. Shortly after World War II we were confronted gradually with the realization that there was a new challenge to our survival, our hopes for being left alone and being left in peace, one that had dimensions that we hadn't seen before. Despite such grand initiatives as helping launch the UN, initiating the Marshall Plan and the Truman Doctrine, which may have marked the beginning of a post World War II foreign policy, we gradually came to realize that there was a need for something more.

There was a demonstrated need to try to graft some kind of political warfare executive onto the established structure of government. That need arose from the simple fact that there was an adversary political warfare executive working very hard against us. And it was needed because the archaic, simplistic national security apparatus with which we entered World War II (which was comprised almost entirely of the State, War and Navy Departments) was hopelessly out of date in the sophisticated world we found from 1945 on. Now, let it be said, we never did accomplish that; we never did accomplish grafting an adequate political warfare executive onto our existing structure. Maybe, given our system of government, we never can.

But we have made some material progress in modernizing the national security machinery to meet the perceived task. Much of this happened during the Eisenhower administration. It didn't begin there, it began in the Truman administration, and with the National Security Act of 1947, and some very important preliminary evolution of the national security machinery occurred under the Truman administration.

But when "Ike" was elected President, you had this five-star general who had commanded the largest invasion forces in history and had been Supreme Allied Commander in Europe, and who was on first name terms with DeGaulle and Churchill and Adenauer and almost anybody else who played or had played a major role in contemporary events. Far from his least important talent was that his experience had made him a master of organizing staff machinery to deal with multinational and global problems. Needless to say he was more than a little interested in seeing to it that the National Security Council and its suborganizations worked in the way he thought those organizations should, in order to help him do his job.

Now there had been established, prior to the Eisenhower administration, a group called the Psychological Strategy Board and some of Eisenhower's people in the 1952 campaign, most notably C. D. Jackson, were great proponents of strengthening its functions in this fancy new world we were entering where the Communists were doing such a good job of orchestrating all their resources and assets. Orchestrating meant so organizing the use of our assets that we were in a position to give a positive and sensitive psychological twist to our activities. But the Psychological Strategy Board, by its organizational design, was divorced from the line operations of the responsible departments and agencies in the national security area. Primarily for that reason it didn't work very well. It really never could have, and it didn't take too long for us to realize that you can't have one person with total line responsibility in State or Defense or USIA or CIA or foreign aid or whatever and then another outsider coming in and telling him how to do his job. So it was dismantled in late '53 and replaced eventually by the Operations Coordinating Board (officially incorporated into the NSC in 1957). I think this was one of Eisenhower's major contributions to finding ways for the President of the United States to get a handle on his government in this complicated area, and this is what I will discuss most today.

The Operations Coordinating Board was established just one step below the National Security Council in level of participants; that is, instead of the Secretary of Defense and the Secretary of State, you had the Undersecretary of State and Deputy Secretary of Defense. And of course, the President didn't take direct part. But the other participants would be pretty much the same as those who attended NSC meetings: the Director of the CIA, the Director of USIA, the Director of FOA and so forth. Having examined the report prepared under the leadership of Bill (William H.) Jackson, having examined the inadequacies and unsoundness of trying to graft something like the Psychological Strategy Board on to the Executive Branch, it was seen by the Jackson Committee that you had to get right into the operations, the actual management of operations, to make sure that they were consonant with the policies decided upon by the President, that they were coordinated with each other and to the extent possible that they were conducted with a view to impact on world opinion in a way most favorable to the United States. That was a big glamour step down from the aspirations of the Psychological Strategy Board, but it was also much more realistic.

But even in that context, of course, there were a lot of growing pains in the establishment of the Board. It was, to some extent, resisted by the State Department in the inexorable struggle between State and the White House. That was perfectly understandable. State saw something being taken away from it, or potentially being taken away from it, and didn't like that much. On the other hand the President was firmly convinced that the problems that had been primarily the sole responsibility of State had now broadened into new dimensions with the Cold War, the growing military threat and the new forms of psychological warfare, and that he, the President, had to have his hands on a vehicle that was more comprehensive in scope.

So you had constant pulling and tugging for a few years; there was some bloodshed between people like Nelson Rockefeller, who in 1955 or so had come into the White House as Special Assistant to the President, and Undersecretary of State Herbert Hoover, Jr. and others. But gradually the system evolved, by the end of the Administration, into a very useful vehicle. And I'll try to tell you a little bit about what it was and what it wasn't. It was, as I said, designed to be the vehicle through which the national security policies approved by the President were implemented. To accomplish that, when a national security policy was approved by the President, say a policy on Ethiopia, it would then be given to the OCB which would assign it an interdepartmental group at the working level within the OCB framework to prepare an Operations Plan. Such plan was designed to have a six-months life. The process involved merely meant taking the policy, containing a broad policy line—of course, the National Security Council policies were always stated in very broad language—and refining it into much more specific assignments for each of the different departments and agencies within the national security area. Once approved, it would become the operational guidance for that area, ending up in the hands of the country team leader abroad, who was the U.S. Ambassador to a given country, and he would thus have in his safe an overall operational prescription for his own diplomats, his military advisory group chief, his economic attache, for his CIA operatives, and all. Most of these ambassadors found it extremely useful, a few didn't. But it at least gave them all something they could refer to for overall policy and operational guidance. They did not have to reinvent the wheel each time or fight over such questions as whether we do or do not recognize Red China when it came up. It settled major policy and major operational matters.

Then at the end of the six months period each such interdepartmental working group, almost always chaired by the State Department, would prepare a Progress Report on the Operation Plan. This would say that the Operation Plan in effect for Iceland, say, is out of date, or the situation has so changed there that we have to have a new Operation Plan or maybe even have a new overall NSC policy, or, everything's fine, the plan is still viable and we can live with it. That Progress Report recommendation would be sent up through the OCB itself. If approved there, then at the next National Security Council meeting it was my job at the end of the meeting to tell the President in the presence of the National Security Council that, in the opinion of his prime operators, things were okay and did not require revision for another six months. Or not; whatever the situation was.

The virtue of all this, of course, (obviously that aspect of the OCB's job was not only not front burner, it was by design back burner) was that it provided a way of monitoring on an orderly basis all the subjects, all the National Security Council problems, and potential future problems, so that when the President and the Secretary of State and Chairman of the Joint Chiefs, and so forth, were occupied worrying about this crisis or that crisis that was keeping them awake nights, the important but non-crisis work was going on back at the store. Iceland was being watched and that Communist legislature in Iceland was not going to kick us out of our bases without us having a pretty good warning. And that was something that the President cared about very much because it made him feel "okay, I don't have to worry about the Philippines or the Mahgreb or wherever; that's all being carefully watched by my Department and Agency heads." The President often expressed his satisfaction with that process.

In addition to this regular OCB function there were a lot of peripheral national security items the primary responsibility for which did not fall under a given department or agency which got dumped on the OCB. Some of these were pretty far out. Our operations in Antarctica, for example; there was no obvious departmental place for them. In its beginnings that was also true of the national space effort. Different departments would have a piece of it. State was upset by the political mileage the Communists were getting out ot Sputnik, for example, parading in the Italian elections with papier mache Sputniks saying, "Look what we Communists can do, what can your friends the Americans do?" State was getting a lot of reaction from diplomats around the world, friendly as well as not so friendly, rubbing it in. But State had no operational capability to do anything about it. Although, in the beginning, Defense had to finance this effort, it was never a favorite of Charlie Wilson's. He thought it rather unfair to give up so many of his pennies to put a "damn orange" up in the air. So though he had to finance it, he wasn't pushing it. Budget was against it too. So it fell to the OCB basically to put all the pieces together and get a policy drafted by the NSC that would establish in a positive way the attitude of the United States toward the beginnings of a national space effort. That was difficult because in the beginning no one had any idea how large to cut the cloth. You didn't know how fast you could spend money effectively even if you were willing to, and you didn't quite know what sort of program you were going to start with. Well, we at least got it started on some sort of basis and then the newly created National Space Council and NASA took over the policy and operational job.

It was much the same with respect to Antarctica. Our growing operations in Antarctica didn't have a home that cared about them much. State was in charge of negotiating the necessary diplomatic treaties with the other Antarctica claimants. Defense via the Navy ran the logistics, the National Science Foundation oversaw the scientific programming, etc., but essentially it had no home. So you had to develop some way to bring together the various pieces of government responsibility, propose an overall government policy for them and get that policy approved. Only then would you have a solid basis on which to proceed.

Thus, in general, front burner crises were lifted out—I'm going to make some exceptions to this—of the NSC-OCB "machinery." But they weren't lifted out of the NSC, itself. They'd be discussed at National Security Council meetings but, by definition, such problems obviously didn't permit of the time to be treated by routine procedures, or even, usually, in an orderly fashion. They had to be treated as the crises they were and dealing with them on a daily, even hourly, basis was what the President gets paid for, what the Secretary of State gets paid for, and the other top executives get paid for. Their front burner work, understandably, occupied most of the time and effort they devoted to national security affairs.

And then there were other matters which were deemed to be too sensitive for exposure to the full formal NSC/OCB process. Some examples: the U-2 wasn't an NSC item until it tore its britches. The OCB had to do some cleaning up after that. Also the off-shore islands affair, when the Seventh Fleet was positioned to discourage Chinese aggression against Quemoy and Matsu and we were constantly moving the fleet around. That's the kind of thing that would be discussed regularly within the NSC as the President felt the need for it, but would not be processed through the machinery for it just didn't permit of the time or the breadth of exposure involved in such treatment. The landing in Lebanon—well, the day I guess it was July 14, 1958, that an Iraqi Colonel, an armored regiment commander, after leaving Baghdad, turned around and came back and assassinated Nuri-Said and thus destabilized the whole Middle East, the President made his decision to land tanks in Lebanon on that same Monday afternoon. That was all done on an ad hoc basis. Contingency planning for a possible invasion of Cuba, by Cuban exiles and refugees, which you recall was much bruited about in the 1960 election, was not exposed to the full breadth of the NSC and OCB machinery. Rather a special committee was established for that. High altitude testing of nuclear explosives at a time when we were trying to get agreement to ban such tests; such things would have special little homes of their own.

Some items were sensitive in other ways—for example, contingency plans for dealing with Middle East oil supplies and other things so diplomatically sensitive that I don't want to talk about them even twenty-five years later. They too had a delicacy that dictated that they not be formally processed within the NSC machinery, primarily for security reasons.

However, the important point is this. The value of the NSC-OCB process in such matters was that all the top government executives in the national security area were well grounded in both the policy and operational factors involved in these different questions, and not only in their own policy and operational factors but in those of their sister agencies as well. Therefore when a crisis arose in some area, whoever was in operational charge could hit the ground running with all of the others. (I call this the "open conference line" effect of the OCB in that these top operators had been working together with respect to such areas for months and when calls for action came in a hurry you could poll them quickly without having to go through a lot of preamble to bring them up to date.)

So the greatest portion of staff effort in the NSC/OCB machinery was devoted mostly to the development of policy and operational plans in, I won't say routine because they dealt with the major policy matters, but rather non-crisis matters.

A final word on how this aspect worked. I don't want to belabor this but take for example, the development of our policy with respect to a major Latin American nation. The policy statements in the NSC paper, approved by the President after presentation and discussion at an NSC meeting, would be quite general. Perhaps, for example, the policy sought to discourage devotion of excessive resources to military development and encouraged reallocation of resources to the development of economic infrastructure. That was a fairly common policy objective of the United States with respect to such countries. Then the OCB's operation plan, much like the NSC paper, would begin with a statement of the general situation in the country and its present and potential impact on U.S. interests. It would translate the general policy statement into much more specific operational guidance to the agencies involved, each one of them. These plans would all be approved on an interagency basis by a body (the OCB) of which their own chief executive officer was a member. So the operative foreign aid officer in Peru couldn't claim that he possessed different instructions from anybody else, because his boss, the director of the U.S. foreign aid program had been sitting right in on the decision.

Again, we took all of these matters up on an automatic, orderly basis to keep the main show going while in no way interfering with the handling of specific crises. Crises don't lend themselves to that kind of deliberate treatment.

But the OCB did many other important things. After all, it was the residuary legatee of the functions of the Psychological Strategy Board. And although the President had concluded that the PSB, as structured, wouldn't work, he never lost his appetite for a means of providing "orchestration," or for a system that would encourage the development of creative ideas in this area. One OCB device to provide that, in addition to the formalized work referred to, was the holding of a special meeting at State every Wednesday for lunch from which all staff was excluded. There was no food service; each OCB member got a sandwich and a glass of apple juice or something, because they didn't want serving staff or anybody else in the room. No OCB staff either, only the board members themselves, were present to kick around the more delicate operational and world opinion problems that were on the President's immediate plate. At these luncheons, this group discussed crises, opportunities, matters of substance and "bright new ideas;" sometimes matters of public relations, often both. This is the place where the USIA Director might say to the Deputy Secretary of Defense, "Your weapons test in such and such a place is giving us fits in terms of international public opinion." The Deputy Secretary of Defense would probably have some choice comments suggesting that perhaps it was the USIA's job to put the best face on whatever was necessary for national security, not "Now let's do what the USIA finds it easy to sell." Or, perhaps, Defense might ask the Director of Foreign Aid, "We hear you're going to end support for the police infrastructure in Pakistan. Is that true?" As you can imagine, the rumors as to what is going on run rampant in so large a government, where on both a vertical and horizontal basis the communication problems are so vast. Such rumors can be disruptive and cause misunderstanding or at least delay. But misunderstandings, misapprehensions, and false rumors usually fell easy prey to the truth at these sessions. Also the candid dialogue about the most delicate issues provided a good insight into the other fellow's problems. It's amazing how little a busy head of one agency will normally know about what's going on in his sister agencies. They usually haven't got the time; they often haven't got the interest; and they almost always have a difference of perspective. But in this informal setting they could sit around and talk freely about whatever the problem was. Very sensitive stuff could be talked out quite fully.

In my opinion, by the end of the Eisenhower administration, after eight years of evolving, there were some quite effective procedures underway. I think the OCB had come to be and was recognized to be even by its early enemies, State particularly, a most valuable and useful device, which would have had to have been invented had it not existed. I know certainly a lot of my pals in State came around to realize that this was the best avenue some of them had for surfacing ideas that they couldn't get up in their own department, ideas that were blocked in bureaucratic channels at one level or another.

Unfortunately the Kennedy group did not agree, but therein lies another tale. I had sessions with McGeorge Bundy and, to a lesser extent, Walt Rostow, during the two months of transition after the 1960 elections to try to convince them that the path of wisdom was to take advantage of the bloodshed we had inflicted on ourselves in the effort to produce a fairly effective working apparatus, to profit by our mistakes as they were perceived, and so forth, but not to take this hard won tool away from the incoming President. With a change of Administration, the President of the United States is the only one who comes into an empty office. Everybody else comes into nearly fully manned departments and in some cases you might hardly notice they come in at all, for all the early difference they make. Whether it was the Foreign Service, the CIA, the military or anybody else, the new top political appointees found the bureaucracy right there, fully entrenched and operative. But you only get a few security people, a few communications people, a couple of switchboard operators, and nobody else when you come in as President of the United States. And every tool he can have to get his wishes and his policies transmitted reasonably accurately, reasonably effectively, down the long line from 1600 Pennsylvania Avenue to some platoon commander in Korea or some assistant commercial attache in Bangladesh, anything he can do to get through that mud pile he needs to be able to do.

But, I'm afraid, during the 1960 election campaign, the OCB got tagged a little bit as an invention of Eisenhower, as a creature of Eisenhower. It fell under the general heading in the campaign of the allegedly unnecessary and excessive staff structure that the "aging general" had imposed upon the government, thereby "stifling creativity and ideas," and all that kind of rhetoric and mindset. Thus it was pretty well doomed from the outset. And I think some of the incoming people really didn't fully appreciate that dealing with the whole world was a little different from what they had been dealing with, or that you couldn't do it on the "old boy" network alone; you really had to have some structured communication channels for firmly developed policies if you weren't going to be banging up against each other all the time all up and down the line.

Perhaps I shouldn't say this with Frank Elliot sitting here because he's an expert on all this much more than I am but the opposition of some of the budgetary and bureaucratic losers during the Eisenhower years—the Army, half the Navy, and some diehard State Department officers—also played a part in the demise of the OCB. But the main loser by this decision was the new President. Within two and a half months of the start of his administration he began to reconsider that decision after the Bay of Pigs slap in the face. But the OCB has never been successfully restored or replaced, and I think that's too bad. I'm not sure nowadays if the world in which our government functions permits enough discipline of thought to set up a structure like that. We seem to want to run from headline to headline every day and let the media decide what our policies should be the next day. I'm exaggerating slightly but that was a different world and Eisenhower was a different President and even the Congress was a different Congress in those days. It was before the days of the Kissingers and the Brezinzskis, and all, making their own personal reputations in a job that was designed originally to be a staff job not a policymaking job. So I'm not sure you could put the genie back in the bottle again even if you wanted to, but that is too bad, in my opinion, because it did a lot of good. By the way, President Reagan seems to be making some effort to work back to the original concept.

A little epilogue—President Kennedy did ask me to come down in May of 1961, because of the Bay of Pigs disaster, which shook him very badly. I had a wonderful session with him alone for maybe twenty minutes and then with him and McGeorge Bundy for another hour or so. The issue basically was would the structure we had had and the procedures we had used have avoided some of the difficult aspects of the Bay of Pigs invasion. I did my best to assure him that each President had to operate in a different way and we weren't about to say that it would have. We would not even have handled it directly through the OCB. We had a separate little group (although made up of pretty much the same people) that was looking that thing over. But he felt terribly disappointed by his policymakers on the way up, that is in formulating policy issues, because they had given him a picture of the situation that did not turn out to be accurate. Similarly on the way down that is, in implementing his decision, he thought they had strayed pretty far from his clearly dictated orders as to how it was to be done. So we were talking primarily about how machinery might have avoided those deficiencies. Incidentally, the Kennedy people shortly thereafter did try to resuscitate something like the OCB in the so-called Tuesday lunch group but it was a much less structured apparatus.

I also visited with Robert Kennedy and Maxwell Taylor on the same subject a month or so later. My credentials were partly that I had some experience in the area but mostly that I was such an identified Republican they knew I had no interest in a job with the Administration. I was very impressed with the candor with which President Kennedy took me into his confidence. Charlie Bartlett had set it up and the President knew exactly where I came from and who I was and that there was no reason I couldn't walk out on the front steps of the White House afterward and bray like a mule. That didn't inhibit him; he told me what mistakes he thought he had made, the mistakes he thought his people had made, and unburdened himself completely. I was very impressed by this candor and trust.

NARRATOR: One of the things that comes into mind—if I could just take advantage of where I'm sitting to ask the first question: Was it the people who came in who made this structure work, the Cutlers, the

Goodpasters, the Gordon Grays, yourself, or was it the President, or was it the interaction between the two? We all know within the university, within the business world, within every sphere in which we work that there are some people that have to ham it up and have to be on shows whenever they can possibly do it. Then there are other people who work away at their jobs. In our Roosevelt Portrait volume, Tommy the Cork said that, "The first thousand men down determine the success or failure of any administration." Within your Administration there seemed to have been at least a number of them who were not so anxious to talk but rather to work hard at their job. Is Ike responsible for that or is it something else?

MR. HARR: Yes, I would think that it was probably traceable entirely to the President. He wouldn't have tolerated anything else very long anyway and everybody knew that. I started out with a rather sentimental statement about how we loved him. Well we did. He was almost a father figure. I have to come back to the one key word—integrity. It was absolute and inspiring. By everyone's standards, he was a good man. Nobody hated him, his enemies didn't even hate him. He was wise and he was sound and he was good to you, but he was also tough. He was not only a career military officer, he was a very dignified man personally. I can remember one time I lost sight of that fact and embarrassed myself badly. I was giving my report at the end of an NSC meeting at some date after Secretary Dulles had died. I said somewhere at the end of my report, whatever the subject was, "Mr. President, Chris (Herter) may want to add something to what I've said." Well, a little while later the President's Naval aide came up to me and said, "Karl, you know, the President doesn't like the Secretary of State to be called by his first name in the National Security Council meeting." And the moment I heard that I realized of course it was so, although I called him Chris everywhere else. So he very definitely had his formal side. Once when a Kennedy appointee was first introduced to him after the Kennedy election he came into the Oval Office smoking his pipe and sat up on the President's desk. This informality was not appealing to the President and you could see the old General's back stiffen. For all his kindness he was very dignified gent.

But to get back to your question. Yes, for instance, people used to kid Bobby Cutler about it. At one point some columnist wrote a very needling article describing Bobby sitting by the President's knee gazing fondly into his face. But there was, I won't say a slavish devotion, but there was a loving devotion of people who (in most cases) didn't have the slightest thought of aggrandizing themselves in that particular context, or if they did, tried their best to keep it invisible. Now, of course, there were exceptions and as long as they didn't hurt the President or get too big nobody ever looked at them. But you take men like Sherman Adams, absolutely self-effacing, a service oriented individual who adored the President. Now maybe there's a little footnote there. Maybe it wasn't just the President, maybe it's the fact that the President picked people like Governor Adams, Bobby Cutler, Gordon Gray, all men of adequate egos, certainly, but men who also saw their role as strictly being to serve the President. They all sought to avoid the press—Bobby Cutler would never even go to a party, he would never go out in the evening. Jim Haggerty's position was clear: "Nobody talks to the press but me." When I first came in, the press was there. Some of them were good friends of mine, like Charlie Bartlett, Roly Evans and Joe Kraft, and they would say, "Why don't we have a little quiet dinner once a month or so and just talk off the record for background fill in?" I raised this with Haggerty who looked at me and said, "Young man, that is the dumbest idea I've ever heard in my life. No, the answer is no." And I must say, in terms of the President's best interests, he was quite right.

But then to move along, just quickly to finish that point. When President Kennedy came into office he said, "We're going to put the onus back on State where it belongs and we're going to make the system work that way." In effect he was saying they were going to dismantle a large part of the White House machinery, dump the overall national security mission back on State and hold State's feet to the fire to make it work. Then, however, he put Dean Rusk, a very gentlemanly non-aggressive type in as Secretary of State and McGeorge Bundy in as Special Assistant to the President for National Security Affairs and the personalities were absolutely out of sync with the concept, so that pretty soon stuff started coming back in to the White House for coordination and leadership. I would argue, however, that even without regard to personalities, given today's world, such a trend is inevitable.

I think it was President Nixon, however, who blew the boat out of the water when he appointed Kissinger as Special Assistant for National Security, because then he was no longer pretending that you just had a staff assistant there working for the President, you had an "assistant president" for national security affairs.

NARRATOR: Before we move on to other questions, could you say just a word about how you got into all this. You graduated from Yale Law School, you were an associate of Sullivan and Cromwell, you had come back from Oxford. How did you get caught up in all this?

MR. HARR: I guess it ties in with the reason I wanted to go to Oxford and the subject I did my doctorate on—the political left in Europe—

specifically the popular front in France. It was really an analysis of Communist and Socialist interaction during the thirties. I was just convinced that the biggest problem in my lifetime was going to be whether we could save freedom or would lose freedom. Our adversaries had become pretty smart working with the prevailing political forces and were way down the road in terms of experience as to how you manipulate such forces. So, I felt, what's the sense of spending your life in the traditional way trying to make money for your kids if they are to end up living in a slave camp. The time schedule of our era just didn't seem the same as it used to be in the old days. There seemed to be a speeded up timetable and the big question had become was anything as important as working for freedom. So, with such a frame of reference, the way those things work I got to know some people who showed up a lot later in government. And we naturally passed each others' names around and all of a sudden I'm called up one day by Gordon Gray to come on down and be his deputy in Defense and the next thing I knew. . .

QUESTION: Did he have a Bradley in the White House?

MR. HARR: Omar Bradley?

QUESTION: No, I'm talking about the concept of a Bradley. It seemed to me, if you read anything about World War II and how he handled the situation, Bradley did the nitty-gritty and it never got to Mr. Eisenhower unless there was a serious problem like firing Patton and that sort of thing. He was sort of the front man for the President and Churchill.

MR. HARR: Well, he certainly believed in organized staff work.

QUESTION: But did he have a Bradley?

MR. HARR: Well, the nearest thing to it was Sherman Adams, when he was there and then Slick Persons, and on the national security side Bobby Cutler, Dillon Anderson, then Gordon Gray, and of course General Goodpaster, the President's Staff Secretary. They really did most of the paper handling and staffing of the issues, getting them organized, and then came to him for final approval or for the resolution of the big issues. Now, the President was very close to Dulles personally. He had great affection for Secretary Dulles and deeply respected his mind. Regularly Dulles would come over to the White House after the day's work and sit down and just chat with the President about world affairs. He never had a free and easy relationship like that with Chris Herter, or, as far as I know with anybody else in his Cabinet. He thought Dulles was the *ne plus ultra*

QUESTION: Yet he could be critical, couldn't he? He said Dulles didn't read other peoples motives and that his presentations sometimes didn't reflect sensitivity.

MR. HARR: I'm not familiar with that, but I wouldn't be surprised. I know that Dulles literally died at the Cabinet table. I don't mean physically died, but you could see his illness progressing at successive National Security Council and Cabinet meetings. He finally had to resign as secretary of state, but they gave him some nominal "assistant to the President" title so he could be present at all of these important things. Dulles' illness really was the hardest thing on the President that I saw during the whole three years I was in the White House, much harder than his own ileitis or heart attack or anything else.

QUESTION: In this forum I've often pointed out that interservice rivalry is a penalty that this country can't continue to carry. I'd like your observations on how the interservice rivalry—if you see it as I have seen it—affects the President's ability to get his policy implemented.

MR. HARR: I've seen it from that angle and now I'm seeing it from another angle. But all I'll say is that when I left the Pentagon to go over to the White House to what, on paper, looked like a feverish activity kind of job on a global scale, it was actually a kind of rest after coming out of that seething five-sided building with each of the Services putting it to the others. I don't know the answer to it. I think the situation has considerably improved; I think there is a degree of maturity that wasn't always there in the early times.

QUESTION: Both General Jones and of course General Brown, felt very strongly that the chiefs had to be redesigned in order to get policy implemented through the service structures.

MR. HARR: I agree with them.

QUESTION: Is there any truth that President Eisenhower's choice for a vice president in 1956 was Robert Anderson?

MR. HARR: No. Well, I can't say absolutely. I never heard that verified, I'd heard the rumor. Of course Harold Stassen was working to get the VP nomination at that point. But I don't think so. Al Gruenther's name was mentioned but I think the President crossed the bridge on Nixon pretty early in that campaign. It would have been disruptive to have to have removed him from the ticket. The President greatly admired Anderson, he respected Anderson, there was no question about that Anderson was another one of his favorite people obviously when he was secretary of the treasury.

NARRATOR: We've been having some seminars on the presidency and the press, and the columnists tell about a dinner where he ran up the trial balloon for Anderson.

MR. HARR: I remember that now.

QUESTION: I had a memory that one of Eisenhower's last public speeches, he made some reference to warning America about the danger of the military/industrial complex. What generated that?

MR. HARR: Well, he was a man, by that time at least, well above any parochial considerations. I think he honestly saw the problem coming. You must recognize now I'm in the other part of that so-called complex, so I'm very sensitive to it. You see we went from a very small defense budget before the Korean War in 1950 to an enormous budget in the following ten years during most of which Eisenhower was in office. And we also went through those years when the country was really scared for the first time in its modern history. The nation started putting in intercontinental ballistic missiles; people started building shelters in their cellars. That's when the country started thinking Atlas missiles and Titan missiles and building up our strategic forces and spending hundreds of millions and billions of dollars on defense programs. As I said if the Army, half the Navy and some of the State Department tended to be against Eisenhower in the 1960 election it was because the Air Force and the other half of the Navy had been getting all the money, and basically people like General Maxwell Taylor had to resign and write a book in order to attract attention back to the ground forces role and the Army. Here was General Eisenhower, greatest living representative of the U.S. Army, doing all this to them. Nevertheless with the enormous amounts of money that got poured into the missile programs, particularly, and aircraft and so forth, we did build up a substantial defense industry, and he truly felt, that if you don't keep a careful eye on it, it would develop a life of its own.

One terribly wise and important thing Eisenhower did—unfortunately we haven't sustained it—was to establish the principle that we had to arrive at a firm concept of how much money we, as a nation, had to, and could afford to, spend on defense and then stick with that figure because he saw we were going to be in the defense business from here on out. For the first time in this country's history we were going to have to have a large peacetime defense establishment, both military and industrial. So the thing we had to figure out was what level of expenditure of resources was adequate to do the job of deterring the Soviets strategically while giving us adequate capabilities to cope with predictable local aggressions, and at the same time was sustainable over a period of time in essentially a peacetime economy. He knew that the expensive course and the wasteful thing was to have peaks and valleys in your defense budget. Building up too fast is expensive and inefficient, and cutting back capriciously you throw it all away; you can't mesh the lead times of weapons systems, you can't order future programs in an orderly way or crank new technologies into the development program. We stayed on that course, set by Eisenhower, pretty well until the Vietnam War. The demands of that conflict tended to defer a lot of major programs that had been part of an orderly plan. Then when the Vietnam War was over, pretty soon all the programs began bumping into each other. It got to be a mess for awhile. I think we're getting out of that a little bit now, but for a while there we weren't getting anything but paper airplanes and expensive paper airplanes, because somebody was always coming up with some technological advance to challenge the deferred programs.

I've been asked about that quote so many times, I used to say just for chuckles, "You know I wrote that phrase (the military/industrial complex) in the President's speech." I didn't, of course, but I used to say I did because it tended to shut people up. When Senator Proxmire quoted it one time, I said, "Senator, why is it that the only people who quote Eisenhower on that subject are people who never quote Eisenhower on any other subject," which I thought was pretty telling. After thinking a moment, he looked at me and said, "Well, that's because that's the most quotable thing he's ever said."

QUESTION: You spoke of John Foster Dulles and I have to inquire about his brother and the CIA during this period.

MR. HARR: He also went to Princeton.

QUESTION: His *entrée* at the White House and in the CIA. Any mention of him during that period with the OCB?

MR. HARR: Well, he was very active in the OCB context. He was also invited directly to be at every NSC meeting at which he would give an intelligence report, informal intelligence report, and also he would be called on for intelligence assessments as required. Of course Allen was bigger than life in many ways. He was a most affable human being; but administration wasn't his *forté*. We used to say, "Well, Allen Dulles, he's not a good administrator òr a bad administrator, he's innocent of administration."

Getting back to the point that was just raised, he had great personal capital and credibility among our allies, particularly the British, dating from his World War II experience and his earlier days with CIA and before that the OSS.

QUESTION: And he it was who held it together, more than anybody else.

MR. HARR: I think he was always "little brother," and I know there was never any question in Foster's mind about that, or in the President's mind either. But Allen was a most competent, intelligent and jolly fellow with a unique wealth of background and experience for his job.

QUESTION: Was there any noticeable impact of Eisenhower's tenure as president of Columbia on the presidency? Did he use any of the Columbia University faculty?

MR. HARR: Well, you see I didn't come into the White House until 1958, and so many of the things done in earlier days, I didn't really see of course. They now have his oral history up there and he always had a picture of himself as president of Columbia University. I can't think of any Columbia faculty coming into the government, can you?

QUESTION: No, I can't either.

MR. HARR. There was a bill called the Kersten Amendment that proposed the establishment of a brigade or a division of central European refugees from Communism as an adjunct to the United States Army, composed of Czechs and Hungarians primarily. Ike thought that was a pretty good idea for a lot of reasons but the top Army brass didn't like it at all. Now these generals were all his old pals of course, fellow generals, so he dropped in one day when they were all sitting around and they started telling him how and why he couldn't do it. Finally Ike said, "Fellows, tell me this, just how high does a fellow have to go in this outfit before he can call the shots?"

The little tiny things. Sometimes they are so revealing of the nature of the man. For example, it so happens that his son John and I are twins, in that we were born the same day, the same year, and that fact worried me some. I asked John never to tell his father because I thought his father would always think of me as being pretty young. But it got out somehow and one very busy morning I got summarily called into his office while we were about to convene an NSC meeting up at Newport, at the Naval War College. And, holding up the scheduled meeting the President said, "I just wanted to say I hear this is a special day in your life. Happy Birthday." A nice little touch, by a very busy, very nice man.

QUESTION: You commented that President Eisenhower didn't have any real enemies and yet President Truman, in his own words, makes clear he didn't admire President Eisenhower. In his book *Plain Speaking,* he was very critical of Eisenhower.

MR. HARR: Yes, I know. He was critical of everybody, though.

QUESTION: And I wonder what led to that, the hard feelings between the two.

MR. HARR: Well, I don't know. I don't really want to be in any way critical of President Truman, and obviously you know what my biases are, but there was never any doubt in my mind as to who was the big man and who was the little man, and I don't think Eisenhower ever sized him up in any way like that.

Well, Ike came along, the hero of the war, Truman was President of the United States, Truman was lambasted to some degree, people didn't think he was going to win the 1948 election.

I think his attitude was a little bit of pique, a little bit of sour grapes, a little bit of having the limelight stolen from him, a little bit of Missouri cussedness. He really took everybody apart in that *Plain Speaking* book. He just didn't like many people.

QUESTION: Do you have any insights into Eisenhower's position in the 1964 election, especially his views on the military/industrial complex?

MR. HARR: I'm not quite tracking the question. You mean the Goldwater national election?

QUESTION: Yes, in 1964. Do you have any insights or thoughts on his thinking in the 1964 election?

MR. HARR: No, wasn't there some public record on that at all?

QUESTION: Well, there is a public record, I guess I was just wondering. . .

MR. HARR: I never saw him around that time. I saw him once in 1963 when I went up to visit him in Gettysburg, sometime just when Nelson Rockefeller was beginning to run his race for the 1964 election.

QUESTION: It was a very divisive period and I think the Republican party looked to President Eisenhower at that time to help resolve some of the conflicts and disputes, and there was apparently some conflict in his own mind and I guess I am wondering whether the points you raised earlier about the military/industrial complex. . .

MR. HARR: If you read that whole speech, he says everything I would like to hear him say except that one phrase, and that was taken out of context. I mean, he also said that we have to have an adequate defense, that our security depends on it. But, of course, the papers that pulled it out of context and used it against him had a lot of fun. He was a little upset by Rockefeller's divorce during preparation for the '64 election. The nature of his disappointment was that, in his view, "Nelson has come before the people all his life representing that he wants to be known as a man dedicated to public service and that such service is his top priority, and now it looks like it isn't quite his top priority." In a purely political sense, in other words, the President thought it tarnished the image Rockefeller had created of being a totally dedicated public servant.

QUESTION: I don't quite know how to ask this clearly but there have been different opinions of how good a secretary of state Foster Dulles was, and obviously Eisenhower thought he was great. But I wanted the perception of those around Eisenhower, whether they felt he had a sound judgment of that matter or was he just bowled over by something in the personality of the man.

MR. HARR: No, Dulles didn't have all that much personality. He was somewhat austere, very proud, he had sort of that owlish look with his mouth down at the sides. He was really a very sweet guy, but he didn't come through in a particularly charming way. However, he was the architect of the system of containment represented by SEATO, NATO, etc., and built the little boxes around the Communists' borders, keeping friendly nations economically and militarily strong enough and on our side. Well, that was a pretty successful formula for quite a few years. Free nations have survived for decades behind that structure, although of course we've dismantled it considerably now. He was very, very creative and effective in establishing those different treaty organizations. But people would get on him for something like the concept of "massive retaliation." without which we had no credible deterrent. But nobody likes to be massively deterred or retaliated against; it's not a happy thought to retain uppermost in your mind all the time. There were those who had a pretty good time making him sound trigger-happy. In fact, more and more, I'm afraid, it doesn't matter what you do in Washington, it's a matter of how it's made to seem.

NARRATOR: Greenstein closes his book by quoting from the oral history, Eisenhower's statement about how you make decisions, you remember:

"I've been forced to make decisions, some of them of a critical character for many years, and I know of only one way in which you can be sure you've done your best to make a wise decision: that is to get all of the people who have definable responsibility in this particular field, whatever it be, get them with their different viewpoints in front of you and listen to them debate. I do not believe in bringing them in one at a time and therefore being more impressed by the most recent one you hear than the earlier ones. You must get courageous men, men of strong views and let them debate and argue with each other. You listen and you see if anything has been brought up, and idea that changes your own view or enriches your view or adds to it. Sometimes the case becomes so simple that you can make a decision right then or you may go back and wait two or three weeks if time isn't of the essence but you must make it."

Kennedy had the opposite view. He said he didn't like meetings that were seminars. How do you sum up your feeling about Eisenhower's approach to this?

MR. HARR: Well, I think the term seminar wouldn't apply to Eisenhower's approach. There would be more orderliness to it. Bobby Cutler, for example, when he would introduce a subject at the NSC would say, "Mr. President, the second item on the agenda, you can see is—whatever—and we have prepared and circulated to members of the Council the policy proposed by the National Security Council Planning Board. There was agreement on most of it but there are splits here between the Joint Chiefs on the one hand and the Department of State. Here are the arguments, and Admiral Radford and Secretary Dulles can correct me if I'm wrong or add to them." So you had a fairly formalized debate structure instead of either a seminar or a wide open discussion. Anybody could say anything he wanted to but he had better make sense most of the time or his stock would go down with the President. Yes, I think that's right, I think he did like to proceed as Dr. Greenstein says, outside the Council too. For instance, on the decision to go into Lebanon in July 1958, he immediately called a meeting of all the people he thought might have any role in it, whether it was the logistics role such as moving the tanks and Marines over there or whether it was the diplomatic role of clearing the way with our allies or whether it was the press role or whatever.

NARRATOR: The best way I think to thank our guest is to say that the late Gordon Gray was right. Gordon Gray, with whom Karl worked, told me, "If you really want to hear somebody discuss the national security policy get Karl Harr," and I think the best thanks I can offer is to say that Mr. Gray spoke the truth.

AN OVERVIEW OF THE
WHITE HOUSE
Bradley H. Patterson, Jr.

NARRATOR: We would like to welcome Bradley Patterson who has been a federal career executive for some thirty-two years and a member of the White House staff for fourteen of those thirty-two years. He is now a senior staff member of the Advanced Studies Program of the Brookings Institution in Washington.

As we proceeded with the Eisenhower portrait one after the other of the guests we had, including most recently at least one or two that we met with in Washington, Milton Eisenhower and Bryce Harlow, mentioned Brad Patterson as someone who understood and had been close to the operations of the Eisenhower White House.

Brad Patterson received his B.A. and his M.A. from the University of Chicago, taught at the Cranbrook School, joined the Department of State in 1945 and served the department for nine years. In 1954 he was appointed assistant Cabinet secretary at the White House and served from 1954 through 1961, the balance of the Eisenhower administration. He was executive secretary of the Peace Corps from 1961 to 1962. He was a national security affairs adviser of the secretary of the treasury from 1962 to 1966. He was executive director of the National Advisory Commission on Selective Service from 1966 to 1967.

He was executive director of the National Advisory Council on Economic Opportunity from 1967 to 1969. In 1969 he joined Leonard Garment as executive assistant in the White House especially concerned with civil rights and Indian affairs. In late 1974 he was appointed assistant director of the Presidential Personnel Office. President Ford shortly thereafter also designated him coordinator for Policies and Programs Affecting the American Indians.

He has received a number of awards for his public service, among them an award in 1960, the Arthur S. Flemming award as one of ten outstanding young men in the federal service. In 1975 he received a special citation by the Civil Service Commission. He has been vice president and president of the National Capital Area Chapter of the American Society for Public Administration. He has been chairman of the National ASPA Policy Issues Committee. He was elected in the fall of 1981 to the National Academy of Public Administration, and has just been elected president of the American Society for Public Administration for its 1984–85 term. His writings include an important paper on the "President's Cabinet: Issues and Questions" and an important article, "The White House Staff" which bears the subtitle "The Bashful Bureaucrat." He wrote an article in December 1980 on the Reagan White House staff which appeared in the *Washingtonian* magazine.

So in every respect through more than three decades Brad Patterson has served the government of the United States in a way that often escapes public notice but for the insiders and those who do the business of the nation is at the very heart and center of public affairs. We are especially pleased that he could be with us to discuss the Eisenhower presidency.

MR. PATTERSON: Thank you very much, Ken. It is an honor, truly, to be at this table among you distinguished men and women. I see many old faces and distinguished colleagues. I'm very pleased and flattered to be invited to join you.

I would like to talk a little bit about what I know best about the Eisenhower presidency which is the experiment with the Cabinet, use of the Cabinet and the Cabinet secretariat. I'll try to give some background about the idea and discuss some of the mechanics and how it actually worked and then talk about the pros and cons of the Cabinet and the use of White House staff that the Eisenhower presidency demonstrated. And I will be glad to have some questions and discussion.

The idea of the Cabinet secretary which I'm sure most of you recognize began roughly around 1904 in Great Britain because they had a Committee of Imperial Defense. The secretary was set up to serve the Committee of Imperial Defense by Lloyd George in 1904 and in 1916 the War Cabinet and after that it became a regular Cabinet secretariat.

I'm going to trace this idea just a little bit because of the importance of its beginnings in the United States.

In the American presidency, of course, we had a very irregular use of the Cabinet. Washington, the story goes, was out of town when the first Cabinet meeting was called. The vice president presided. My memory is that he tried some consultations on the Hill. He went up to the Congress to get advice and found he was somewhat rebuffed up there and then came back to holding his own Cabinet meetings. He often said, however, "These public meetings with reference to and from different departments are as much if not more than I am able to undergo," so he found himself beleaguered with meetings. Jackson didn't call a Cabinet meeting for two years after he took office. Harrison and reportedly President Pierce were rather spineless, even polled the Cabinet with the President's vote counting as only one among the others. Lincoln of course reversed that. President Polk wrote, "I have not had my full Cabinet together in council since the adjournment of Congress on the 14th of August last. I have conducted the government without their aid. I prefer to supervise the whole operations of the government myself rather than entrust the public business to subordinates. And this makes my duties very great."

Then in the Roosevelt period, Ickes said of the Roosevelt Cabinet, "The cold fact is that on important matters we are seldom called upon for advice. We never discuss exhaustively any policy of government or question of political strategy. The President makes all of his own decisions and, so far at least as the Cabinet is concerned, without taking counsel with a group of advisors. It is fair to say the Cabinet is not a general council upon whose advice the President relies. . . . Our Cabinet meetings are pleasant affairs but we only skim the surface of routine affairs." Then Henry Stimson, referring to the Roosevelt Cabinet said, "the same old two and sixpence, no earthly good."

In fact, they called the Cabinet often, as some of you I'm sure recognize, the President's "Amen corner." That is, the members of the Cabinet would try to corner Roosevelt in the room after the meeting and take up their own individual matters with him and attempt to do this privately.

In Jefferson's time he had an interesting quote about how he used the Cabinet. Comparing the two modes of consultation, that is, one on one separately and then the assembly form, namely the Cabinet form, Jefferson said after he had left the presidency, "I practiced the last method (namely the assembled form of Cabinet) because the harmony was so cordial among us all that we never failed by a contribution of mutual views on the subject to form an opinion acceptable to the whole. I think there was never one instance to the contrary in the case of any consequence. Yet this does, in fact, transform the executive into a directory and I hold the other method to be more constitutional.'' Jefferson is saying that he considered a Cabinet, even as harmonious a one over which he presided, he considered possibly not even constitutional because it derogated the role of the President as an individual executive. An interesting discussion at the time.

A couple of other little quotes from American history. Here is one from the White House secretary in Jackson's time. This is an excerpt from the letter from Major Jack Downing dated August 17, 1833. That's about 150 years ago. "The gineral [sic] says he likes things simple as a mousetrap. There's enough of us to do all that's wanted. Everyday just after breakfast the President lights his pipe and begins to think pretty hard. I and Major Donaldson begin to open letters for him and there was more than three bushels every day and all the while coming. We don't git through more than a bushel a day and never trouble long ones unless they come from Mr. Van Buren or Mr. Kendall or some other of our great folks. Then we sort them out and jest like Zeke Biglow does the mackrel at his packing yard; we only make three sorts and keep three big baskets; one marked 'Not Read' and another 'Read and Worth Nothing' and another 'Read And To Be Answered.' And then all the President has to do is say, 'Major, I reckon we best say so and so to that,' and I say, just so or not, just as the notion takes me and we go at it. We keep all the secretaries and the vice president and some district attorneys and a good many of our folks and Amos Kindel moving about and they tell us just how the cat jumps. As I said afore if it weren't for Congress meeting once a year we would put the government in a one-horse wagon and go just where we liked.'' That was the White House secretariat vintage 1833.

Going back to the First World War about the British Cabinet secretary. During the First World War—this is a quote from a book called *The Clock with Four Hands* by James Leaser:

> Hankey, who was, of course, the great Cabinet secretary was said to be the only man to attend every political and inter-allied conference and afterward he was given the thanks of both houses of parliament, praise galore, and more usefully the gift of 25,000 pounds. Lloyd George declared he was the best chief of staff he had known. Mr. Baldwin called him 'the ablest civil servant any country could possess.' A. J. Balfour gave him the highest praise of all. 'Without Hankey,' he said, 'we should not have won the war.' Hankey owed much of his success to his ability to draft superbly good minutes of meetings and to record clear-cut conclusions and to

prepare memoranda on a variety of subjects as required by the government. All this when the ministers themselves were not always very clear about what they had resolved.

At the peace conference in 1909 for instance, when many controversies and much friction disturbed the atmosphere, Clemenceau would arise from the table and say, 'Gentlemen, it is luncheon. Let us leave Monsieur Hankey to tell us later what we have decided.' After lunch, Hankey would table a list of 'conclusions' to all of which all the delegates would exclaim that was exactly what they had been trying to say all the time.

And one little quotation from a book entitled *The Turn of the Tide:* "And so while the great ones depart to their dinner the secretary stays growing thinner and thinner racking his brain to record and report what he thinks that they think that they ought to have thought."

The Second World War, as the literature that I've been able to be discover when I came to Washington just at the end of 1945 reveals, demonstrated some very great gaps in the coordination of American policy in the use of the Cabinet and the policy coordination in the presidency. In an excellent case study which my good friend and colleague in the State Department at the time, William McHenry Franklin, did in *World Politics* in October of 1963, he traced how Berlin got to be divided up the way it was—it was a separate city and was divided into four zones of occupation—how the zones were divided into the American, British, French, and Russian zones; how this agreement was reached. (The agreement about access was the occasion for a great crisis in 1948 and the Berlin airlift.) The Council of Foreign Ministers meetings in Paris resolved the issue in spring of 1949. (That was my first trip abroad as a secretariat officer in the Department of State for the American delegation to the conference in 1949.)

Anyway, Bill Franklin's article points out that under Roosevelt the Pentagon and the State Department were absolutely on different wave lengths on this very vital issue of the zones of Berlin and the occupation of Berlin and how any agreements with Berlin were reached:

> The War Department representative seemed reluctant to participate very actively on the ground that the whole problem of German surrender, including zones of occupation, was a military matter to be decided in due course by the appropriate military authorities. In response to the arguments of the Department of State this attitude was relaxed sufficiently to make possible the preparation of an agreed draft instrument for German surrender. . . . But this document said nothing about the zones of occupation because this was a subject which the military representatives would not seriously discuss with the State Department.
>
> The question was still on the agenda of the combined chiefs of staff. War Department offices at the level of a working security committee had no authority to discuss or share this problem with the State Department,

civilians who were not even familiar with its background. This awkward dilemma resulted from the fact that the prime minister in England had allowed the subject to be brought up in the European Advisory Commission while the President assumed that the combined chiefs of staff still had sole responsibility in the matter. The lines of authority were now completely fouled. This made little difference on the British side where the military and civilian elements were closely meshed in the War Cabinet and subordinate committees. But in Washington, with its sharp dichotomy between the State Department and the Pentagon, the effect was paralyzing. No agreed instruction on zones of occupation could be sent to Ambassador Winant for weeks and weeks during which his position became increasingly embarrassing.

Bill's article has an excellent point about the confusion and the lack of coordination in the 1944–1945 period.

Then came the beginnings of some discussion that was impelled by such lacks of coordination and Ickes' comments and others about a possible White House secretariat in 1945, 1946, 1947.

I have some memos I was looking at. Here is, for instance, a memo dated December 19, 1946 from Vannevar Bush to President Truman talking about the possibility of a presidential and Cabinet staff and recommending, "the possibility of a secretariat in the White House to prepare in advance the matters which should be taken up at Cabinet. The preparation of the agenda should include not only the subjects on which the President wishes Cabinet advice but also matters which the secretariat should raise on its own initiative, prepare minutes and record the meetings, see that the decisions rendered by the President are executed and so forth. But they are all executive orders. Review the status of legislation and so forth."

Then Harold Stein, a few weeks later wrote a memo to William Y. Elliott of Harvard warning against copying the British system. "My own experience," he said, "indicates that any attempt to focus the basic staff work of the American President on the Cabinet meetings is doomed to failure. The parallel with the British system is misleading..."

Then came the beginnings of the Hoover Commission. Don Price was at the center of this attempt to begin to discuss these questions within the context of the Hoover Commission. In March of 1947 he sent Jim Webb a note from the Public Administration Clearing House. I was interested in seeing the stationery which I've got here. The board of trustees included Robert Hutchins and Herbert Emmerich. But Don Price wrote this note for Jim Webb, who was at that time the director of the Bureau of the Budget, summarizing and making important warnings again about the British system and not to make too close a comparison. In the end, in fact, he said, "We should really build on what we have. A much safer approach would be to build from the present system. Possibly have one of the President's administrative assistants—(you remember those were established by the Brownell Commission in 1936)—head a small secretariat to serve each of the most important present interdepartmental committees." Don Price in effect was cautioning a great deal of modesty.

Now at the same time General Marshall took over in the State Department. He created the executive secretariat in the Department of State in 1946 and 1947 and I was part of that secretariat beginning in 1948. We served the committees of the Department of State; there were two kinds: the internal or intradepartmental committees and then those interdepartmental committees which State chaired (a large number of them.) And we were about ten of us. We used to have regular luncheons together although we're somewhat scattered now. And we were the secretariat for these committees, reporting to Acheson and Webb directly or informally through the director of the secretariat, Carl Hummelsine, lately at Colonial Williamsburg. Acheson liked that very much, Webb did, and the Hoover Commission I think had an eye on the successful creation of the secretariat in the State Department as it began its deliberations. I think Don Price's memo was building on some of that experience.

The secretariat in the State Department was greeted with a good deal of skepticism within State at the time. The line officers in effect said, "What are these characters doing up here in Acheson's and Marshall's office? Are they going to get in the way of communications between the secretary and us?" All the old issues which were again to be raised at the White House level had been raised and fought out in the Department of State. I think State's experience which set the groundwork stemmed largely from the modesty of that secretariat: the fact that it did not in any way try to second-guess in a policy sense the line officers. In other words, they created and maintained a reputation of career professionalism, anonymous professionalism. We in no way tried to get out and interpose ourselves between the line officers of State and Mr. Marshall and Mr. Acheson. So through the experience in the State Department we proved that you could have a secretariat which was modest and behind the scenes, professional, quiet and anonymous. If we had not been able to do that, I think the White House, even in the Eisenhower time, would not have been so receptive at the time Eisenhower took over. We proved it could be done.

Here is Roger Jones writing a note to the director of the Bureau of the Budget (that would be James Webb again) in April 1947: "In my concept a coordinating staff should be small, mature, flexible, and even more selfless than the administrative assistants; it would be the nerve center of information available to presidential offices." Then here's a note from Don Price to Mr. Hoover, December 1947, mentioning how it began in England: "The principal arguments against the Cabinet secretariat idea are that the President should not be required to handle a policy problem through any set procedure or to consult any fixed group of officials, or to take up problems except at the time he chooses. A Cabinet secretariat might reduce the flexibility with which he could direct his subordinates. And then a Cabinet secretariat might formalize Cabinet procedure which could invite legislative interference with the method by which the President directs his department heads." Interestingly, that note must have been written just after the President signed the National Security Act, which was arguably a legislative interference with the way the President manages the machinery because it set up the national security machinery by legislation. I think at the time there was some concern although in my opinion, the example of wartime coordination, or the lack of it, was so egregious that the National Security Act sailed through when the President signed it. Even with his having signed it, Don Price is advising Mr. Hoover to watch out for the creation of any kind of a Cabinet secretariat in addition to the National Security Council; that was December 1947.

Then in May 1948, Don Price sent Mr. Hoover a long memorandum about the possibility of a secretariat, but he said he could do several things which would greatly extend the President's ability to guide the policies of administration. Don went on to describe the White House in its most advanced concept. It could help the President identify principal issues he must decide; it could decide whether the problems should be handled by direct staff work, by holding an ad hoc meeting, and so forth. If the meeting seems desirable it could arrange for the President to consult. And there was a concept of a secretariat, a very advanced concept, which was really describing the chief of staff function in the White House more than just the Cabinet secretariat at such but then in effect warning again not to copy the British model.

What happened was, as you know, the Hoover Commission recommended a White House staff secretary. It did not recommend a Cabinet secretariat. The Hoover Commission backed off from a Cabinet secretariat idea and recommended a staff secretary. Here's an excerpt from the report, "A New Staff Secretary." Said the Hoover Commission, "At present there is no one place in the President's office to which the President can look for a current summary of the principal issues." (Now that's more than just a secretary in the narrow sense. That's the secretary in the broad sense.) To meet this deficiency the Commission proposes the addition of a staff secretary. "He would not himself be an adviser to the President on any issue or policy nor would he review in a supervisory capacity the substance of any recommendation made to the President by any part of the staff." That of course was the idea of the secretariat which we had personified and developed in the State Department. And you remember who the vice chairman of the Hoover Commission was? It was Dean Acheson who brought into the commission, I think, his own experience with the secretariat there. "And if possible," says the Hoover Commission, "the staff secretary like the executive clerk should be a career public servant." I'll comment on that a little bit later.

So, recommendation number ten: "The President should be given funds to provide a staff secretary in addition to his principal secretaries to assist him by clearing information on the major problems on which staff work is being done in the President's office or by the Cabinet or interdepartmental committees." That was the Hoover Commission recommendation. So what happened to it? Mr. Truman as you know rejected that recommendation. I've often wondered why.

I had lunch with Don Price in the White House some years ago and I've made a few notes from the luncheon. I'll just quote from some of these notes. Some of this idea (the origin of the Cabinet secretariat idea) goes back to Marshall's relation with Roosevelt. Marshall, according to Don Price, felt that Roosevelt was very secretive. Marshall's bias tended to be in the direction of creating systems or institutions which would help combat such secretiveness on the part of the chief executive. A Cabinet secretary with the implication that the Cabinet would be used was such a system or institution. I made a footnote here to myself, "Marshall of course was the one who set up the secretariat in the State Department." Forrestal inherited the same bias from Marshall and he, too, favored the systematic use of the Cabinet somewhat as a way of making sure that the President had better communications with his senior subordinates. Forrestal was said to have considered Truman as "little but a haberdasher from Missouri," implying little experience or intellectual weight. When Forrestal was secretary of defense, and again this was according to Don Price, he began convening Cabinet meetings without Truman. Now I checked the Forrestal diaries and I couldn't find any quote about that and I checked the new book on Truman, Bob Donovan's book on Truman, and I couldn't find any reference to that either, and I quote you this as having it from Don Price and if any of you know any differently I'd like to know. And I really ought to do a little more research on it. But anyway this is the statement Don made: "When Forrestal was secretary

of defense he began convening Cabinet meetings without Truman.''
You remember in the Wilson presidency, the secretary of state was
convening Cabinet meetings without him and I believe Seward did the
same under Lincoln. And of course you can imagine the reaction of
Truman. Truman considered the Cabinet, therefore, as an enemy and
he changed most of them in 1949.

So when the Hoover Commission came in with its recommendations
about a staff secretary, Truman reacted with some of that original bias
about not wanting to be tied into any Cabinet or staff system and he
did not accept the Hoover Commission's recommendation. Truman
even had the same suspicion about the NSC and he often let the NSC
meet, I remember this, without his being there. He often let Acheson
chair the National Security Council and he absented himself from
those meetings. Hoover, during the discussion of a possible Cabinet
secretariat, shied away from the title himself since he was very
suspicious of any European-type bureaucracies.

Then came Eisenhower. Let me give you one wonderful quote from
his book *Crusade in Europe*. He points out, and I give you the quotation: ''In modern war battle areas frequently extend over hundreds of
miles of front and are equally extensive in depth....In the same region
dwell civilian populations, sometimes friendly and sometimes hostile,
sometimes neutral or mixed in attitude. All these units, individuals and
activities must be carefully controlled, so everything is coordinated
toward the achievement of the commander's strategic plan.'' And to
go on, ''The teams and staff through which the modern commander
absorbs information and exercises his authority must be a beautifully,
interlocked, smooth working mechanism. Ideally the whole should be
practically a single mind.'' That was Eisenhower from his experience
in the war.

And then immediately in the post-war period: I have an interesting
copy here of a memo that he sent the secretary of war in January 1946
when he was the Chief of Staff of the Army. ''Although I knew your
views on the matter of a joint secretariat for the executive departments
of government, I have agreed with the proposal put forward by the
Navy Department that Admiral Nimitz and I would each forward to
the two secretaries a brief memorandum on the subject.'' And here's
his memo dated January 4 of the Nimitz memo 46: ''A system of coordination in the executive branch of the government.'' And it recom-
mends: ''A system of committees similar to State or Navy coordinating committee with a common secretariat appears to be the most
practical method of coordinating the functions of the executive
departments and agencies for the formulation of policy and for plann-

ing. And therefore it is proposed that a Cabinet secretariat be established as a separate division of the executive office of the President to provide the necessary secretarial services to committees [we always avoided *that* adjective] charged with coordinating functions. And that a Cabinet secretary be appointed by the President to direct the activities of the Cabinet secretariat to act as secretary to the President at Cabinet meetings and to recommend to him the establishment of coordinating committees." That was Eisenhower in 1946.

So when he became President he obviously was much more favorably inclined than Truman was to buy the idea of a Cabinet secretariat and he already had in 1952 the National Security Council. He held a meeting in the Commodore Hotel, pre-inaugural and post-election in December of 1952. I had the notes of that but I can't put my fingers on them right now. I wasn't there but he in effect told the Cabinet that this was the way he was going to run the Cabinet when he was President. He was going to have all the major questions of domestic policy laid out on the table in front of him and he didn't want anybody coming around the back fence and making an *ex parte* private presentation to him, and he was going to run the National Security Council the same way. And he laid down the rule on it and he referred to Cabinet meetings that he'd attended under Truman and he added, "If you could call them meetings." He had a rather derogatory phrase for the Truman Cabinet meetings because he really felt that there was poor coordination in those days. So even before his inaugural and the first meeting of the Cabinet, pre-inaugural, he said, "This is the way I'm going to run my government."

On February 19, 1953, Gabriel Hauge who was administrative assistant to the President, has written a memo to Harold Stassen saying: "In order to place the planning of the agenda for regular Cabinet meetings on a firm basis, I would appreciate your forwarding to me by Thursday noon each week any items which you wish to have included. Gabriel Hauge, administrative assistant to the President." So that was the very first act of the Eisenhower secretariat.

Then in July in the summer of 1953, here's a note from Paul Carroll who was the acting staff secretary: "The functions previously performed by Dr. Hauge in preparing the agenda have been passed to the recently created White House staff secretariat. It would be very much appreciated if you will in the future get in touch with this office to make any suggestions or requests you have for placing items on the agenda. The secretariat will make every effort to inform you. . ." So in July it shifted to Paul Carroll. This was the creation of a staff of the secretariat in the White House and of the staff secretary. It was not only a result of the Hoover Commission recommendation to Truman, but the result of a study done by Carter Burgess who was a distinguished member of the Defense Department and then overseas with Eisenhower. Carter did a study of the White House for Eisenhower in the summer of 1953, and there was a quote from the Cabinet proceedings of July 31 that Governor Adams had announced that Mr. Carter Burgess will do an exploratory study of government organizations at the sub-Cabinet level. Here is a copy of the original Burgess study in which he called for the creation of a staff secretariat, and this was done and Paul Carroll was named.

Then something went wrong; I don't know exactly what it was and Eisenhower asked that another study be done. And Carter came back in the summer of 1954 to look at it again with a little more energy, a little more pizzazz, and a little more pointed focus. And at that point, he and I teamed up because he had been helping Dulles reorganize the State Department secretariat in the spring of 1954 and he and I had gotten acquainted with each other. So he asked me to join him in studying the White House secretariat, and that was the real beginning of the organization.

One thing we did was to send a communication to the embassy in London asking for information about the British Cabinet secretariat. Simply, how was it done? How was it organized? What was it like? It came back stamped Secret, and as you know it was British practice to say in effect that the British public had no business in asking about the organization of the prime minister's office or the Cabinet secretariat. We had a series of charts and some information, all classified. So we looked it over and on August 3, 1954, after two months of study, consultation and research, we gave a presentation for the President, and here's a copy of what we call the presentation script. I'll read a few quotes from it: "How can a White House staff office fit into this picture and at the same time not violate the original proviso which the President laid down when he asked for this study, that nothing should restrict the President's direct contact with this Cabinet and agency heads?" We said: "It will work with the existing coordinating mechanisms that the President shall designate: the Cabinet, Cabinet committees and the National Security Council." We met with him in his office on August 3, 1954, and we proposed a little booklet and some charts—I have donated the charts—the big 30 x 40 charts—to the Eisenhower Museum in Abilene, and they're out there.

Incidentally, the very first version of the charts we had was a chart with a British flag, the Union Jack, and the American flag and a big black line down the middle comparing the British system and the

American system and saying in effect the American system is very different. The President is the executive branch, the executive power, and Eisenhower said, "You're right, and I'm glad you put it in there, but don't you put in the booklet. I don't want any reference to the British cabinet secretariat or UK or anything," and the chart was removed from this booklet—not removed but just was not included. Eisenhower was so sensitive and so aware of constitutional differences that he refused to have any reference made in the study to the British system even though one of the actual charts which is out at Abilene had the comparison.

Our booklet said this staff was intended for "supporting but in no way altering the direct line of authority in communication which the President has to each agency head." We described the way the system would work and we talked about the staff secretary, too, even though Paul Carroll was there and then we talked about a possible Cabinet secretary saying here's the Cabinet agenda, here's how it would work. And in the Oval Office I held the charts and Carter did the presentation. We proposed to have this a Cabinet and liaison officer in each of the departments tied in to the Cabinet secretariat, and we recommended post-session briefings, oral debriefings, the way the NSC had been handled.

And let me say one more thing. In our presentation to the President we said: "It's the final admonition that the Cabinet operations office is not a policy group, it cannot be repeated too often. In 1924 Lord Hankey laid down three maxims about the secretariat: it was not to interfere with the responsibility of the departments; it was not to issue statements to the press; it was not to laugh at the jokes made by ministers, though a smile was permissible." That was the tone and the presentation to the President and he bought the whole thing. "Absolutely," he said, "that's exactly what I want. Now I've got to sell it. I want to sell it. I want my Cabinet to know about it. So you are to come back to a Cabinet meeting." The next Cabinet meeting was, you remember, the famous hot dog roast at Camp David on August 13, 1954. Eisenhower said, "We are having a Cabinet meeting and you are to make a strong presentation to them and I will tell them that's the way I'm going to do it." So I remember riding in the truck with the charts (they wouldn't fit in a car), and Carter rode in the limousine. We went up to Camp David and Laurel Lodge with the Cabinet, not a lot bigger than this room at Faulkner House, a little bit bigger but not much bigger, and the width, it seemed to me, was much narrower. We were just squeezed in but we put the easel up and we did a little staff work. Carter got hold of General Bedell Smith, who of course was

Eisenhower's aide during the war and Harold Stassen who had created a secretariat in AID precisely paralleling the State Department secretariat. They promised they'd speak up with personal endorsements. Then we put on this chart presentation, and handing around the printed version of this book called *Staff Work for the President in the Executive Branch*. The President made it perfectly clear that it was exactly how he was going to have his Cabinet work. Then Sherman Adams turned around to Max Rabb who turned to me and said, "Patterson, if you know so much about all this, will you help me?" and that was the way I was hired in the White House.

(I remember a personal footnote. Charlie Willis came to me later and said, "Patterson, we're going to hire you at the White House, what's your politics? Do you know your Maryland congressman or senator?" I said, "Let me see, I'm not even sure who they are," and he said, "Well, if you don't know who they are, will they have any objection to your being here?" I said, "I don't think they know who I am either." That was my "political clearance" for the White House at the time.) So Max Rabb and I started out. Max was designated as Cabinet secretary but I want to point out one difference. You remember the original booklet said there would be a staff and Cabinet operations office, but the printed booklet has a chart which says "Staff and Cabinet Secretaries." One interesting thing was a decision, which may have been a mistake, to keep the staff secretary and the Cabinet secretary separate. Now the staff secretary was already there in being, with Paul Carroll. We had suggested that it and the Cabinet secretariat be the same office, which I think the Hoover Commission had in mind in its recommendation. All previous discussion of the idea of a White House secretariat, as you've seen is in the language that I read to you had implied that the secretariat idea would be staff secretary and Cabinet secretary combined. There was to be a dual function in a single office.

In the Eisenhower White House in the summer of 1954, with Paul Carroll already there, they decided to separate them and Paul remained as staff secretary and Max Rabb and I took over as Cabinet secretary and the dividing line was there and it stayed there. When Max left in 1958 and the Cabinet secretariat job was vacant, I remember going to Andy Goodpaster and saying, "Andy, shall we unify it now as we originally thought? " and Andy said, "No, let's keep it separate." So the staff secretary and the Cabinet secretary were physically separate and functionally separate, although obviously we worked very closely together all during the Eisenhower period.

My job was to take this presentation, charts and all and copies of this booklet, around to the departments in the fall of 1954 and present it to their staff meetings and tell them "this is the way everybody is going to be working." It was a very interesting communications device. Talk about feedback from the White House and a President letting his whole administration, not just the Cabinet who were there at Camp David, but letting everybody know how he was going to run things. I remember some of the comments. Oveta Culp Hobby was all gung ho for this. In fact, she was one of the early ones to create a secretariat in her agency. Marion Folsom, on the other hand, took one look at the staff briefing with just a few people there and said "My God, you could never run a business this way." I disagreed with him but that was his comment. So that was the communications device in the fall of 1954.

The Cabinet functioned in this way for all those years. In the time we were there it met 227 times—22 times with the vice president in the chair and the rest of the times, 205 times, with Eisenhower presiding. Of course he'd make trips and would not be there.

One of the problems we faced right away was the problem of secrecy and privilege. We recognized there was a difference between "secret" in the national security sense and "privileged" in the sense of discussing domestic issues, and if we stamped Cabinet papers "Secret," we were in a certain sense violating the executive order and the intent of the classification authority. So what would we do? We solved this problem by printing special stationery and I kept one copy of it, and here it is. "Cabinet Paper—Privileged," we said. "Property of the White House—for Authorized Persons Only." So that's the way we handled it. Everything was privileged though not necessarily secret. Occasionally we would have some papers which were in effect classified national security and we put "Confidential" or "Secret" top and bottom. But this was the stationery preprinted. The White House had a very efficient White House reproduction office and they would reproduce. We gave them large quantities of the stationery and they would reproduce the Cabinet papers from mimeographed stencils.

A little word about process and procedure. In the first place I can state as a basic principle that Cabinet members don't like Cabinet meetings. Particularly they do not like having their favorite subjects brought up on the table for everybody to shoot at. They much prefer the "Amen Corner" philosophy, coming individually to the President and saying, "Mr. President, look what I've got here, please sign here and don't let anybody get in my way." Eisenhower, of course, was not going to conduct his government this way as he made clear to them but the problem of forming the Cabinet agenda was a difficult problem from the beginning and we ran into some reluctance for all the seven years that we worked the system. Max and I had what we called a radar set. He was succeeded, of course, by Robert Gray in 1958 so Max and Bob and I were a radar set. We soon discovered one of our principal duties was to work this radar set and, as the Hoover Commission documents predicted, to identify issues, which ought to be presented at Cabinet meetings. But they did not come walking into our office. Only Arthur Flemming would be the kind of a person who might bring something into the Cabinet of his own volition, a person like that with an unusual sense of staff work. But everything else we had to reach out and drag into the Cabinet agenda.

The way we did it was the radar set. We would call Cabinet departments and say, "This subject is important," and they'd say, "Yes, it's important." We'd say, "We want it on the Cabinet agenda." "Well, I'm not sure about this." So what we would do is go to Sherman Adams as chief of staff with a list of potential Cabinet agenda subjects every week. And Adams himself, first of all, would often strike off the list some of our favorite ideas and so we would lose with him. And then he'd say, "Well, what about this one?" and we'd say, "Well, we think that's an important thing. The attorney general ought to present this." He'd say, "Does he want to?" and we'd say, "Hmmmmmm, no, he doesn't want to," or Adams would say, "Well, let me talk to him." He'd reach for the phone and say, "Give me the attorney general," and he'd get Brownell on the phone. He'd say, "Brownell, Patterson and Rabb want to have you discuss this at Cabinet." You could hear the expletives coming out the phone and Adams would sometimes overrule us and, as I say, we'd lose. Sometimes he'd say, "Well, I think you ought to" and bang that was it, and it would be on the agenda.

The question is did Eisenhower have anything to say about the Cabinet agenda? The interesting thing is, no. Adams made all the agenda decisions. Sometimes we'd ask shouldn't we have an agenda planning session with the President? "Mr. President, here are the things we see." And also at the same time we'd be going over the record of action. "Here's the record of action from last week, here are the plans for next week or next month," and then be able to walk out of his office and pick up the phone ourselves and say to a Cabinet member, "Damn it all, you are on the agenda, the President says so." Couldn't we have that kind of a session? Bobby Cutler had them for the National Security Council. He'd go over the record of action of *his* meetings and he'd go over the plans for the NSC agenda for *his* meetings. Why couldn't we have one for our meetings? No, we never got anywhere. Max and Bob didn't really want to push it and Adams certainly didn't want to push it.

So for all those years Sherman Adams (later General Persons) was the final say on the agenda. Well, that sort of made me nervous.

At Cabinet, Eisenhower would open his Cabinet book; we'd send the material to him on Wednesday maybe for a Friday meeting. He'd open it up and he'd look through his spectacles and say, "Well," and I thought "My gosh, suppose he sees something there he doesn't want?" But never in those seven years did he say, "What the hell is this doing here? Max?" Never. So that is a good measure of Adams' skill and sense of staff work and our sense of staff work. He often added one, but he never subtracted one and he never fussed about something being there. So the system in that sense worked smoothly.

We had these legal size black loose-leaf binders and we'd send each Cabinet member the agenda and also the papers and send them one set of pre-punched papers with four holes. We had them punched in the White House and one was actually pre-punched with four holes because the big four-hole legal size papers were not very common even in a stationery business. Then we'd make two and three copies of each Cabinet paper for circulation in their department. We trusted them to handle that privilege and just send it around and get comments and get briefed. There was a lot of trust in this system.

The papers and agenda would go out and everything would be on blue stationery which meant they'd be for consideration; the white ones were for action approved; and the yellow stationery for information items. The meetings would be held on Fridays from nine to eleven, and the President would walk in. We'd all rise, of course, in that beautiful Cabinet room. He'd sit in the center, Adams and Persons would be there, I'd be in the back, Max Rabb would be on the corner, Henry Cabot Lodge would come down from New York. We'd define Cabinet membership as whoever sat at the table. That's the way we defined being a member of the Cabinet, who sat at the table. If you didn't sit at the table you weren't a "member."

The next thing that was surprising was the number of White House staff who came to Cabinet meetings: eighteen to twenty-four people of the White House staff sitting around the room. I thought, "Good God, the President talking with all those people listening? Shouldn't this be a restricted meeting?" But interestingly, my observation was not apropos. In all those seven years they never really interfered with the candor of the meeting; they never bothered the President, and they never bothered the Cabinet members. We never, with one exception, had any leaks from Cabinet and the White House staff members. All senior people, all were greatly informed and educated by sitting in on these meetings because Hagerty and all the others could talk to the press or to whomever much better and deal with the departments with incredibly good information having just walked out a Cabinet meeting. The National Security Council, I think, was more restricted for security purposes but the Cabinet had all these White House staff people all around the room, about fifteen or twenty senior people.

Eisenhower liked charts. Arthur Burns would often come in. In June for instance we would have an interesting trilogy. We would have Arthur Burns come in with an economic forecast, then Treasury would present the revenue forecast based on economic forecasts and then the Budget Bureau would come in with a discussion of the budget problems, the overall budget not any specific budget questions, but the overall totals. You'd see these three subjects fitted neatly—the economy, revenues, and the budget. In June we had this presentation and then the Bureau of the Budget would do its instruction to the departments that summer based on this presentation.

Incidentally, at the very beginning, I'm going back to Harold Smith, I guess, there was some question, and I think Harold Smith raised the question, whether it would be even appropriate for the director of the Bureau of the Budget to attend Cabinet meetings because by sitting there he might be obligated to follow what was discussed at the table. He always wanted to have the ability, presumably, at the end of the meeting to come around privately to the President and say, "Mr. President, you don't want to do that. You've got to do this." I believe it was Smith who wanted to or thought it was more appropriate to absent himself from Cabinet meetings. Under Eisenhower they soon found out that if by any chance anybody in the Bureau of the Budget, Joe Dodge or anybody, felt that way about it from previous traditions of the bureau, that tradition died because if you weren't at the Cabinet meetings the President would say, "Well, that's the way I'm going to do it." If they weren't there to holler they would be committed by the record of action and wouldn't have their chance.

I should add that two things never came to Cabinet, quite appropriately. Never did we discuss reorganization and never did we discuss individual departmental budgets. The reorganization matters as you know were brilliantly handled by the Rockefeller/Flemming/Eisenhower Committee, and I guess you've probably talked with Milton and maybe with Arthur about how they handled it. It is a fascinating experiment in American public administration in which those three gentlemen, of whom you could find no finer in terms of their intellectual powers and knowledge of government, handled all of those questions quietly and came in to the President on a Saturday morning and got the decisions. So neither of these two subjects ever came to Cabinet.

But lots of policy issues did come up and some information matters. The President would jump into the discussion, he would not follow what I've heard is a Supreme Court rule, withholding his comments until the junior-most person has spoken or all the others. He would jump in right away. He may not have read all the papers we sent him on a Wednesday but Ike was very sharp. He'd be right on top of those subjects. He had been through them in the war, he'd been through them at Columbia, he'd been through them as a candidate; he needed very little briefing. He was on top of issues.

The Cabinet members would present their papers. One thing we did not do as Cabinet secretary is write any of them. I guess I wrote one maybe for the subcabinet on the committee management system. The Cabinet members presented their papers. We had no role in writing any of them.

Nor did we at Cabinet have what they did have in the National Security Council—a planning board. Under the NSC you had a planning board which was a group of assistant secretary level people who met prior to the meeting and who combed over and thrashed over the papers and debated them. Sometimes they cut the papers up—State, Defense and Joint Chiefs—three columns literally, and then sent that to the NSC and have a meeting on it. Not so the Cabinet, we had no planning board. We often thought we might but Eisenhower and nobody else ever wanted one. So we had no planning board.

Nor did we have an OCB (an Operations Coordinating Board). That was the follow-up coordinating mechanism also on the NSC which Elmer Staats himself chaired at one point. None of that—we had no formal Cabinet follow-up coordinating mechanisms. The NSC of course came under fire from Jackson in the Eisenhower administration. It was much too cumbersome and Kennedy wiped them all out at Jackson's recommendation. He issued a publication on this. Eisenhower and his Cabinet had only the Cabinet itself.

Papers would be presented, chart talks would be given, occasionally slides would be shown. We had a screen and I'd have to run around and pull the drapes closed and that would take a couple of minutes. The Cabinet room was incredibly poor for modern-day presentations. There was no soundproof booth for the projector, it would sit there at the end of the table and rattle away. There was no place for the screen to come down from the ceiling; easels had to be trucked in and out—it was really a primitive thing in terms of modern facilities—but it was a beautiful Cabinet room that you didn't want to monkey with. Occasionally you would have a motion picture if it were pertinent to the subject. At the end Eisenhower would make his decision. And he was a very effective head of the Cabinet.

A Cabinet, as you know, is a group of very contentious people. I don't think I need to lecture any of you on the makeup of the Cabinet, probably you've read Richard Fenno's book. As you know, the Cabinet, as they used to say, is the enemy of the President, subject to enormous centrifugal forces. To understand how a Cabinet is put together you have to go back to the convention at which the President receives his nomination. Think of the factional debates at the convention.

In Eisenhower's time, for instance, at the convention of 1952, it was Eisenhower versus Taft. MacArthur was the keynoter and he gave a pro-Taft speech. Lodge and Adams were the floor managers. There were delegate fights on credentials—you remember all of this? Eisenhower got the nomination, the election and then turned around, as most Presidents do, to the Taft wing of the party and brought several prominent members of that wing into his Cabinet: Sinclair Weeks, George Humphrey, Ezra Taft Benson and Arthur Summerfield, and even brought in a Democrat, Martin Durkin, as secreatry of labor. (That broke up after a few months and he resigned). A Cabinet can no longer be (although there is nothing in statute about it) of one sex, of one race, of one profession, of one religion, or from one state or from one or the same faction of the party, and probably a couple of other factors I haven't mentioned. It has diversity built in. Now Fenno says it is so diverse that it can't help the President and there Fenno and I part company. He was doing his thesis at the time while I was there and we talked a couple of times. I sent him a long letter and said, "You crucified us, you misjudged us. Yes, you're right about all those centrifugal forces but the way you overcome them is that you recognize them and overcome them as you put these people at the same table and have an effective President at the helm, and we did." But he's still right in the sense that it is subject to very strong centrifugal forces which often make that impossible.

In any case Eisenhower was not one to let those centrifugal forces overwhelm him; he was a positive, strong, forthright President. The stereotypes which have come up about Eisenhower include "What if Sherman Adams died and Eisenhower had to be President?" and so forth, are all a lot of balderdash. I can testify to you that in those days, Ike really ran the Cabinet. He would swear like an old army mule sometimes and bang the table. I'll never forget a subject came up once about the student exchange program. Dulles was talking about it in some kind of a context and Eisenhower banged the table and said, "For crying out loud, remember the B-36 bomber costs billions and just a few millions for student exchange when that's the future and really building America's roots for friendships in foreign countries, and we wasted all that money on the B-36." Having been in the student exchange program briefly in the State Department, this was music to my ears. But here was Ike, and he was very keen on that particular program, and I remember he was so furious he banged the table on that. I took shorthand, not really like a pro but reasonably well, and when he spoke I would try to catch him as much as I could in shorthand. The rest of it was notes, also in shorthand, but only notes.

Ike was also a very humble man. Many, many times he would stop and say, "Well, now, what would the man on the street in Dickinson, Kansas, think about this?" I'll give you an example, You remember the famous case of the gas bill when the Congress had passed a bill to deregulate natural gas, a subject incidentally still much before the Congress. Senator Case had reportedly received a $5,000 bribe in the process, and the bill was sent to the President and was on his desk, and the question was would he sign it or veto it? There had been a Cabinet committee on energy policy chaired by Arthur Flemming and the question was whether to sign or veto, and we didn't have Cabinet meetings very often on a specific bill, although we talked about legislation a great deal, but on this one we had one. Ike called a special meeting on Monday. We almost never had a meeting on Monday. And he did another thing we never did—we went around the table. We never did that before, but he started right here and went right around the table. Of course Flemming presented the views of the Cabinet committee, and so forth, but we generally worked toward deregulation and toward recommending signature. We went right around the table and finally after they all got through talking, he said again, "I have to think what would the man on the street in Dickinson, Kansas, feel about this bill?" He said, "I think he would say it stinks because of the alleged bribe," and the next day he vetoed it.

Interestingly enough, Drew Pearson wrote a column a few days later, "Inside the Eisenhower Cabinet," in which he pretended to report the discussion on that bill. It was a matter of great controversy and he went around the table saying how each member voted. And he said of Arthur Summerfield, for instance, you could see his mind work here from Michigan, that was generally a consuming state rather than a producing state, they'd be interested in keeping prices down. So, says Drew Pearson, "Arthur Summerfield said, 'You should veto it,'" Arthur Summerfield was absent that day, he wasn't even there, and that gave some illumination to me about how Drew Pearson worked. With some intelligence but some whole cloth he would put together something that looked like a leak from inside of the meeting. Interesting anyway.

Though Eisenhower sometimes swore and banged the table, he never lost his temper. He never got personal to anybody. He was one of the most dignified and gracious Presidents in the sense that he never made his disagreements personal. He never cut anybody down, ever, although he could be very firm.

QUESTION: They told us about one speech in which Eisenhower deleted the word "deliberately" and Bryce Harlow argued about that and said, "Well, this conveys the meaning." And he said, "All through my European experience I learned that you never try to judge people's intentions and if you try to judge them you are almost always wrong. And if you try to condemn them, why then the consequences are often beyond your scope." And he told the story about the fall of the Belgium government when he went back in NATO. He made some condemnatory statement and the government fell. A couple of us were speculating exactly what this example was. We hadn't heard it before.

MR. PATTERSON: Bryce was right and he could be very firm and very positive because my point is this. You have to be *very* firm, *very* positive, and *very* commanding to run a Cabinet meeting. And Nixon, when he took office—and I served five years under his presidency or however long he was there—hated Cabinet meetings because he didn't like to have people quarrel in front of him. Bill Safire has written about this. He didn't like advocates arguing back and forth. He wanted everything in writing and so we had developed an option paper system. That's another presidency and another lecture. Johnson or Kennedy or Reagan have had different styles and I must say I very strongly want to preserve the freedom and flexibility of each President to choose his own style of running his White House and be held responsible for it but not for Congress or anybody else to tell him how to do it. But Eisenhower liked it this way and it fitted his style perfectly.

The next thing that would happen at Cabinet would be they would break at 11:00 and at 11:30 I would rush back to my office. (At first we had our office in the west wing and later the east wing. A major problem was carrying a whole bunch of briefing books, Cabinet papers, some of them stamped "Secret," a rather large armload, and rushing back to the office halfway through the White House basement and through those curtains and all of a sudden coming on hoards of tourists. You would have to weave your way back and forth. I was always reminded that the White House belonged to the American people. I'd wish though it would be a little bit less thronging with people because I wanted to try to get back and get to my typewriter and start to type out some notes.) Then at 11:30 we'd go back to the Cabinet room and the elite Cabinet assistants (—each was a special assistant to one of the Cabinet members—) who were always the recipient of all Cabinet mail and always the ones who made sure their secretaries were briefed and prepared, would be called into the Cabinet room. They would sit in the still warm chairs of their bosses and Max Rabb and I would give an oral debriefing of everything that had taken place. Now when I say everything we often withheld the attribution of specific remarks but we always talked about the issues pro and con. In other words we often kept to ourselves *who* said what but *what* was said on the issues was summarized and, of course, naturally the decision. And we would say: "Okay, Rod O'Connor or Johnny Hanes, Dulles has this assignment" or "Bill Parsons," who was the Cabinet assistant for Treasury and an interesting and distinguished career executive, "Bill, Humphrey has this assignment by next week" and we would particularly point out the assigments that were given. Meanwhile Mr. Humphrey had taken off for San Francisco, Parsons could then go to the under secretary and say, "Look, we've got this job." So that would be done.

I would sometimes have a very rough draft of my record of action ready in half an hour but often not quite. But always the assignments and the decisions were reported and sometimes, always in fact, we would have a presentation done again, a chart presentation. Sometimes Arthur Burns would come back and do it again. Slides—we would run them again. The movies— often oral audiovisual material— we would run through again for the Cabinet assistants so they would have a full flavor of the meeting. As I say we would withhold only the most privileged things and the attribution of discussion. This was very helpful so they could go back, and they were very senior people: Bill Parsons from Treasury, Rod O'Connor in State, John Lindsey—*the* John Lindsey who was Mr. Brownell's Cabinet assistant. In each case they were the executive assistants to the Cabinet member. We took them into total confidence and gave them the full flavor of the whole session.

Then the rest of that Friday afternoon I would spend drafting the record of action. The record of action would be concise and would refer to the Cabinet paper, like Cabinet paper 57–46 was approved or was amended following understanding or I would put in often some of

Eisenhower's language. Example—one of the things we discussed in Cabinet was a continuing issue in the government and is even today: the problem of surplus government real estate. Eisenhower would keep telling his Cabinet, "Get rid of it! Sell it! Get it off to surplus!" And then he told them one of his little homilies. He said, "Why, you folks around here are like my mother back in Abilene, she was a string-saver." And he looked around and said, "None of you know what I'm talking about do you? Well, a stringsaver is somebody who takes the string that comes on packages to the house and cuts it off and puts it in a ball. And another package comes, she saves the string, ties it on the ball and the ball gets bigger and bigger and that is called a stringsaver. Now you know what I mean don't you?" He said, "Well, you folks are all stringsavers of real estate." I thought that was pretty interesting so I wrote that language right into the Cabinet record of action: "The President admonished his Cabinet members not to be stringsavers of real estate." We tried to use his language and use the sense of his priorities and his wonderful human way of looking at public policy issues and reflect that in some of the most official documents of government.

I would check the record of action as a courtesy, only as a courtesy, with Cabinet officers. I remember in the State Department when I was there under Acheson, he would come back from Truman Cabinet meetings and call in his secretary, and say, "I'm going to give you the Cabinet dictation." Then she would come out with typed papers of a couple of paragraphs on a page, one page on each different action the State Department should do. I always thought to myself, particularly when I was working with Carter working on the Cabinet secretariat plans in December of 1954, how improper and how unconstitutional a procedure that was. You could have twelve different versions of what happened in Cabinet and damn it all that was a White House function and not a Cabinet member function anyway. So one of the first things we did was to make sure the record of action was our record of action and not that of Cabinet members. However, sometimes the Cabinet members could come around for lunch and by the end of the luncheon I would pull them by their coattails, or go see Bob Anderson or somebody across the street and say, "Does this language fit with your conception?" If it was something they were deeply interested in I'd change a word or two as a courtesy to them, only a courtesy. And Friday night it would go to the President. Monday morning it came back with a "DE" written on it. In the seven years he never changed a word. I was pleased at that. Then it would be circulated.

We had a very nifty facility in the White House. We had a group of typists who worked all night long. We had a night shift. The people there were just wonderful people and they would give good attention to us and if necessary they would work the night shift to cut our stencils. I could go home at night at 8:00 p.m. and say, "Here's the stuff for the Cabinet paper or the agenda." The typists would do it and send it over to the reproduction room. We would have a sheet which would list how many copies, how many punched, how many unpunched and so forth and they would all be in envelopes and off via courier the next morning. It was a very efficient system.

I remember suggesting to Ken Cole in the Nixon White House that when Metro was being built in Washington, we have a tube system built into the Metro tunnel. Why should we use a horse and buggy system of White House cars going out and driving all around town. Ken thought it was an interesting idea but never did anything with it. Now, of course, it is done electronically and I believe many Cabinet papers are sent around by electronic means with the privilege included in the electronic means.

Anyway the record of action would be distributed, again two or three copies to each department. We trusted them. Our trust was well placed. If we had had the same kind of system we have these days of everybody arrogating to himself the right to leak anything that came to the White House you couldn't run that system. You can't run it now and as the President is pointing out "he is up to his kiester in leaks," many of them of course from the senior White House people. You *could not* run a Cabinet system like this without trust. And people who are career or non-career people or who have White House privileged material and don't keep that trust are detracting from the ability of the President to have a good communications, a good policy delivery and followup system. You couldn't do it without that trust. I worry about it today but in the Eisenhower period it was a matter of trust.

Then at the end of our meetings on Friday morning, we would have a discussion of next week's agenda so there would be a planning meeting and we'd say, "You're going to be on the agenda next week and that Cabinet paper from you, is it ready? That will be there won't it or will it?" Then followed some grinding on them to get it ready and discussion of the plans so they would know ahead of time before the actual papers arrived. It was a very useful session and very fine men and women made up that group. They were full of information in terms of feedback from the White House and we were on the phone with them all week long. "What's happening here? What's happening there?" They calling us, we calling them. So the nerve network that was portrayed in a political science book really worked. It worked superbly. They would be calling us constantly and we dealt with business all the time. We limited it to them. We would never call elsewhere in their departments on Cabinet matters. We made that promise that all our contacts would be through them.

The most interesting Cabinet discussion I remember in those years, and maybe Arthur Flemming mentioned it, was a remarkable meeting in 1959 when Flemming came out with a proposal to try to match the Murray bill for aid to education. The Democrats and Senator Murray had a very expensive plan and the question was what would be the Eisenhower administration response to aid to education. It was in the fifties and schools were running out of money and out of classrooms. Flemming came in with a proposal to have a guaranteed program for bonds of local school districts. I guess what happened was he had been talking with the President about it on Thursday evening and Eisenhower said, "Arthur, damn it, bring it to Cabinet tomorrow morning. I'm not convinced. I'm skeptical but I'll let you talk to the Cabinet about it." We get a phone call late Thursday night, "You've got one more big paper coming up for your agenda. Change it." "Yes, sir." So we went over to Flemming and he had the paper right away. We circulated it. It needed distribution right away and we had it reproduced within an hour and then came Friday morning.

I'll never forget that meeting. That was one meeting that I wrote out my notes. And that was one meeting for which I have a full, almost verbatim text. Eisenhower said, "Well, now Arthur, you know you and I have been talking about this and I must say I respect the American federal system and it means so much to me to have the states play their proper role. I'm really apprehensive about this. All right, now that I've put the noose around your neck, go ahead, Flemming, make your presentation." Well, that was a pretty tough introduction for a Cabinet officer. But you know Arthur Flemming; he was his old self, articulate, vigorous and full of force and he made his presentation. Of course the conservatives in the Cabinet had seen the opening that Eisenhower had given them about his apprehension and his not being sure and they jumped all over Arthur. Summerfield and Benson gave him an awfully hard time. Then Mr. Nixon spoke up. He was of course in 1959 somewhat the heir apparent. He said in effect that if the Democrats get away with it we've got to come up with something. He talked about education as a national resource, that the national government is responsible for education in that sense. That was a very important comment and it sort of tipped the discussion. In the end Eisenhower said, "All right, Arthur, we're going to do it," and he turned them all around and Arthur turned the President around. It was very interesting and it illustrated the openness and the vigor of the debate and honesty of the debate and how it went.

One of the Eisenhower associates has said that he was bored with the Cabinet and I've seen some comments like that. Well, Ike wasn't bored with Cabinet and he really enjoyed these sessions.

Finally, one piece of the system that's interesting is the Cabinet Action Status Report. All the things in the record of action we'd keep tabs on, of course, and we would keep on the phone and we'd say, "What are you doing? What's happening with them?" Every three months or so on the yellow stationery for information we would sum them all up. Each department—Justice, State, Treasury, Defense, and so forth—would have all the Cabinet items for which they were responsible, all of the decisions, and a little paragraph on what they had done with them. And that would be circulated to the Cabinet as information. And everybody would see who hasn't done what and who was behind the eight ball. We would send a private copy early to Sherman Adams and he would pick up the White House phone and say, "Where are you on this?" Eisenhower would flip through it and say, "It's a great satisfaction to me as a wartime commander to make sure that what we discuss here doesn't evaporate."

So, it just fitted him. It corresponded to his own personality, to his own way of running the White House and way of running the Cabinet and fitted him to a tee. At the end of the Arthur Flemming meeting he said, (and I'll end this session with the same remark)"We've had a good growl!"

QUESTION: You spoke of the responsibilities of the staff secretariat. I'm not clear what they did. Did this survive all through the entire Eisenhower administration separately?

MR. PATTERSON: Yes, it was separate. General Goodpaster of course took over in the fall of 1954 when Paul Carroll died and you could not find a more skilled, more dedicated, more brilliant, more anonymous, more responsible professional person than Andy Goodpaster. He is one of the great White House servants of all time. He ran that staff secretariat with tremendous skill. He was helped by Art Minich, and by John Eisenhower and Bill Hopkins. They handled the day-to-day business of the presidency all during the week. And of course Art and John and Andy all came to Cabinet meetings so they were clued in on the Cabinet. But Andy also handled the national security side and attended NSC meetings and we did not. They were held separately but we worked closely together.

I forgot to mention one thing to you. I said no minutes. I said *I* didn't take any minutes. We had a separate set of minutes of the Cabinet taken only for the records. Art Minich did those out of Andy

Goodpaster's office. This was something begun before we even got there and it continued. And those went privately to Ann Whitman's files. Occasionally when he was sick or away, I did them because I could take shorthand and that was four or five or six pages of full minutes of the Cabinet meetings.

Now when Donovan wrote his book in 1954 they showed him those minutes. Of course, we said "the Cabinet had no minutes," just Patterson's record of action. Then he quoted from the minutes of the Cabinet meeting, and we were all afraid about that because we had some Cabinet members who said, "Why, I thought you guys didn't take any minutes." But Minich did and they are all in Abilene now with my notes of all those meetings. When 1961 came I called up Andy Goodpaster and said, "Andy, what do I do with all these shorthand notes? I can hardly read then anymore myself. I'm going to pitch them out." And he said, "Don't pitch them out, send them to Abilene." So they are all out there and maybe some day we can decipher them but the minutes are there also but they are the "Minich Minutes" as we call them.

QUESTION: To what extent do you think Eisenhower's style was attributable to his military background?

MR. PATTERSON: I would say greatly. Although in saying that I would say his style came from his experience but I *would not,* clearly *do not* believe that the secretariat is a military idea and is only applicable in the military services. The secretariat in fact is a very applicable idea to all running of big institutions and in fact it has flowered. It spread to AID under Stassen, to HEW under Mrs. Hobby, and now it has spread, I am pleased to report, to almost all the departments and agencies of government—they all have an executive secretariat. It has varied in its effectiveness from handling paper flow and mediocre things to very important functions in the departments. And so we are pleased to have planted the idea. But Ike's style, I believe his experience with working with de Gaulle and with Mountbatten and his diplomacy and his requirement for coordination as indicated in "running a war" clearly influenced his style in running the government and I think much to our benefit. In no sense was he a militarist as you know by his famous quote at the end.

QUESTION: You mentioned Nixon's participation in regard to education. In the seven years, to what extent did he participate? Did he participate actively and consistently?

MR. PATTERSON: Yes, actively. He was there at every meeting, right opposite the President, making many comments. Some of them were a of political nature in the sense of "We have some opposition up there and we have to do this in order to meet that." That was one of his major comments on the education bill. But he made very intelligent and helpful comments. He had a Cabinet assistant, too. All the agendas and the black books and so forth he had, he was included in all of that. He also came to our debriefings, that is, his assistant came. His comments were very helpful and generally on the liberal side of things. We had some very conservative members of the Cabinet. But at no time did anybody put anybody down. The closest we got to this was one interesting comment, quite by accident, when we had discussed something and the President said, "Now I want to do this," and Henry Cabot Lodge said, "Well, we've got to sell it. We've really got to sell it to the people. We've got to sell it to the lowbrows, too—the Elks and the Lions." Summerfield rose straight up from his chair and said, "I'm a Lion! What's this stuff about lowbrows?"

NARRATOR: I wish we had all afternoon. I wish we could be sure that Brad Patterson will come back. We'll certainly look for other ways to bring him back. What may well distinguish this discussion is the infusion of details, specifics, and very large amounts of particulars. I think all of us deeply appreciate that. All of us appreciate the clarity and well-documented form of your presentation. We are deeply indebted to you.

III.
EISENHOWER
AS POLITICAL
LEADER

THE "COMPLEAT" PRESIDENT

Bryce Harlow

MR. THOMPSON: What we've been asking people to talk about, if they would, is the political leadership of Dwight D. Eisenhower, how it took shape and where it received its impetus; what Eisenhower's concept of presidential leadership was; how it changed if it did change at all; what you think of revisionist thought as it has developed. Professor Fred Greenstein did part of his work at the Miller Center. It is quite a departure from the the media view that President Eisenhower paid very little attention to the politics of anything that came along. I think that's one area we'd like to explore.

Another area is how you became involved with President Eisenhower; what your preceptions were in the beginning; how they evolved and developed. Did you change your mind at all about him and about the problems of the office—anything that could be brought in, in that respect. In your case, of course, one of the things that would interest us a great deal is President Eisenhower's relations with the Congress and with the party as you saw it.

We have had people who've hit pretty hard on two or three points. We had Richard Strout visit us the other day for another purpose and he said some nice things about President Eisenhower but then he immediately reverted to the McCarthy thing in Wisconsin and the speech, and you undoubtedly have insights on that.

MR. HARLOW: I wasn't with him then.

MR. THOMPSON: Well, any thoughts, first of all, just on Eisenhower and your association with him—how that began, what you expected of him and what he expected of you.

MR. HARLOW: Shall I just start talking free-style?

MR. THOMPSON: Surely, that will be perfect.

MR. HARLOW: You are going to regret it.
   I came grudgingly to the White House. I tried hard not to come there. It is hard to believe that in 1953 I had already been in Washington for fifteen years. I had served in the Congress and I had served General Marshall during the war. I'd had five additional years on Capitol Hill after the war with the Armed Services Committee of the House. I was already a burned out bureaucrat by the time the President got elected. I had resigned from the Armed Services Committee and gone back to Oklahoma City which was my home. I did *not* want to come back to Washington, D.C. But General Persons, for whom I had worked during the war (he and I had worked on Congress for General Marshall), wanted me to be one of his two major reliances in the White House for Eisenhower. He called me and talked about it and I started sparring with him for six weeks, trying to stave him off. I figured that White House jobs are so precious, so eagerly sought after by people, that some campaign contributor's son or daughter would seize upon that slot, so if I just stalled long enough Persons would be forced to take someone else. Well, six weeks later he was still badgering me. I stalled through the trip to Korea, thinking that by the time he got back it would be over with. But the day he got back he called me in Oklahoma City, and I was back to square A. My father was sitting there with me when the call came in and he finally interrupted me and said, "Son, give up. You can't keep saying no to the White House; a good citizen just can't do that." So I gave up and came back.
   So you see, I came into the thing grudgingly, but not with any hostility, not angrily, not antagonistic to the President. I admired him enormously and had strongly supported him for President in a region where it was somewhat costly to be a Republican, in Democratic Oklahoma. So it wasn't that. I just didn't want to stay in the government. When I came back, I was used in the White House congressional

section as a special assistant on the White House staff by General Persons who was then deputy assistant to the President. I remained in that configuration for some nine months, then became Ike's speechwriter. I did that a couple years and then went back to congressional work and speech writing, which is what I did the rest of my time in the White House. Thereafter, I stayed with him as his Washington representative, you might say, throughout his retirement, and was his Washington "commissar" until his death. I'd say it was a very wonderful experience, that he was an extraordinary person, whom I came to regard as utterly admirable.

I was contacted early in Nixon's time when I was back in the White House by some reporter who was doing a special anniversary story on Eisenhower. He was going around the country asking people who knew the President best, most intimately, for one single word that would best characterize him. I never saw the article that he wrote. It was for the *Saturday Evening Post* or some such publication. I responded instantly—it came to me instantly what the answer should be, and I've never changed my mind. I said, "Oh, that's simple. It's the old English word 'compleat'—that's Eisenhower." He was the most completely rounded American I shall ever know. Not a perfect man. He's more like the Olympic all-around athlete, decathalon—not the best in everything but best in most things, and therefore the finest athlete of all. That's Eisenhower. Personality-wise, ability-wise, motivation-wise, he was about the finest leader we've ever had.

I put together a montage of pictures I had of him taken in Paris when he was commander of NATO. I escorted some thirty congressmen over there, and of course each of them had to have his picture taken with this hero. The man's face mirrored his feelings, you know. He had this majestic face that went from a five-star general's cragginess to the Kansas grin and to the captivating boy-like quality of the grin, almost a mischievous thing, and then that five-star look which was far from mischievous. I captured all that in this wheel of snapshots showing his face breaking into this big grin, then sobering up into the five-star sternness, then coming back up to the grin. I had enough pictures to make it come alive. It shows the real Eisenhower in his various configurations pretty well.

He was a marvelous person. No hang-ups. He was at peace deep down inside, deep in the psyche. He never felt internally insecure. He wasn't defensive in any aspect of his life that I know about with the exception of certain isolated experiences. There was nothing personal in this, but he was very defensive about General George Marshall; he was ashamed of the McCarthy episode. He thought he blew that. There is no question that he thought he blew it. He felt he was put upon by aides who induced him to blow it. He gave in to them in a season when he was still getting his sea legs in politics. I think my beloved General Jerry Persons was one of those who made him blow it, probably. I cross-examined Jerry about that and I doubt not that he had a big hand in it. He and Sherman Adams and James Hagerty and so forth. I can understand their doing it, but I can also understand Eisenhower's hindsight that that was a terrible thing they had him do. He never quite said that to me but he said its equivalent to me several times.

MR. THOMPSON: Did he ever feel he ought to take the advice of the political professionals even though his own instincts pushed him in another direction?

MR. HARLOW: Well, sure he did. He knew he wasn't an expert in everything. He was a great commander; he would depend on the corps commander to tell him what was going on in the corps. That's the way he believed, the way he was trained in delegation. It was one of his great skills. That's one of the hardest skills to master—how to delegate.

He was not pleased with how the Marshall affair came out at all. Neither was he pleased with the stories about that English girl. I know that just bugged the daylights out of him. I never discussed it with him, believe me. I didn't know anything about it and I didn't care to try to find out from him, so I can't say anything about it except I know about it. I know that because he never mentioned it, and he would have mentioned it. He and I became trusting friends and talked about everything, and he never mentioned this one thing, so I didn't mention it.

He had a kind of interesting temper. You've talked about that to many people, I know. Of course there came a time when he put it under control, after his heart attack. It was marvelous the way he controlled his emotions after that. But he blew up at me once in 1954, and I relished it because I saw it close up and it was like looking into a Bessemer furnace. It was exciting to see it, and so dramatic, so spectacular a sight, that it didn't effect me in the least. I wasn't bothered by his anger, I was simply fascinated by what I saw, and I leaned forward to see deeper into that furnace. It showed the enormous, vital force in him.

MR. THOMPSON: Was there any warning sign?

MR. HARLOW: Yes, he'd look beet red. He'd put out all kinds of signals. I might add that it was like an Oklahoma thunderstorm or tornado—whish, and it was gone.

MR. THOMPSON: No grudge.

MR. HARLOW: Just gone, amazing. He jumped on me because I had rewritten a speech that he didn't want rewritten. He thought I had deliberately violated his instructions. He wanted to know in very explicit terms, very fast, why I had done that. I was busy looking into that flaming furnace. I almost didn't hear him because I was so intent looking at that! Then I realized I had better answer because, after all, life is short at best. I said I had been up all night doing the speech over, I hadn't been to bed, and I hadn't had hardly any sleep for almost a year, and I was so tired I didn't care if he fired me or not. I never wanted the job anyway, so it was to me a matter of relative indifference, which was the greatest strength I had with him. So I leaned forward in the Oval Office and I said, "Well, Mr. President," in almost inaudible terms because I was so exhausted, "goodness knows, I would not have spent all night doing this if I had thought you didn't want me to." I just looked at him, and if he had said the wrong thing I would have picked up my papers and walked out and quit. I think that was manifest. Then I saw the furnace door clank shut completely and totally, the fires all turned off, and he said, "Why, of course that's right. Let's get this all straightened out now." Just that and it was gone. But that was a manifestation of the man. He was capable of losing his temper on things important to him, which I think is an aspect of strength and not weakness.

MR. THOMPSON: Editing and writing were important to him?

MR. HARLOW: Oh, yes. As you know, he edited with great enthusiasm. It's well nigh impossible to write effectively for a writer, and he was a writer. It was no picnic writing for Eisenhower, not if you have editorial pride. He edited, edited, edited at least half of what he saw. He edited everybody, and he was very good at it. He was a very good writer. Many people didn't think so, but he was.

MR. THOMPSON: What about his press conferences? The people who say he is a good writer say that either of two things happened there: either that he confused the press deliberately and that's why the syntax was so bad; or the other view was that he was confused.

MR. HARLOW: Well, assuredly he was not a confused man. He was a man of great confidence and intelligence and I note that Greenstein believes it was a calculated move to put off the press and keep them befogged. I don't believe that either. I think he openly groped for the right words in talking on complicated matters, protecting the presidency as he did that. You can't do those broad and pearly expressions if you are conscientious about it. I believe you can't, some think you can. At any rate, I think he was being careful, trying to be very careful, to protect the presidency. They knew what he was saying but wanted to pick at him anyway. If he had been glib, they'd have said he was glib, didn't mean what he said. That's what we would have had if it had been the other way around.

MR. THOMPSON: If he was protecting the presidency one of the interesting things is that Truman got so much credit for his love of the office and respect of the office. A lot of the journalists kept saying Eisenhower really was more proud of being Commander in Chief than he was of being President.

MR. HARLOW: Well, that could be. The last job he had me do for him of major size was to get that bill passed on the Hill restoring his generalship so that in retirement he would be called General instead of President. That seems to answer your question precisely. That was his object: he wanted to retire as a general not as a President. You may not like that answer but that's the right answer.

Again, I remind you, this was an uncommon experience in the history of our country involving the presidency. We had a career public servant as President. You get those only rarely. To get a comparable generalship situation you have to go back, I suspect, all the way to George Washington in order to discover this kind of selfless approach to the presidency. It was a matter of public service, period, that he was in there for. He didn't want a damn thing personally. All he wanted was to get out with his reputation intact. He wanted to serve the country, to do a good job for America, and he wanted to do that the best he could. He had certain convictions about that. He was a deep-dyed, true-blue conservative, far more than people credited him or knew, and most notable including Bob Taft, who was dumbfounded when he sat down with him and saw what Ike really was. In some ways he was more conservative than Taft was, and to Taft's consternation because Ike lit into him all over the place about his housing bill. He said Taft was being socialistic.

He didn't want anything for himself from the presidency. He was a career public servant, and he had a great sensitivity about the dignity of the presidency. He was extremely sensitive about it, so much so it almost was a hang-up of its own kind. An incident I recall as an amusing little aside: We were out at Frazer, Colorado at that little retreat of Axel Nielsen's, a nice, secluded, rustic place up in the mountains. I had to go up and work on some speeches with the President and so Howard Snyder, the President's physician, and I drove up in the

White House car from Denver. This was 1954. We were getting ready to go on a campaign swing that congressional election year, so this day I was to finish off his speeches for that trip. General Snyder and I got there at noontime. We were going to lunch with him, then go over his speeches. Then General Snyder wanted to check him out physically. We parked in a clearing, between cabins and there Ike was in front of a grill, cooking. He was having great fun, dressed up in a chef's hat and apron. He was cooking a huge rainbow trout on the grill, wrapped in tinfoil and over hickory chips. Oh, he was just having fun.

A group of men were standing around, friends and Secret Service and so on, while he fixed lunch. I don't remember who the people were specifically, but all of us noted a big herd of cattle sauntering down the mountainside, all of them registered Angus cattle. They were following an absolutely huge bull. There is nothing that looks erotically more puissant, as you know, than a bull, and down he came, and this bunch of lacivious men looked at him, and you know what happened—someone had to make some obscene remark about the animal. Well, a fellow did that, and this was intended to be heard by President Dwight David Eisenhower. The General did hear, and he looked up, those blue eyes of his turned crystal cold, off came the hat, off came the apron, down went the spatula, and without a word he wheeled and walked into his cabin. It was devastating. The man turned, left the group, and broke into tears before he got to his cabin.

Now this involved the dignity of the presidency, in Eisenhower's view. You did not talk smut in his presence while he was President. Not that he was a prude, but you just did not talk coarsely around him while he was President of the United States. This contrasts with Harry Truman who loved barroom talk all the time, in such a measure that the press had been known to walk away. That happened at the Press Club one night. I remember the language got so bad even the press couldn't take it. So you see, two different guys, neither of them bad. But that dignity of the office was profound in Ike.

MR. THOMPSON: What about his dress? Would he have held a televised speech with a sweater on or would he have walked down Pennsylvania Avenue? Was there any of the populist at all in him?

MR. HARLOW: He wasn't much of a populist. He was a trained senior officer in the armed forces, and he had great poise and reserve. He was not nearly as reserved as George Mashall or Robert E. Lee or George Washington, but he was more reserved than Bryce Harlow, more reserved than you are, more reserved than most, and it was the reserve of a leader trained not to fraternize with the troops. He was an

extremely popular leader, as you know, during the war and his relationship with the troops was very good. He'd mix with them and they
would love it as he'd go down the line with a friendly and happy face,
yet with that gravel voice and obvious leadership force. They admired
him, they liked him. But he wasn't one of the boys; that would have
eroded effective leadership. I don't recall that he used to run up and
down airport fences shaking hands. I don't believe he ever did that.
Lyndon Johnson "pressed the flesh" and so forth, which is today par
for the political course, but I don't believe Eisenhower ever did that.

Another vignette may give you a measure of the man: In 1958, I
believe, there was a senatorial election in New Jersey, and Jim Mitchell
was running. He had been a very, very popular and very good secretary
of labor, widely respected in New Jersey. Well, he was doing very poorly
so Eisenhower and I and Bob Shultz went up there; I helped him with
his speech and he came out swinging for Jim Mitchell, rode in the
parade with him, waved his arms, and all the rest, doing all he could to
help Jim Mitchell. The night before he did the parade, Jim Mitchell,
Eisenhower, and I and General Bob Shultz had dinner at the hotel,
and had a nice and enjoyable conversation. Then Ike pushed back
from the table and said, "Jim, I want to tell you something. I've been
watching you. You've got to change the way you're going after this
thing—you're too wooden. Now, Jim, tomorrow in this parade, I
want you to do something. I want you to move your lips, I want you to
be talking to the crowd, wave your arms and talk to them, look at
them and move your lips; you don't have to actually say anything, just
look like you're talking, look like you are genuinely interested in them,
Jim." Well, I sat there and almost went ahem-em-em. Here's this nonpolitical general who reputedly doesn't know a thing about politics,
one who came up with the biggest landslide in American history just
two years before, lecturing his Irish friend. Nonpolitical and didn't
know how to be effective politically! Possibly that's an example of his
political sensitivity—his populism, you might say. He was telling Jim
how to relate to the public.

Let me give case number two: In 1961, it must have been, Bill Miller
was chairman of the Republican National Committee. He had me
drive him to Gettysburg to see the President to entreat him to go to
Texas and campaign for the open House seat in the first special election since Miller had become chairman. Miller wanted badly to win
that to get the Republican party going again after the Kennedy disaster.
So he talked the President into going; the President grumbled mightily
about it, groused like he always did, but then did it as I was sure he
would. So we flew there, and our candidate was a Marine Corps hero,

which fact has something to do with Ike accepting the assignment. The Democratic party's candidate did not serve in World War II and was left-wing politically in the Texas legislature. He is still in Congress. His district is in San Antonio. On top of all that, thousands of the retired military of the United States live there, so it was a great place for Ike.

We went there to campaign and Ike rode up and down the streets of San Antonio waving his arms for this candidate (I don't recall his name), a nice, handsome Marine who was inexperienced in politics but an attractive candidate. So the President sat down to reassess things after our first sally at campaigning, which was rather unsuccessful. This was about two o'clock in the afternoon and we hadn't produced the large crowds we expected or enthusiasm either. So he had a little emergency review in the hotel. Ike asked the campaign manager and the candidate and the national committee woman to be there. Ike said, "I want to ask a question. I've been over this campaign plan. Where's the Catholic college? I don't see a Catholic college on this list anywhere. Why am I not going to a Catholic college?" Well, they just waffled—didn't know what to say. Ike said, "Well, this is a Catholic place, isn't it? So let's get busy showing a concern for Catholics." Now, this is our reputedly nonpolitical general telling the politicians what to do! So there was a rush, calls were made, and some poor college president was scared half to death as suddenly Dwight David Eisenhower was thrust right down his throat. We went racing out to the campus with a presidential caravan. They let the classes out and put on a warm reception and so the President rubbed off on the Catholic university.

He had reserve, poise, and, yes, he didn't like ordinary politics much but, yes, he was very, very good at it himself. Once he got into it you had to head him off; he'd get too excited with it. He loved it once he got started. So as a matter of fact, he had trouble at first relating to his new career. You see, in 1954 he was starting his first congressional campaign year. It was very important to him because he was trying to salvage a Republican Congress. But he began by refusing to make a political speech—this was in his pre-presidential configuration. He just wouldn't make a political speech. I knew, I was then his speechwriter and I had replaced Emmett Hughes. Indeed, I was his one and only speechwriter at that point in time.

He called me in to say they were to have a big speech in the Hollywood Bowl, very important. It was the theme-setting, take-off speech for the entire campaign. I wrote two speeches—one, the kind I wanted him to make, all fire and brimstone. The other he ordered me to write, which was professional and deadly dull, on foreign policy. It was like a kimona—it didn't touch anything. For him to get up before a fired up political audience and deliver that as his take-off speech for the campaign would be, in my view and the view of many others, an absolutely irretrievable disaster. Some 5,000 to 10,000 Republicans were to be there eager to scream, wave their arms and stamp their feet, not sit there woodenly and be preached to about foreign policy.

Well, I did, I must admit, what the President told me to do. I put my asbestos, firey address in my desk drawer, and I proceeded to draw up lilies of the valley. This I sent along with violins to the White House for Sherman Adams and his crew to go over and make all right for the President to give it, and to make sure it was factually right and let the State Department pick at it. Then I get a call from Sherman Adams on the phone. "Bryce," he said, in his crisp way, "this is a conference call, just so you'll know." I said, "Bully for you, Governor—who is on the phone?" "Leonard Hall, Herb Brownell, Jerry Persons, Jack Martin, Jerry Morgan, Gabriel Hauge." All were sitting there, all the White House staff brass, and I said, "Yes?" I knew, of course, what they were calling about. I knew perfectly well and was elated. I was in Denver all alone and couldn't do anything with this teeth-clenched leader dead set on being nonpolitical. I put on that I didn't know what they were up to. "We have a copy of this address that you've written for the President," Sherm said. I said, "Yes, what do you think of it?" "Well, Bryce, it's awful." I said, "Yes, it is, isn't it?" And that disconcerted Sherman, he didn't know quite what to do with it. He thought I was going to say, "Oh come now, you are hurting my feelings." Instead I said, "It sure is, isn't it?" "Well," said Sherm, "I didn't expect that answer. If it's so awful why did you send it out here like this?" I said, "Because I had to." I said, "Look, we can save lots of time, Governor. You and your buddies there—I know what you're talking about. You don't like that speech; I don't like that speech. You want him to make a hot political speech. I want him to make a hot political speech. I have written him a hot political speech; it's right here in my desk drawer. You would love it. You'd want to tone it down, it's so hot. I just haven't the guts to give it to the President. You give it to him. You come out here and give it to him if you want short service in the White House." He said, "Oh, you can make him believe it." "Oh, no," I said, "I've broken my pick, he will not let me do anything even a little like that. This speech you have is exactly what he has ordered. He has been over it; he thinks it's jim dandy. But it will be a political disaster, Governor. So you come and talk him out of it, I can't." He said, "That's exactly what we will do."

He hung up and next I knew an airplane arrived at the Air Force base and here were all those men, so we had what was tantamount to a summit conference with the President. It was even set up like one. To me it was funny as hell. There was Ike, sitting at a desk in one of the briefing rooms for the Air Force, and in front of him we were all lined up, looking with great solemnity. Here was Sherman Adams and all his staff making speeches to the President, and he was just sitting there looking grimly silent, motionless. And they told him, "Mr. President, you have to make a political speech. You cannot make a soaring foreign policy speech at the Hollywood Bowl. That's a group of our party members wanting to cheer, and shout and roar and give the party a charge for this campaign. You can't go in there with that kind of an address. You'll ruin us, you'll just ruin us." The President just listened, obviously displeased. There were some thirty or forty-five minutes of this.

We all took turns and when one was done we'd say, "It's your turn, boy," and up would get the next one to make a speech; and Sherman spoke, and Jerry Persons; they all spoke, and it was in sum a gutsy performance. When it ended, he said, "All right, Bryce, have a draft ready by seven o'clock tonight. We'll meet in the basement of my house. All of you are coming," and he turned around and strode out of the room, leaving a trail of smoke behind him. I turned and they said, "Can you do that?" and I said, "I've got it already done. It's in my desk drawer," and I said, "We just need to clean it up. Just let's come to my office, clean it up, and there's no problem."

So we got to the President's house, Mamie's house in Denver, and down to the gameroom downstairs, and spread ourselves out around the table and started working on this speech until midnight or so. Eisenhower had a ball. As I said, you would start him into one of those political exercises fighting against you all they way, then you'd have to catch him by the coattails. He'd start putting in things you wouldn't dare say, and it would be tougher and meaner than you should say even as a bitter partisan, because he didn't know the metes and bounds of politics. So we created a torchy speech. He went out and delivered it at the Hollywood Bowl and was resoundingly cheered by Republicans nationwide.

But now you see, politically we normally had that experience of his resisting the making of political speech. Then making it with great gusto and enjoyment. He loved doing it but hated getting ready to do it, an odd behavior.

MR. THOMPSON: Did it hurt when it came from the other side? Frank Pace, I think, and someboy else said that when Truman played the political game he had been playing all his life and made statements in the campaign against Ike in favor of Stevenson, why, Ike never forgave him. He couldn't forget that somebody who had once admired him had said bad things in the campaign.

MR. HARLOW: Well, I think his relationship with Truman went much deeper than that. Truman jumped him on the McCarthy thing. I think he never forgave Truman for his attacks about the George Marshall relationship. That's number one; number two, Truman tried to make him run as a Democrat and he turned him down and Truman never forgave him for that. Truman thought it was an act of apostasy, as did Sam Rayburn. To accuse Eisenhower of apostasy is unforgivable in Eisenhower's context, and the Marshall thing hurt very deeply too.

I might say something else about this Truman relationship. Late in the adminstration, 1958 it must have been, I went to Sherman Adams and said, "Governor, there is one thing about the President that's got to be cleaned up. He has never invited the Trumans to come here. I understand why; it's because he despises them, I understand that. But that's going to plague him in later years because he should have invited them. He just shouldn't do that to a former President. And there's no point in his going on in later life saying; 'Ah, that was a fool thing I did and unbecoming. I should have invited him over and maybe held my breath while he was around but, the heck with it, I should have done it.' " I said, "Let's make him do it so it won't trouble him in later years. I know it will." And the Governor looked at me and said, "Are you kidding? Do you expect me to go in there and tell him to invite Harry Truman in here? You've got another think coming." I said, "All right." So I went to Jim Hagerty and made the same request. Jim said, "You think I'm going in there and tell him that? Great God, I'm not crazy." So I went to Tom Stevens, and I went to Jerry Persons—no takers. So I went to Ann Whitman and said, "Honey, let me in that side door now. Is the boss busy?" Ann said, "No one's there right now." I said, "I'm going in. You leave that door open so when I skid, I won't hit the wall." I said, "I'm going to do something to him that's going to infuriate him, and I just want not to hit the wall when I come out skidding." She said, "What are you going to do?" I said, "You wait and see."

So in I went and the President looked up at me and said, "Hello, Bryce, sit down," and I sat down. It was late afternoon, he was putting on his golf shoes. He was ready to go out to hit some drives on the South Lawn. He said, "What's on your mind?" I said, "Mr. President, I want to make a comment to you that I think you will dislike. I am suggesting it, I think, in your own interest. I think you will see later that, if you will let me finish what I am trying to say, I am correct in making this proposal to you. So I want to ask you, before I tell you what I am going to say, please let me finish." He started to look at me with that five-star look. But then he said, "All right," and he looked at me hard and questioningly, and I went into my recital. I told him, "I think you ought to invite the Trumans to come here. I think you should clear this deck so you won't be harrassed by this in later years. I think you should not have the country feeling that you did never invite him here. It won't hurt you to do it; it will be unpleasant, but you have done other unpleasant things in your life that you've thought you had to do. Truman is going to Europe; we can intercept him and ask him to drop by here on the way and bring Bess with him and they can spend the night." I said, "Mr. President, I talked about this in confidence with one of Mr. Truman's closest associates in Washington. He is delighted; he feels the same way. He says Mr. Truman can't turn it down." Ike said, "How would you say this?" I said, "I just happen to have a telegram draft right here," so I handed it to him, he read it, and said, "He'll never do it." I said, "Let's try it, Mr. President. Mr. President, really, I hope he doesn't do it so you won't have the mess and the unpleasantness to go through, but then that's great. If he turns it down, that's fine. That's best. That's what I hope the answer is. Send it." He told me to go ahead. I walked out of there and thought, "I hope I did the right thing." In the end, Truman didn't do it. The trip to Europe was the excuse, saying this and that, a sloppy response. It was his way to get out and he got out. The President never told me "I told you so" but he had every right to, but that was all right. I felt very good about it.

As a matter of fact, I went back and did it all over once again, I did it again to him on the day that the second unknown soldier—the Korean War one—was honored at Arlington Cemetery. I told the President that's Harry Truman's—that's his war. What's more proper than to have him there, riding with you in the car to Arlington Cemetery? Perfect. And Bess and Mamie in the follow-up car— perfect—and you will be hailed from coast to coast for doing it." I thought, Truman can't turn that down, but he did. Then he was asked on the gangplank of a ship as he was boarding, after the second invitation, "Why hasn't Eisenhower ever invited you to the White House, Mr. President?" He said, "I don't know, I guess he doesn't like me." That even though this was the second invitation he had turned down. But the point is, Ike overcame his revulsion about Truman, his intense reaction toward Truman, to proffer those two invitations, and I can tell you that's factual because I personally did that with him. I don't know why no one has probed into it, but there it is.

MR. THOMPSON: It will be there for the future in our little book. I think that is a terribly revealing story.

MR. HARLOW: Have you seen it written anywhere?

MR. THOMPSON: No.

MR. HARLOW: It's one honest, unwritten story of two Presidents as far as I know.

MR. THOMPSON: Could I ask just one more question on his political attitude? Greenstein advances the idea of the hidden hand. He states that Eisenhower was continuously involved politically but he didn't want anybody to know it and that he studiously avoided any public perception of him as being politically engaged.

MR. HARLOW: I disagree with that. I don't like to say it. I think the world of Fred Greenstein, but I tell you why I disagree. There may be some truth in it, but the best way to answer that, I think, is to refer to a press conference answer he gave one time. He was asked why it was that he was not truly a Republican, apparently, as far as the American people were concerned. Was he trying not to be, or what? That was the inference—you really are not a Republican, are you, Mr. President? He answered somewhat testily. He said, "I don't know the answer myself. I'm a Republican President. I send Republican programs to the Congress of the United States. I request Republican support. I advertise for Republican support. I go across the country and speak for and demand Republican help. And still they say I'm not a Republican, that I don't try to be a Republican. You answer that, I can't." This is an approximation of his response, and it was true. In 1954 and 1958 he campaigned harder from the White House, on the road, out in the country, than any President for a Republican Congress, for the Congress of his party, more so than any of the political Presidents. He never was so regarded, that's true. He nevertheless participated very actively but got little or no credit for it, one main reason being that the Republican party itself never quite felt he was one of them. That was a tough problem. He wanted to be an accepted Republican; he tried hard to be; he tried hard to rebuild the party that had been decimated by the New Deal years.

MR. THOMPSON: One of your predecessors in our Portrait series said that he was actually hurt that Dick Nixon didn't call on him more to speak on his behalf.

MR. HARLOW: Well, I know a good bit about that. I was jerked off Nixon's campaign. Eisenhower and Nixon threw me into Nixon's campaign where I didn't want to be because I was burned out by eight

White House years. I had tried to quit, but I was thrown into the campaign with Dick Nixon, to whom I was very close. I was made his speechwriter and we careened around the country back in that campaigning business again. What a way to go! Then comes the time for Eisenhower to make his coming-out speech. It had been carefully timed by Leonard Hall and Dick Nixon and Bill Rogers and Fred Seaton, I guess. I don't know for certain, but mainly it was by Rogers and Hall and Nixon; they had carefully timed it. They had timed it late in the campaign on purpose so Nixon wouldn't appear as Eisenhower's little boy. He had a serious problem with that, he thought, and he did not want to appear as Ike's lackey. Understandably he wanted to be his own man, a mistake, I believe, in hindsight. One can understand that he might make that mistake in foresight. So when it came time, Ike was going to make his coming-out speech on a Friday in Philadelphia according to their plan. Ike called up and told me to get right back to the White House and write the speech for him. So he snatched me off the Nixon campaign, much to Nixon's distress. I told Nixon—he was upset over it and said I shouldn't leave until midweek—something like that. And I said, "Dick, you know better than that. You don't write a speech for Ike in a day or two. He'll edit the thing ten times. I'll be working all night every night from the time I start doing it. If you think this is a trip I'll enjoy, you're mistaken, it's going to half kill me." But I said, "You ought to be very glad I'm doing it though, because he'll get a good hot speech for you which I'll write for him, and he'll deliver the speech I write for him, so you'll get a hot speech. This is worth far more to you than my wandering around the prairies with you. This will do you some real good."

So I went back and reported to the President at about 7:30 Monday morning. The President said, "We sure got to have a good speech, I don't like the way the campaign is going at all. Something isn't going right. We've got to get this going." He was so eager to get involved he could hardly stand it. And he said to me he couldn't get in earlier because, "It is Dick's campaign, not mine. I'm very sensitive to that. I will not do anything he doesn't want me to do. He's going to have to tell me what he wants me to do, and I'll do that." He was almost pathetically eager to do it. So we wrote a hot speech which he gave in Philadelphia, and it went over very well with a stodgy audience in tuxes—a horrible political spectacle. Then Nixon used him more after that, used him in fact much more than he expected to as he realized his fortunes were endangered. By this time, though, he was running headlong against Mamie Eisenhower who had turned into a tigress protecting Ike. She wasn't about to let politicians destroy her President, so she would scratch and scream every time they tried to put him back on the road. I agreed with her. It wasn't an easy time.

The story, you see, is correct. Eisenhower was desperately eager to get into the campaign and would have liked to have helped much more than he did. Dick Nixon writes about that. He says he didn't lean on Ike because he was asked not to do it by Ike's doctor and Mamie. I must accept that as true.

MR. THOMPSON: You used the phrase "rebuilding the party." One of the things that has absolutely baffled me is that we've held numerous sessions with the people you know who have come in and who give us very perceptive accounts of Eisenhower. Our Forums are part university and part community leaders who have come together with our visitors. The only community people who have stayed away are the far, far right, and to them a discussion on Dwight Eisenhower is more repugnant than a discussion of Harry Truman, Franklin Roosevelt—you name the President. They quote *Human Events* and other papers carrying the John Birch line on Dwight Eisenhower. Did he ever have any view of how you might deal with the far, far right?

MR. HARLOW: He thought they were kooks. That's why they don't like him. He said there were extremists in both parties which were necessary to make the parties find the middle.

MR. THOMPSON: So he let them alone.

MR. HARLOW: You've got to have perimeters to find a center. He had little patience with political extremists. He thought they endangered our system. He had little patience with the left. He was surprisingly conservative. The only time he was relaxedly happy in the presidency was 1958 to 1960. He was never really happy before. He liked the last two years because he just threw bombs at will, he was himself. He was not going to run again, he was getting out of the troublesome business. He was Ike straight away, and he turned out to be a hard conservative. He said what he thought ought to be done in this country, to what and to whom. He stood for what he thought he should stand for; he didn't shade it. He whaled away. He had a bully time. He was his own man. He was still under the doctor's orders to keep Cabinet meetings absolutely quiet, so he'd go to meetings with agendas so watered down it was ridiculous. You couldn't so much as hiccup because everybody said you shouldn't upset the President. So what did he do? Leadership meetings with the Congress became his out, first because the doctor hadn't thought about that, and second, because we couldn't control the agenda very well. We had to let the leaders participate in the agenda, and we'd prepare a red hot agenda and sit down and fight it out and Ike would love it. He'd get in and throw his weight around and argue to beat the band and Dirksen and Halleck and everybody would have a wonderful time.

He enjoyed those last two years that way and he didn't like the hard right. He thought they were counterproductive. He didn't like the hard left, either, for the same reason. But I don't have to remind you that he never attacked anybody by name of the right or left because he had too much sense. President Truman didn't appreciate that, and he created the ogre of Joe McCarthy out of a political nobody. I rode with Joe McCarthy to Quantico in a bus, side by side with him the whole distance, thinking he was a Senate staff member. Not until we got off the bus at Quantico did I realize he was McCarthy from Wisconsin. Even so, then he didn't amount to a hill of beans. I was the senior veteran in a bus ride discussion; he was the junior. I had been around Washington endless years and he didn't know much. Truman attacked him personally, by name. Thereby he created a monster. Eisenhower killed him and he did it by ignoring him. The press almost went wild trying to force Eisenhower to attack him. There was White House staff friction over this, but Ike didn't bite. He wouldn't attack McCarthy by name. The result proved him right.

MR. THOMPSON: That was his own idea and own style—no one had to tell him?

MR. HARLOW: That was his style. It was again this business of understanding the use of power. He had had a lesson in this—he attacked the Belgian government once and it fell, when he was in NATO. He told me about that. It frightened him. It was the first time he realized what he had become. He was no longer Dwight D. Eisenhower—he was a figure of immense influence. He never did that again. So he learned that he had to be careful in using such power.

MR. THOMPSON: He got that from experience. He didn't read Acton about abuse of power?

MR. HARLOW: No. It wasn't that absolute power corrupts absolutely. Great power can be benign. Acton was too severe with that. Great power can do immense good. He said it corrupts absolutely; it can but he says it must. It doesn't have to.

There is one experience I had with Eisenhower that I treasure, which I'll give to you. It's a window into the soul of Eisenhower and to his motivation on things. There are three of these. They were all in 1954 when I was doing his writing.

The first one was in respect to Dixon-Yates, the first "scandal" Ike had to deal with in his administration and it involved, of all people, his own budget director and it was a very embarrassing, troublesome thing. Everyone cried, "Let's not get Ike in the mess." So we came to him, Jim Hagerty and all of us, with a press release on Dixon-Yates. It was a mealy-mouthed thing, sort of lame, sheer bureaucratic blather. The President read it. Hagerty handed him this proposed release, and he threw it across the room. He said, "Now, listen boys. You go out now and sit down and write exactly what happened, whatever it was. You bring it in to me and I will issue that, whatever the facts are. The story will be dead and gone in three days. You issue this thing and it will destroy us all." Nonpolitical? An insensitive general?

Number two: I wrote a press item for him. It had to be issued quickly, and I wrote up a legal-size, double-spaced statement and we came running to give it to him as it was a rush item of some kind. I rushed in and sat down beside him, and he then picked up his pen and struck out a word, put it back, handed the paper to me and said, "Bryce, I want to explain what I did there. I struck out the word 'deliberately.' Let me tell you something: don't ever attack a man's motives. Don't ever attack a man's motives because he will never forgive you for that. You can attack his judgment forever, you can argue with him forever, and he will respect you for that. Remember that in the future writing for me."

The final example is this: I came to him with a "last" draft of a speech and we went through it for about the tenth time. I thought it was all wrapped up and ready to go, but suddenly he came to the end of it and said, "I can't say that, and I want to explain to you why so you won't have this problem in the future. You said that "with the help of God"—I never say that. I won't say that. I don't believe that. I believe that the Lord deals us a hand, that's right, but he expects *us* to play it." That's almost an exact quote; that's an insight.

Again, decentralization of power, under him a reflection of the fact that he was a public servant. His approach to this was very different from other Presidents. He was selfless in the presidency and we only rarely see that. His White House staff was a reflection of it, too. Here was a man who had forty-five years experience in government before he became President. And for aides he brought in seasoned people.

You see, Carter could probably have been reelected. Reagan might have lost if Carter had done similarly, for two reasons: number one, his staff would have protected Carter from his difficulties. Every President has them, his seasoned staff would have protected him; number two, if Carter had done it he would have had enough sense to have been presidential. I don't mean to kick him but he manifested himself to be a small bore politician and he beat himself in 1980.

FROM CAMPAIGNING
TO GOVERNANCE
Herbert Brownell

NARRATOR: Welcome to the Forum with Herbert Brownell, attorney general of the United States from 1953 to 1957. One personal reference: About six months ago, maybe a little longer, I happened to be in New York at a meeting of another group concerned with constitutional reform and met a man with whom I had worked for twenty years, he as a trustee, I as a laborer in a foundation. We struck up a conversation again and he said, "Ken, why are you sending me all this stuff from the Miller Center?" Later I met Herbert Brownell with whom I had not worked for twenty years and immediately he plied me with questions about what the Miller Center was all about. I thought of that yesterday when, in a discussion with General Andrew Goodpaster, he spoke of the fact that President Eisenhower particularly liked, as he put it, "to tug and haul" with people on the great issues that the Eisenhower administration had to deal with.

As many of you may know, or some of you may not know, Attorney General Brownell is a native of Peru—Peru, Nebraska. He received his A.B. from the University of Nebraska; his LLB from the School of Law at Yale University; he was admitted to the New York bar in 1927; and from 1927 to 1929 was an associate at the firm of Root, Clark, Buckner, Howland and Ballantine. In 1929 he joined the firm of Lord, Day & Lord and continued with this firm up to the present, with the exception of his government service. He became counsel to the firm in 1977. He is a former president of the American Judicature Society; a member of the American and New York State Bar Associations; a former president of the Association of the Bar of the City of New York; he's a member of the Pilgrims Society; the Order of the Coif; Phi Beta Kappa; Sigma Delta Chi; the Century Association and the Recess Club, so you know where to look for him in New York.

It's a very great pleasure to have him with us. Several of the people with whom we have talked about the Eisenhower presidency have, on certain issues, issues having to do with relationship between the President and the Republican party, issues having to do with the transition, for instance, from the Truman to the Eisenhower presidency; issues having to do with a great many difficult, political and legal questions, all have said, "Why don't you save that question for Herbert Brownell?" So we have saved some questions, and we are very grateful that he is willing to open our discussion with comments of whatever length he may wish.

MR. BROWNELL: Thank you very much. It's nice to be here in Charlottesville and meet with a distinguished group of this kind and talk about Eisenhower, which is my favorite subject. My personal relationship with him was as close and satisfactory as my official relationship. I can see around the table many who knew him so well and worked in one capacity or another for him. It all makes it especially gratifying to be here. I'm going to plunge right in to the subject if I may and hope that it won't be too long before we can have the questions and answers.

I met President Eisenhower for the first time in any serious way when I was sent over to SHAPE headquarters near Paris to discuss with him the possibility of his running for President. I was sent over by a small group that was interested in getting him to run against Senator Taft for the Republican nomination. That included Governor Dewey of New York, General Lucius Clay, Senator Frank Carlson and Senator Harry Darby, both from Kansas, and Senator Jim Duff from Pennsylvania.

Well, this was perhaps the most interesting day that I ever spent in my life getting acquainted with President Eisenhower and discussing the motives which made him consider running for President and the attitudes he had toward various issues of the day. He was undecided at that point whether or not to run and you can well see why he should have been because he was at the peak of a distinguished career, having led the Allied forces during the war and now being head of SHAPE, carrying on the chief interest in his life, that is, the development of a working relationship with our allies in Western Europe and their relationship with the United States. That was his prime objective in his life at that time and was the chief reason if not the only reason I think that he considered running for the presidency. He made that very clear at this all-day one-on-one session that I had with him.

He had not the usual motivations for running for the presidency. He seemingly had all the honors that anyone in public life could ever have. It was only because of his interest in seeing the country turn its eyes outward and away from isolationism that caused him to seek the presidency, and he made that very clear. He told me about a talk he had with Senator Taft some years before at which he had, in effect, offered to support Taft for the presidency if Taft agreed with him on the development of a close working relationship with our allies in Western Europe and a general internationalist outlook toward free trade. Taft, as you remember, did not see eye to eye with him on these issues. In fact, there was a sharp clash in their attitudes toward the relations of the United States with the rest of the world. And this clash proved to be the cause, above everything else, that made Eisenhower get into the political arena despite the fact that he had sworn many times he would not do so.

The thing that impressed me that day at SHAPE was that his entire career prepared him for the presidency. It was unique in many ways and has never been matched by any of the modern-day Presidents. He started out, as you remember, as a young man in the military and was sent to the Philippines under General MacArthur. This was of course before the war. He developed there a detailed knowledge of the relationship between the United States and the Far East. He not only knew in a military sense what our relationships were with the various countries in Asia, including Japan, but also our trade relationships with that part of the world. And after that he became Chief of Staff of the Army in the years leading up to the war. Unknown to almost everyone, I think, was the fact that he spent several years there developing the Pentagon budget and presenting it to the Congress. He came to know on a first name basis most of the leaders in the legislative branch who carried over, as it turned out, into his own administration. He learned there the relationship, which I may mention a little later, between the Pentagon budget and the general economic welfare of the United States.

Then after that, of course, he had the command during the war and came to know on an intimate basis all the leaders of the free world. What a benefit that was to the United States as it turned out when he became President. Then came his leadership in SHAPE and his role in the development of our postwar policy toward Western Europe. He did not have the handicaps that so many of our candidates for President have in that he was not limited by a strong partisan background, nor was he brought up in the log-rolling atmosphere of Congress or in any state house. He was free to take a national, indeed an international viewpoint, a national viewpoint.

I sensed this in one day in my meeting with him in the SHAPE headquarters in Paris. For all practical purposes, he then decided to run. We discussed the details of what would be necessary for him to do to obtain the nomination and get into the race for the presidency. He started out by saying that he wasn't going to change any of his views—his views were well known and he was going to try them out on me to see whether or not I thought they could be fitted into a political framework that would result in a successful campaign. We had the opportunity to review the issues which were likely to come up in the presidential campaign and also to review the personalities in the Republican party with whom he would have to deal.

It was a comprehensive review and exciting from my standpoint. He gave me an opportunity to size up his assets and liabilities as a candidate. At the same time, I found out later, he was sizing me up to see whether or not I should take an active part in his campaign. It was the beginning of a friendship which lasted for all the years thereafter.

When election day came, I am skipping over the campaign now, he called me up to his temporary office which was in the president's office of Columbia University. They had given him his former office quarters to use during the election campaign. He was up on the fourth floor painting. He had his smock on. He was dabbing away at some picture. He said, "Well, do you think we're going to make it?" I said, "Oh yes, it's going to be a landslide." "Well," he said then, "maybe we better think a little bit about what we're going to do when we get down to Washington if you think it's so certain as all that." And then he described to me the way he was going to organize the White House with a chief of staff. He had evidently given it a great deal of thought. There again his experience as Chief of Staff of the Army and his relationship with Congress was a valuable asset in preparing his own plan for how to run the executive branch. He said, "So this chief of staff is going to be an important office and I want you to be chief of staff." Well, I was almost bowled over. He'd paint a little bit and then he'd go on and talk about what he was going to do. I said, "I'm overwhelmed at the thought of it. But I don't think I want to do that. I'm a lawyer and that's all I know about and that's what I want to make of my career." He painted another branch or something on the tree and then he said after a while, "So you want to be a lawyer." I said, "I'd made that decision." He said, "Well, how about being attorney general?" So I said, "Well, that certainly meets the qualifications that I had in mind." And while returns were coming in on election day I knew that I was going to be attorney general in the new administration.

There again it sealed the bonds between us in a way that was characteristic of the man. He depended very much on personal relationships and friendly contact to get what he wanted. He could make up his mind fast and he had a wealth of experience in back of it, as I've tried to describe. Those characteristics showed many times during his presidency.

I went down to Washington and found out the first thing that had to happen to me was confirmation by the Senate. I went before the Senate Judiciary Committee, and Senator Pat McCarran of Nevada was quite a force at that time and he questioned me. He said, "Mr. Brownell, have you resigned from your law partnership?" and I said, "Yes, Senator." He said, "Did you take your name off the door?" "Yes, Senator." "Did you take it out of the telephone book as a lawyer?" "Oh yes, Senator." He asked, "From now on you have no direct or indirect interest in the profits of the firm?" I said, "That's right, Senator." "Well," he said, "Mr. Brownell, what investments do you hold?" "Oh, such few as I had I disposed of before I came down here." "Well," he said, "what did you do with the proceeds?" I said, "I put them into government bonds." He turned around in front of the TV cameras and said, "Say, Brownell, you're in a hell of a fix if we don't confirm you." So I learned some of the facts of life of an official in Washington on that occasion. But it taught me one of the lessons that Eisenhower tried to teach all of his associates: the importance of cooperation with the legislative branch of the government. And I suppose, as we look back on it, in recent years there has not been more cooperation with Congress. That doesn't mean there was submission by any means but there was cooperation in the best sense of the word during his eight years in the White House between the executive and legislative branches.

Then when I was sworn in as attorney general (I'm going to make this rather personal in the belief you meant what you said when you wanted *my* perspective on the presidency during the Eisenhower years), I think the first contact I had with the President officially was when I took in a list of pardons recommended to him. I started to go into the details of all the applications that were before him and he said, "Say, listen, this is your job. You're not supposed to put all that burden on to me. I'm going to rely on you. What are your recommendations?" He pulled out his pen and said, "I'll sign them." Then I turned around after I'd gotten what I wanted and went out, and he said, "But say, by the way, it's your responsibility, you know, as well as your authority. Now if anything goes wrong, you know who's going to get it, don't you?" That was the way he operated with his close associates. He delegated a maximum of authority, keeping an eagle eye on what was going on. I always said that Cabinet members were dispensable and it was their job. They should do their job the best they could but if it turned out that they were a liability to the administration and they lost public confidence in any way, they could be changed. He believed that and he operated in that sense as a benevolent boss, but a strict one. You measured up to his standards or else you got out.

He helped me in the selection of associates but without interfering. I had the opportunity to choose all of my associates—by that I mean the deputy and assistant attorneys general—but when I was stumped I went to him. For example, he recommended the selection of Earl Warren to be solicitor general of the United States. That was before Warren became Chief Justice. He admired Warren for the way he had operated the government in California on a nonpartisan basis. This very much appealed to Eisenhower. And then I had troubles over finding a commissioner for the Immigration Service to cope with the invasion of what we used to call "wetbacks" from Mexico. He recommended General Swing who was a classmate of his at West Point who came in and for the first and only time in modern history, stopped the flow of illegal entrants from Mexico. I wish we still had him there. Those were two cases where he gave me help in filling out my team in the Justice Department.

In the antitrust field—you never think of Eisenhower as being interested in the antitrust field—but he authorized me to appoint a commission to study the antitrust laws. He did not veto any of the recommendations that I made as attorney general for that commission, which developed some significant recommendations in that field, including the use of the civil investigative demand for the commencement of antitrust suits, thus providing the government a procedure for a thorough investigation, with the power of subpoena before legal action was started. The commission made several other useful recommendations, all of which were adopted by the Congress. It was typical of Eisenhower not to interfere in any way with the work of a commission of that sort, but to consider its recommendations and if he approved them to furnish the executive leadership that enabled the recommendations to go through the Congress.

He took a personal interest in the Eastman Kodak antitrust case, I remember. He said, "What are you doing over there in the Justice Department? I see you are suing the Eastman Kodak Company for having a monopoly on the processing of colored films (which were quite new at that time). They're the best films that there are. I use them every day. What are you up to?" He made me prove every detail of the case. A couple of years later when the case was decided in the government's favor, and many new competitors entered the field as a result and the prices came down, I made it a point to go over and give him a briefing on that so that he'd know the prosecution had been justified. Those little examples of the way he worked and the interest that he took and in the encouragement that he gave to his subordinates, I thought, were illustrative of his methods of operating his presidency. My chief contact with him of course was in the field of the civil rights where we developed the first Civil Rights Act since Reconstruction days. He supported us in presenting that measure to Congress even though the Cabinet was split. Time came when the opposition in the Senate was too strong for successful passage of the original bill. Senate leadership of course was in the hands of Lyndon B. Johnson who later when he was a presidential candidate became a strong civil rights advocate, but at that time he was bitterly opposed to the original bill. We didn't get everything we wanted. We did get the voting rights part passed through the Senate by arranging a bipartisan coalition which developed a process for avoiding the filibuster. For years, the House used to pass a civil rights bill every two years, which would go to the Senate. There it would be filibustered out of existence. We worked out a procedure in which we bypassed the graveyard Senate Judiciary Committee and were able to bring the House bill directly to the floor of the Senate.

I've always thought the significance of it was not only that it was the opening shot in the campaign to assure voting rights to the blacks in this country but also the development of a legislative procedure that killed the age-old practice of filibusters that had so long prevented civil rights acts from coming on to the floor of the Senate. I mention this incident only very briefly, for the purpose of illustrating the type of leadership that President Eisenhower showed by standing up even though it meant a bitter opposition to some of his other legislative programs by some Senate leaders. He capped that attitude by sending the troops into Little Rock afterwards, you remember, when one of the governors, Governor Faubus of Arkansas defied the Supreme Court school desegregation decison. Although he was not at all personally strong for the Supreme Court decision in *Brown vs. the Board of*

Education, he recognized his obligation as chief executive to uphold the law as defined by the United States Supreme Court. Of course that action proved to be the turning point in the enforcement of the Brown decision. It is one of the lasting accomplishments, I think, of his administration.

Finally, I had the opportunity to sit in the National Security Council meetings and see the way in which he organized that council and exercised his leadership there. I think now that his papers are open to the public, for the first time people have seen how he worked day in and day out as the chairman of the National Security Council to develop our security policies affecting the whole world and guarding the development of his program for intercontinental ballistic missiles, quietly done without partisan rancor but effective. When the charge was made at the end of his eight years of peaceful presidency, that there was a missile gap, it turned out to be false. The careful development of the missile program under his administration is, I think, generally accepted as being one which was not only good from a military standpoint but done with regard to the overall budget in a way that would not overburden the domestic economy.

So those were the experiences I personally had with him and gave me my perspective on his work in the presidency. If you ask me in closing what I thought were the greatest accomplishments of his administration I would say turning the Republican party from a party of isolationism into a party that had a world outlook not only in military and diplomatic areas but in world trade. Never again did we have isolationism. Since that time, although there are disagreements from time to time, neither of the major parties favored the isolationist point of view. That has really had a great effect, I think, on the development of the United States as a world power.

He ended the Korean War; he gave us seven and a half years of peace. It was interesting the way he ended the Korean War. Within a few weeks after he had been elected, he went to Korea and he conferred with the generals there. General Mark Clark gave him a military plan for invading China; General Van Fleet gave him a plan for carrying on the war within the boundaries of Korea. He came back and decided that the public would not support a full-scale war in Korea and he got out of it fast, which is an example of his decisive type of leadership.

Then he had many fights against the isolationist point of view which I only recite to you to refresh your recollection. There was the fight over the confirmation of Ambassador Bohlen as ambassador to Russia; the defeat of the Bricker Amendment; the cooperation with

Congress in formulating our policy in the Far East, centering around the Formosa Resolution; a very controversial decision to not support aggression, even though the aggressors were our friends in the case of the Suez; his especially strong support for NATO; and finally his recognition that the Pentagon budget must be framed with a view to the general economy of the country and his warning in his farewell speech that we should look out for the military-industrial complex that sometimes went too far in supporting the Pentagon budget.

As to his domestic policies that had a lasting influence on the country, I would only mention the admission of Alaska and Hawaii as states; the development of the interstate highway system; and the creation of the Saint Lawrence Seaway. These were cases where he succeeded in having the national point of view overcome state and sectional differences and opposition. Many of these things have come to serious public attention in the last two years since the opening to the public of the Eisenhower papers at the Eisenhower Library in Abilene, Kansas. This event has given scholars the opportunity to judge from original documents rather than secondary sources the facts of Eisenhower's personal leadership. I think I would say that his crowning achievement to me was his behavior as President in maintaining the dignity of the presidency. Somehow or other he made everybody proud of the United States. The development of that spirit in the White House was of lasting benefit to our country.

QUESTION: Mr. Brownell, I'm particularly interested in judicial selection and presidential choice. I wondered if you would care to comment to what extent, if at all, the President actively participated in the selection or decisionmaking involving the five successful nominees to the Supreme Court that were appointed during his administration.

MR. BROWNELL: Let's see, there was Earl Warren as Chief Justice; John Harlan and William Brennan, Charles Whittaker, and Potter Stewart. It was an unusual opportunity for a President. Of course he's the only two term President we've had for so long. We haven't had a repetition of that experience. He worked out with me a formula at the beginning of his first term that I was to follow in making recommendations to him for the federal judiciary, including of course the Supreme Court. There are many stories that have still to come but let me to try to focus on your question. He was very active in the selection of Earl Warren as the Chief Justice. He sent me out to California to get the answer to certain questions before he passed on the final recommendation. As I said, he tried to get Earl Warren to come in as solicitor general to "touch up his legal experience" because he had been out of the legal field for several years as governor of California. Earl Warren had accepted the solicitor generalship and then unexpectedly Chief Justice Vinson died and then the question came up as to whether or not he should be considered for the chief justiceship, or merely for the first vacancy of an associate justiceship. I reviewed with Eisenhower at least four other possibilities, including some persons who were on the Supreme Court at the time before he settled upon Governor Warren.

As for the associate justice vacancies that came along, he relied on us in the Justice Department to screen the persons who were mentioned for the Supreme Court and then we would present to him the alternatives and he would make the final selection. He wanted to have a Democrat on at one time, I remember, because the idea of public support for the Supreme Court was foremost in his mind in making judicial selections. He felt that a partisan balance on the Court was one way of accomplishing that. That's when William Brennan was chosen. In the same way, perhaps influenced by my own feelings in the matter, he felt that there should be a geographic distribution on the Supreme Court so that all sections of the country would feel represented and would support the Court in times of crisis. There had been a strong attack on the Supreme Court at that time and much of that continued during Earl Warren's time as Chief Justice. He always felt that judicial selections should be made with a view to encouraging public support for the Court as an institution.

QUESTION: In reading about Eisenhower, both before he became President and afterwards, I was always struck by the charisma that he had that you have mentioned, and I must say I always found it curious that, although he could write very well—the book that he wrote about World War II was a wonderful book, well written and he wrote it himself I was told—and he could speak wonderfully, that famous speech that he gave at Guildhall in London—and yet, I always found that he was a curiously flat figure when he spoke. He read a speech very badly. He didn't seem to take any effort with it. He wrote pretty badly. Those memoirs after the presidency were very bland and unhelpful documents, and I wonder if you could tell me why a man who was such a charming man, who could speak and write so well, often did both badly when it was very important to do them well.

MR. BROWNELL: Well, you remember that story that came out in the papers the last couple of years. He had pre-press conference meetings with his associates in the White House and he had one particular difficult question that involved foreign relations. He knew it was going to come up at the press conference. He said that if he discussed the problem openly he would ruin his relationship with Churchill. So he turned to Jim Hagerty, his press secretary, and said, "Well, Jim, we'll just fuzz it up." Of course it was in the best interests of the United States for him not to answer the question. Then when he went into his press conference the question came up. A third grader could have done better. He stumbled all over the lot and ended up by giving no answer at all. So there was that element of shrewdness in some of his press conferences. Each question, I think, should be examined with that point in mind.

I was talking to Jack McCloy the other day about this exact subject. He said that in his experience in the Pentagon and in Germany that he found that Eisenhower wrote the sharpest, most concise, and to the point letters and memos of anybody that he ever dealt with, but his public presentations were often so bad that you just couldn't believe it. Now, I haven't answered your question. What's the reason for it? I think some people can write and not speak; others can speak and not write; and others are smart enough to avoid embarrassment when the embarrassment is to the country itself. Se he was a combination of all of that.

QUESTION: You point out how skilled he was in his bipartisan relationships and relationships with all kinds of people in getting things done. That being so, how do you explain the missile gap fiasco, the missile gap accusation?

MR. BROWNELL: I think the missile gap accusation, later disproved, was strictly partisan in origin and developed for use in a presidential campaign. The fact of the matter was that when he went into office there was a missile gap and the Russians were far ahead of us in planning for an intercontinental ballistic missile programs. It was only by careful speeding up of that program over a period of three or four years that we caught up with the Russians in that particular area. I think it was President Kennedy who acknowledged, or people very close to him, perhaps it was McNamara, that there was no missile gap when they got in and looked at the records and examined the facts. So I always thought that the missile gap accusation exploded into thin air.

QUESTION: Is that partly because he did it so quietly?

MR. BROWNELL: Yes.

QUESTION: In that sense that wasn't wise was it, in this particular case.

MR. BROWNELL: Well, that of course is a subject for fundamental debate as to whether the proceedings in the National Security Council should be discussed contemporaneously in public. He felt very strongly that if he had discussed them publicly that it would have created almost panic in certain quarters, especially in Western Europe, and that his job was to develop that secretly, if you will, on a confidential basis. He did that and that story never became public at the time. It was his belief that it was best for the country if we recognized that there were certain things in the military and the diplomatic arena which should not be disclosed to the public contemporaneously.

QUESTION: I can't resist asking you to elaborate a little on the Mexican immigration difficulties because of what went on yesterday with Attorney General French Smith.

MR. BROWNELL: I didn't see that because I've been on vacation for a week.

QUESTION: He made a trip to the border.

MR. BROWNELL: Oh yes.

QUESTION: Is the situation beyond help of another General Swing or is it eternal?

MR. BROWNELL: I think the flow of illegal entrants can be stopped again. Of course ours was a controversial way of attacking the problem. When President Eisenhower selected, in effect, General Swing for the immigration commissioner, I went down to the border with him. It is interesting to note that William French Smith is doing that same thing, to watch the Mexicans come over the border. It was open and no great secret about it. They came over in droves. They went to the big metropolitan centers and they were living outside of the law and they accordingly were subject to blackmail in various ways. It was a tragic situation. We felt that the only way to prevent it was to do two things: one was to establish a military atmosphere on the border that prevented the wholesale entrance of the illegal immigrants; and the other was to establish a legal employment program for those who should legitimately come over, the so-called Brazero program. That program allowed the Mexicans to get a certificate to enable them to come and pass freely back and forth across the border and openly work for American firms and American agricultural employers. The two together—I don't want to be held to the figures—but the curve of illegal entries for those years, as you will see in all the history books, now drops from about 250,000 illegal entrants a year to a pittance.

And then when they repealed the Brazero program and adopted other methods of preventing entrance, the numbers went right up again where it is today.

QUESTION: Mr. Brownell, did President Eisenhower play a significant role in the defeat of the Bricker Amendment?

MR. BROWNELL: Yes, indeed, he did. Ordinarily the delegation of authority to do the frontline work would have gone to John Foster Dulles, secretary of state. But he had made a speech during the presidential campaign in support of the Bricker Amendment. So he had the written record against him and Eisenhower delegated it to me. I had day-to-day contact with it for several months. He was the boss. Together we would formulate the different compromise proposals. We got Professor Corwin of Princeton and John W. Davis and Erwin Griswold as our advisers. We met with the American Bar Association which was in favor of the Bricker Amendment and numerous other groups. We organized a public relations campaign. But every policy decision along the line was always taken up with President Eisenhower and he would say yes or no. I must say that he depended on the lawyers a lot for advice because the language of the proposed constitutional amendment was pretty tricky. But he got the point which was that the amendment would destroy the powers of the President to deal effectively in the international affairs. He said he was not going to give up the powers of the presidency. I'm sure he would have fought the War Powers Act just as vigorously because he felt that the President should not be hampered unnecessarily in the execution of foreign policy which was his primary duty as President.

QUESTION: Mr. Brownell, I'm interested in the subject of Eisenhower's habits of thought. I gather from what you've said that delegation was very important to him and that he liked to have a recommendation presented to him, and he would often accept it and then go on to support it. But when he was initiating something on his own, did he have a characteristic way of setting up a question or problem, or was his habit to turn to somebody who could give him a recommendation, or who could define the alternatives?

MR. BROWNELL: In the field of foreign affairs, he initiated; in the domestic field he did not initiate, generally speaking. Of course there may be an exception to both instances. In the field of foreign affairs there were many basic problems with which he had dealt either during the war or in his role as first head of SHAPE. There he did initiate, as in the Status of Forces Agreement. He was really the leader in that. In the papers that have recently been opened to the public, I think that you'll see from his correspondence, especially with Churchill, that he initiated and then transmitted many of our policies to Mr. Dulles for execution especially for Western Europe. In the legal field, I must say that he depended almost one hundred percent on some of us.

QUESTION: If you go back to General Eisenhower when he was a general in England in the summer of 1942 and having Churchill to his right and people like de Gaulle and the Polish delegations and all, here was a man who a few months before had been a brigadier general on maneuvers in Louisiana. We had no TV in those days, but watching him in operation there, you would have had great confidence, I think, in his thought processes because he didn't have a board of directors. He was there pretty much on his own and he had to make his way at that point. Second question: On decisionmaking, he made the greatest decision in life and that was the one to invade France on the day he chose. If he had waited a little while he would have had problems. That's luck, but he knew how to take advantage of it.

QUESTION: You mentioned that one of his strategies for dealing with the press was to have a pre-press conference with his experts. Did he have other strategies and how did he control so-called leaks to the press? How did he deal with the press from your perspective?

MR. BROWNELL: He used to get furious about the leaks to the press. At one time he asked me to make a study of the British War Secrets Act, which is well known to anybody who has studied in this field. So I did and made a thorough study of it and wrote out recommendations to him and he decided that that was the wrong way to attack the problem. He had to deal with the media carefully as potential opponents, but also as people who are absolutely necessary to have in his camp in any educational campaign that he wanted to embark upon. So he rejected the criminal law approach to punishing leaks. I never knew him to discipline anybody that leaked except under the regular civil service procedures. He thought it was one of the most difficult aspects, I think, of the presidency.

QUESTION: And perhaps it still is.

MR. BROWNELL: It still is. There is no question about it.

QUESTION: We have heard that President Truman wanted General Eisenhower to run on the Democratic ticket in 1948. Did he actually consider that? And if so, why did he choose the Republican party?

MR. BROWNELL: Well, of course there were four years in between the two decisions. I think there is no question about the fact that President Truman asked him in 1948. At that time he said, and he said it as late as early 1952, that a military man had no business mixing into civilian affairs in government and that he wouldn't touch it with a ten-foot pole. At that time it wasn't so much that he was rejecting the Democratic nomination, which I guess he could have gotten with Truman's support, but he was rejecting the idea of a military man being the President. And then when it came around in 1952, as I think I referred to in one remark that I made, his experience at NATO, especially, made him feel that if we didn't handle our alliance with Western Europe in the proper way, if we went back to isolationism, that it would be tragic for this country. Then he was faced with the fact that Taft was the leader of the Republican party and that he was in essence an isolationist. He did not agree with Eisenhower's views as to the place the United States should take on the world scene. Eisenhower felt that if he could swing the Republican party over to an internationalist point of view, it would assure that position for the United States in the years to come. In a way it was a 180 degree turn. He withdrew his opposition to the idea of a military man being President. As to the selection of the Republican party, he thought he could do the most good in solidifying the country behind an internationalist policy.

QUESTION: We've seen a change in perspectives of Eisenhower in the public mind and certainly of some historians since the opening of the papers in Abilene. We saw the same thing with Truman some years ago. Is this a surprise to you since you enumerated many of his accomplishments?

MR. BROWNELL: No, not at all. It is a surprise to me that some of the media would rely so heavily on the secondhand sources. I've nothing against secondhand contemporary accounts. How else can you report the news of the day? But history should depend on firsthand accounts and documents. I'm sure the problem is not confined to the Eisenhower administration. I think in the Eisenhower case, however, there were certain people like Arthur Schlesinger, Jr., who accepted the secondhand reports, the news accounts, as being gospel and attempted to write history on the basis of that. That attitude seemed to have gone rather far in the case of Eisenhower to a point where I think the political scientists one time took a poll of who was the best President. Eisenhower was about next to the last or something like that. I think that was due to the fact that the original sources weren't available. Now of course that has all changed and he has a very respectable rating in political science circles as I understand it. But I agree with you that I don't think it is unique in experience or that this happened only to Eisenhower. I'm sure it happened to other presidencies with which I am not as familiar.

QUESTION: Mr. Brownell, Presidents usually have very little to do with our vice presidents and I think that was probably the case with Eisenhower. Was it?

MR. BROWNELL: Well, I always thought the most significant thing was that he called Nixon in at one point in his first term and told him if he had any ideas of running for President he should get some administrative experience. He said that he lacked that completely in his career. He tried to get him to take a Cabinet job to give him that experience, and of course Nixon turned him down. So I know that was a very important element in his relationships with Nixon.

NARRATOR: We certainly thank Mr. Brownell and we hope that he'll plan to come back and visit us again and that we can remain in the closest touch with him in the future.

THE EISENHOWER PRESIDENCY
Sherman Adams

GOVERNOR ADAMS: Let's start at the beginning. You run through this the way you want it and I'll try to be as brief as I can. I get off into the branches of the discourse, away from the trunk of the tree and I find myself sometimes out on the end of the limb with nowhere to go except, as Robert Frost said, "To swing myself down", and I have to look out for that but that is one of my failings.

MR. THOMPSON: It is a strength, too. Governor Adams, we've asked each person with whom we've met something about the origins of their relationship with the Eisenhower administration, with General Eisenhower if their relationships antedated the presidency, with him as President if it began as candidate Eisenhower. We would be interested to know when you first met Eisenhower, what were the circumstances of your meeting, how did they lead to the relationship which you were to play, some say as Chief of Staff, some say Assistant to the President in the Eisenhower administration.

GOVERNOR ADAMS: The beginning of your question—I was elected Governor in 1948. I served until 1952 at which time I severed my connections with New Hampshire and went to Washington. The Governor of a State at least *ex officio* makes known what he wants to see happen in a presidential election. This is not invariable but it is very often the case. Logically the people look to him as the person who is expected to assert some leadership in regard to New Hampshire's early primary and by his own preference of a candidate.

What got me really interested were two visits, one of Republican leader Senator Norris Cotton who had been over and talked with Eisenhower; and the other was Robert Burroughs of Manchester who had been Chairman of the State Committee and was generally looked upon as a conservative Republican who was also sufficiently interested in Eisenhower's possibilities as the Republican candidate to take the time to go to Paris to visit with him personally.

Both brought back glowing accounts. The significant thing about their reports for me was that here were two people, respected and well known throughout the State who were persons experienced in the art of candidate selection, interested enough in Eisenhower's qualifications to go to Paris at their own expense to persuade him that he, and he only, could win the election on the Republican ticket. The thing that impressed me greatly, I think, and perhaps the principal thing that decided me in my own mind that this was a reasonable thing to do was the conviction they held that Eisenhower was the only man who could be elected on the Republican ticket.

In addition we had a lot of important people—I say important in the sense of their activities in life. Bill Robinson, for instance, was the General Manager of the *Herald Tribune*. He had great influence on the editorial policy of that paper. He came up to throw his weight behind Eisenhower and he said, "I'll get you what money you need. You don't have to worry about that."

I thought about it and agreed that an Eisenhower candidacy was the logical approach to a successful campaign.

We had fourteen votes in the convention and had fourteen alternates. I set up with some of my staff a list of people I thought might get elected and tried it out on some of them. They all said, "Well, whatever you say we'll do." I was amazed at the interest outside of New Hampshire that was expressed and the extent to which people would go. They were very much impressed with the possibilities of Eisenhower becoming a successful candidate. You didn't see that sort of enthusiasm and the extent to which it was shared by people of knowledge and experience in the field of diplomacy and foreign affairs.

I gave a lot of thought to the contribution that Eisenhower could make to the peace of the world. I never met the man until after I had made up my mind about what I was going to do and had organized a campaign in his behalf in New Hampshire. We had the nation's first primary, of course, which was no more significant than anywhere except that it was the nation's first.

I put together, with a good deal of help, a slate of delegates and alternates. It was at that time Herbert Brownell, who was then on the early management team, asked me to come down to New York and make some appearances in a dozen western states. They were political things, not in themselves very important. But, Eisenhower was back at Morningside Heights and receptive to seeing people. So I went down with the fourteen delegates one day and was invited up to Morningside Heights to meet him and Mamie. That was the first time I ever saw him. With informal geniality he said what he thought about a number of important public questions. It was a fairly light-hearted discourse and no hard sell at all. I had to find a way through one obstacle in our statutes which provided that a person who ran in the Republican primary had to be a declared Republican. Ike wasn't. So I had to go to the clerk in Abilene, Kansas, and ask if he had ever heard or had any record of Eisenhower's party affiliations. I have his reply hung on my wall in Lincoln, New Hampshire. I found it very interesting. In effect he said, "No, Eisenhower never voted in this town. I don't know about the young fellows nowadays. They go off and come back with strange ideas. I know his people always voted Republican and probably he might have but I can't say for sure." While it was a very interesting letter it obviously didn't prove anything.

Meanwhile Truman was after him to run as a Democrat though this was a matter of no public concern. It wasn't an issue in the campaign but the Democrats did speculate about using him as a candidate to keep their hold on the presidency.

Having discussed a few issues with the delegates Eisenhower said to us, "I want you to meet Mamie," and then asked her to meet with us. We had a little tea and then the delegation left. Then Eisenhower tapped me on the shoulder and said, "I'm going to have Frank Carlson (who was then a senator from Kansas) for lunch. Why don't you join us?" I talked with the delegates and said, "I guess I probably ought to do this, don't you think?" They said, "By all means." So I did.

At that luncheon there were only three of us at the table. We had a general discussion about some of the issues that would occupy the attention of a candidate. It was in the nature of a political discussion but quite friendly and oriented toward the wheat belt. During that year the Midwest and cattle country suffered a severe drought. On one occasion a delegation from the Northwest Cattlemen's Association came in to talk with Eisenhower but their spokesman insisted that all they wished the President to do was let them alone. They wanted neither subsidies nor handouts of any kind. I happened to be in Bend, Oregon during the convention of the Cattlemen's Association which was held in Prineville, quite near Bend. I was in Bend to speak to some Service Clubs and the head of the Cattlemen's Association asked me to come over to Prineville in support of the Eisenhower candidacy. Earl Warren, then Governor of California and a declared candidate on the Republican ticket, had been asked to address the Association and I found myself in an embarrassing situation for I knew that Governor Warren would not be happy about such competition. It was arranged to satisfy Warren's objection to my appearance by asking me to come over in the evening, but I wanted it clear that I wasn't an intervener and had not asked for the privilege of the platform. In addition I made up my mind that Eisenhower's representative could not share the platform with another Republican candidate at that particular time because the General would immediately become Warren's adversary. When asked, Warren said he did not think it appropriate to have other candidates during the time he was invited to address the convention.

I finally did appear at the evening session, resurrected a few old Yankee anecdotes, and spoke in behalf of my candidate. I'm uncertain whether I got him any votes or not, but I guess I didn't lose any.

I was with Eisenhower through the uproar about the private fund that turned up in California. I remember the long wait at the Wheeling airport, waiting for Nixon's plane to come in from Seattle. Eisenhower had called him so that they might discuss the political implications in the fund imbroglio. It was cold that night. We had to stay up until midnight. Neither of them knew how the other was going to respond to the situation. Driving back from the airport they sat in the back seat and I sat with the driver and listened to the conversation they had. Eisenhower was all sympathy. "You've had a hard time, young fellow. It was a hard thing for you to go through and I want you to know I understand that. . ." It was an understanding greeting. Eisenhower said, "With the politics in the thing, I don't know how this is going to come out really, nor what the effect on the public will be."

I had a long telegram from the publisher (Sulzberger) of the *New York Times,* who was telling me what I was going to have to do. Nixon, the New Yorker said, would have to be dropped from the ticket. This alerted the Eisenhower people early on to the politics of press coverage. Especially did it shake up the Nixon partisans. After long and fruitless discourse Eisenhower finally closed the matter by saying, "I hope very much that Richard Nixon stays on the ticket and we go on to victory."

This was a brave statement. When the story broke we were at the Commodore and Eisenhower said to me, very quietly but with some emphasis, "I do not see how we can win unless Nixon is persuaded to withdraw." But Eisenhower's statement to the public quieted the uproar and what he had to say about the matter was confined mostly to answering questions at the press conference. The public reaction after the Checkers Speech changed considerably the adverse public impact, but nevertheless the whole affair left an indelible impact upon the campaign.

MR. THOMPSON: He was impressed with the Checkers Speech.

GOVERNOR ADAMS: Yes. He sat there with a few of us before the television (at Cleveland). I saw it along with them and it was an effective appearance. Anybody would have been impressed because what obviously came through was the sincerity of a guy that found himself in a jam. He wasn't at that time hiding any essential fact. The speech was something that his friends and the National Committee people had pulled together for him to help him out of a tough situation.

MR. THOMPSON: You mentioned the early meetings and the meaning of the session that the President and Nixon had in the back of a cab and the light that threw on the subject. One of the things that has interested us was what each of the intimates, so called, thought about the President as political leader when they had their first contact with him.

GOVERNOR ADAMS: You recall in your research the name of Robert Humphrey? He was the chief architect of the campaign document. The best way to answer your question is to recall our efforts to get this document to meet the need for an articulate campaign plan, but to play down the partisanship since Eisenhower wanted the plan to reflect his own personal positions. It was a comprehensive and complex confrontation. The document was well done in terms of the business of politics as it was then practiced. So it came time for the National Committee to tell the candidate about the document. Arthur Summerfield and his cohorts came up from Washington and a meeting that lasted over three hours ensued. Since Humphrey was the principal architect he was the spokesman. There were probably seven or eight representatives of the National Committee with Summerfield and three of the Eisenhower staff. The conference room was at the Brown Palace Hotel and called exclusively for the purpose of conveying to Eisenhower what the campaign plan was, how it was going to be run, the topics and positions that the party was going to take and how they should be presented, together with some reference to the itinerary that should be laid out.

During the Humphrey presentation which went on for a couple of hours, there was some interplay and exchange of ideas between the chairman (Summerfield), Humphrey and two or three others of the National Committee group. They were knowledgeable political people and it was an interesting discussion. But Eisenhower sat there impassive and mute. During the presentation nobody asked him if he wanted to say anything about any particular matter. When the presentation was finished Summerfield asked Eisenhower if he had any questions. "No", was the blunt reply. He got up to leave the meeting and I could see that his color had heightened somewhat. Later we discussed the program and he expressed some opinions about it. One of the things he said was, "These people come up here from Washington with a well laid plan. But I didn't know what the plan was going to be. I didn't have any comment to make about it nor how it would work. I admit that. Until they had it all wrapped up they didn't ask me if I had a thought or a question. In fact, I never had a chance to express an opinion and as I sat there I didn't think they had any interest in the fact that I was going to have to win the election for them." That is almost exactly what he said.

When Meade Alcorn came aboard things began to change. A Connecticut Yankee, he and Eisenhower got along well. Alcorn had more of a sense of what Eisenhower's position was on many questions. The fact that they communicated well together made it much easier to handle the political questions at the staff level. Alcorn was well informed about the campaign speeches and promises and he also knew that the chairman of the party during the campaign had traditionally been offered the job of Postmaster General if he wanted it. Eisenhower never quibbled over that political fact of life.

Eisenhower had no enthusiasm nor any antipathy about Summerfield's belonging to the political world whereas Eisenhower lived in a world of people and the humanities. When it came to discussions about the principal issues, for example the matters relating to price supports for the products of the farm and grain fields, irrigation and reclamation, the economics of the farm and the ranch, Eisenhower understood the impact of federal policy upon this large segment of the Midwest and plain states. He became involved with many of these issues with his Secretary of Agriculture, Ezra Taft Benson. Benson was opposed in principle to every single one of the subsidy programs and plead with the President to support a free market for all agricultural products. He expressed his opinion often to Eisenhower that farmers were capable and ought to have the opportunity of getting support for their product off the backs of the American taxpayer.

MR. THOMPSON: Are there subjects that fairly early on you did have an opportunity to deal with, to channel them, to be the gate keeper as these ideas came to the President?

GOVERNOR ADAMS: The term is hardly an appropriate one. I was continually being accused of making arbitrary decisions about who should see the President. Let me give you an example. We had a senator from Nevada, Molly Malone. What is your impression of him?

MR. THOMPSON: I've got a vague impression—eccentric and right wing.

GOVERNOR ADAMS: Way to the right of right field. He came from out in the bleachers. Here is a typical incident. I'm not telling you this just because it is an interesting story. It is a good lesson when thinking about the answer to the question that was just posed. Malone came in one day and said, "I want to see the President." In his case I used a mild blandishment, asked him about his health, and then asked him what he wanted to see the President about. "Oh," he said, "I've written a book." I said, "As a matter of fact, the President will see any United States Senator any time it is mutually convenient for them." So that question was settled. "But", I said, "you are going to find that there is a lot that you have written that Eisenhower is not going to get up and cheer about." I thought that might cool off his eagerness about the visit. But Malone said, "That isn't what I came here for." I said, "All right, relax a moment." So I went into the Oval Offices and said, "Mr. President, do you want to see Senator Malone alone?" Eisenhower said, "What does he want?" "Oh, he's going to get you to endorse his book." The President said, "I'm not going to endorse a single thing he has written." "Well," I said, "I didn't expect you were, but you're going to have to handle Malone yourself because you're President." I reminded him of one explicit directive he had given me to the effect that any Congressman could see him any time, and so I showed Senator Malone into the President's office. They both got pretty red faced about the argument, but they didn't actually explode. Eisenhower said afterwards, "I told him that between the first page and the end of the last page, there wasn't a damn thing in there with which I would agree." Surprisingly they ended the discourse in an amicable exchange that an onlooker would hardly have expected.

MR. THOMPSON: Bryce Harlow referred to Eisenhower as the "compleat" President. Would it be totally unfair to say that you did at the very least complement him if not compleat him on such things as the example you just gave? He wouldn't have known himself, would he, what you were able to tell him about some things?

GOVERNOR ADAMS: As I look back upon some of these discourses I must say that I had an intuition which gave me some understanding of what Eisenhower's reponses would have been under any given condition. If I made a mistake, I wouldn't have been there long.

Take tariff policy, for instance. Decisions relative to import duties were sometimes terribly important. Bicycles for the English, for example; watches for the Swiss, and a great many others; these being matters of international significance, the adjudication of cases sent over by the United States Tariff Commission were matters for presidential decision.

Gabriel Hauge was a man recommended by Tom Dewey as advisor to the President on economic matters. It was his duty to review the recommendations of the Tariff Commission and to prepare position papers for the President's consideration. These papers came to Hauge, who referred them to me for a review preparatory to making recommendation to the President. These cases were sometimes important enough to give attention to the diplomatic considerations involved in the President's decision. That meant that attention had to be given in the case of the watchmakers who complained about the competition that the Swiss made by reason of being able to undersell the American manufacturer. Another, as I have mentioned, was bicycles. The establishment of quotas on items like these were not only avoided but actually were often matters of serious diplomatic negotiation since it was understood that the United States simply had to find the ways and means of not only fostering, but actually promoting, international trade. To cut off the import of foreign goods by reason of the harm that this competition later on generated for the automobile industry were matters of the highest importance. Above everything else, these questions must not be the subject of punitive legislation by the Congress, for such a situation would involve us in deep trouble.

The papers that Hauge prepared based on the recommendations of the Tariff Commission were submitted to me and Hauge and I discussed the merits of each particular question preparatory to sending a recommendation to the President.

To the best of my recollection these recommendations were never edited by me or changed in any respect whatever. They were simply passed along to the President for his signature and again, to the best of my recollection, the President never returned them with any negative responses or questions concerning the merits of the recommendation.

The difficulty that the staff occasionally ran into was more often political in nature than economic.

An extreme example of this problem came up during the campaign when we left New York for a trip to Wisconsin and subsequent stops on the way back in Indiana and other places. Eisenhower had given me instructions not to go into Wisconsin at all. The reason for this was the unavoidable confrontation with Senator McCarthy. A speech was prepared for General Eisenhower to deliver in Milwaukee after a long day campaigning which began at Green Bay, where we arrived after a long night in the sleeping car. At this point Senator McCarthy had boarded the train some time during the night, along with Governor Kohler and members of the National Committee. In the speech the writers had made specific reference to the fact that McCarthy had publicly referred to General Marshall as a traitor to his country. This had incensed Eisenhower. When Governor Kohler got hold of a draft of the speech, he and his staff were upset. Kohler appealed to me that such a statement as was contained in the manuscript represented poor grace for a candidate soliciting votes of the people of Wisconsin, and actually their guest during his campaign visit. After discussions with Eisenhower's staff, I decided that it was my responsibility to discuss any change in the text with the candidate. It was my opinion that the Governor of Wisconsin was correct in his contention that the remarks were gauche and awkward and, from the Governor's point of view, a slap-in-the-face of a senator whose state was our host for the day. I felt duty bound to take the objection up with Eisenhower.

"You have spoken on this question before," I said to the candidate. "I think my question is, 'Is the remark you make about General Marshall necessarily desirable or politically expedient, keeping in mind that this is the first time the subject has come up, probably, during the campaign? You have not been defending Marshall in your speeches in other states, but you wait until you get to McCarthy's home state, and in Milwaukee, before a great gathering to put this record on.' " Eisenhower thought a minute and then said quickly, "I guess you're right. Take it out." For the moment that ended it, but unfortunately the manuscript was then in the hands of the press and was instantly played up as a capitulation.

Hauge was angry when I saw him. Some others of the staff were extremely unhappy also. I received a sound drubbing from Sulzberger of the *Times* and the New York crowd. While the issue was never forgotten, it faded into the background almost entirely for the rest of the campaign. As I thought about it afterwards I knew there was no love lost between these two gentlemen. I reasoned that they could have their differences if they wanted to, but they could do it without coming to blows on a platform in a state that he needed to win in the election.

MR. THOMPSON: Did you know when you advised him that the text was already out?

GOVERNOR ADAMS: I think I may have, and certainly ought to have assumed that it would be of public record if it were not already.

MR. THOMPSON: Would there have been any way to come into Wisconsin before the primary and did that ever come up?

GOVERNOR ADAMS: No. He wouldn't go. Earlier I had been called by Tom Dewey, then Governor of New York and an important Eisenhower supporter, who maintained city offices at the Roosevelt. He said, "Why don't you come on over? I have some people here who would like to meet with you." So I went over and there were the big guns from New York State and his National Committee people. I was invited but I thought, knowing what they were going to talk about, it would probably be desirable to have some National Committee people there. Indeed there was. I made it clear to the meeting that Eisenhower had given specific instructions that we were to avoid Wisconsin. It was difficult to find any support for this attitude outside of New York. With as much patience as I could muster I supported Eisenhower's position but I do not recall that I had a single supporter in the whole meeting. I came to the conclusion that I could not be held responsible for every decision and that if Eisenhower, knowing in advance that the schedule for this particular trip included Wisconsin, wanted to eliminate the Wisconsin visit he could do so. The candidate did not become reconciled to the schedule and made it clear to the National Committee people that it was they who took the responsibility of failing to carry out his order.

MR. THOMPSON: These two examples and other examples that are sometimes mentioned suggest that there was a tutoring process and educational process on politics going on in your relationship with him. You were the person that helped him in making hard political decisions because you know more about politics and the press than some others did. Now there are people who say that one of the eternal problems in politics is a tension between doing what is right in terms of individual morality and doing what is right for the Republic and the people.

GOVERNOR ADAMS: You know who expressed that? You remember Ralph Flanders, a senator from Vermont? Vermont had two very special senators and the junior senator came from Springfield, a machine tool town. He was the one that had a supporting role when the Watergate resolution was brought up in the Senate. The author was Senator Watkins of Utah. It was his resolution.

Well, the senator from Vermont said this, "Sometimes you have to lay aside your conscience and do what's right." That is essentially what you were talking about.

MR. THOMPSON: But David Hume's grave was desecrated after he died because he had written about the balance of power and other people from Machiavelli to the present have been attacked. I guess what I'm really asking is if seventy percent of the people we've interviewed say the McCarthy thing, the Wisconsin business was wrong and a mistake and Ike regretted it to his dying day why are you more inclined to say that it was the iron law of politics that was necessary in Wisconsin, at least as you saw it at the time? Does that tell anything about it?

GOVERNOR ADAMS: There is another point. If I were to ask you, "Do you understand what senatorial courtesy is?" you would say, "Of course I know." If you have a man in your state unfavorable to the senator you don't appoint him because you know you're never going to get it through because he'll say that he has a personal objection. That's sometimes an insurmountable obstacle.

MR. THOMPSON: But you knew more about senatorial courtesy in politics than Ike, more about the campaign than some of the others did and you came to this conclusion. Was that a conscious role you played in the administration to channel information from a lifetime of politics to the President who might have been a little bit naive about some of these things?

GOVERNOR ADAMS: I had been in the Congress. I had been chairman of a state committee. I had had a variety of different exposures. I don't think that I was exposed to the point where I could say that I was a political expert. That would be a little too much emphasis to put upon it. I used to look at myself in the mirror and say, "How did you ever get here with what you know, coming out of New Hampshire?" What would you say if the President said to you, "I'd like to have you at my right hand. You take the staff and set it up and you have a chance to work with me; there's a lot of people would like this." At that point I asked myself about the quality of judgment that a candidate had in making any such statement as that. If I had been in his place, looking at a relatively young political figure from New Hampshire, it would have occurred to me that I had all the bigwigs around me in politics and would expect that the knowledge that they had would have enjoyed a strong comparison to the knowledge that I had. Look at two other possibilities from the Northeast, Warren Austin, for example, or Ralph Flanders, or even George Aiken. All of them were able people with more political experience than I had.

MR. THOMPSON: Eisenhower picked good people.

GOVERNOR ADAMS: I was about to say something to you about the job of President. The question has come up again that the presidency as it is presently constituted is a position which no man can fill. No man has the talents to meet the demands of the people or the authority to see that those measures are passed that need to be passed in order to provide for the national interest.

That's not true. It makes logical sense but I was there long enough to know that it can be organized. But the crux of the matter is who you get around you. He was really on a land mine when he took on that job with no more experience than he had had. But he was smart enough to take the advice of three people on the question of who he should have in his first cabinet. Eisenhower in his book tells who they were. I was not one of them. It's in *Mandate For Change.*

I came into the picture and was called back to Morningside Heights on the question of the cabinet. He said, "Now, I've talked about this with Lucius Clay, with George Humphrey and Oveta Hobby." In addition to those he had the best advice the Republican Party was able to give any candidate in Herbert Brownell.

MR. THOMPSON: Was there anything common to all of you who came into the White House and who organized this administration?

GOVERNOR ADAMS: The common attitude or common character-istic was that they were completely sold on the ability of Eisenhower to get politically oriented sufficiently to be able to run the country and to get us out of the imbroglios that we were in. We were then in a war with Korea. Eisenhower made up his mind the first thing he was going to do was to get us out of it. And he did. When the confrontation with the Chincoms came up with regard to Quemoy and Matsu he met the issue quickly and effectively.

MR. THOMPSON: You don't hear much about leaks in the Eisen-hower administration.

GOVERNOR ADAMS: None except intentionally. Eisenhower was a party to the exception. I was given credit for having put together all of the history that I could assemble on John Adams, Counsel to the Army.

One of the most baffling situations arose when McCarthy went after certain individuals in the Army and held them up to ridicule, calling them traitors and communists. It was decided that this kind of invective was outrageous and simply had to stop. We had a discussion in the President's office about how this might be accomplished. You might say this was a conspiracy, but only to the extent that what you were conspiring to do was to bring facts before the people, exact facts, and to say nothing that was not so predicated and absolutely right down the middle of the road. That document was held to be sufficiently factual to warrant the knowledge of it becoming public. But we couldn't release it. But we could create the means of having it released, which we did.

MR. THOMPSON: What about his trip to Korea? Milton Eisenhower told about his appointing a small committee to evaluate foreign policy and it was announced they were to meet the President but that was a cover for his going to Korea at the time.

GOVERNOR ADAMS: That wasn't very important though.

MR. THOMPSON: In trying to draw a portrait of the President but also a portrait of your role one question is how you did these things. John Steelman in our Truman portrait said he served the President in the way that he did by working until two or three in the morning. In some of the biographies you are credited with having contributed because you worked terribly hard. You really made it your business to master the last detail and to see the last person. But is that an explanation of why the President depended on you as he did? He knew you would have given him the facts.

GOVERNOR ADAMS: I never gave him any wrong information. I never glossed over a problem by making it appear casual or any different than it actually was. I got up early in the morning, but I was accustomed to that anyway. I would get to the White House at 7:00 and sometimes earlier if he had a press conference. Hagerty was there at the table and we went over every point that he thought was newsworthy and on which the White House should have a position. Eisenhower wanted me to be at all meetings of the National Security Council. The latter was the straw that broke the camel's back. I just couldn't do that because of the demands made on my time. He finally understood that and said, "When you can." I knew what the policies were and how everything should be worked out.

One of the interesting things was the appraisal of the military capability, constantly changing. All of those were top secret items with a code name that we had that was important to the security of the United States.

MR. THOMPSON: One of the things one associate said is that you sometimes protected him.

GOVERNOR ADAMS: I don't know what instance they were referring to but I don't think we need to go into that, but if you say so, we will.

MR. THOMPSON: For instance, if there had been a Brzezinski or Kissinger in the NSC who wanted public attention would that have been something you would tried to put a stop to or you would have called it to the President's attention?

GOVERNOR ADAMS: Well, not without orders, obviously.

MR. THOMPSON: You were mentioning Governor Stassen.

GOVERNOR ADAMS: At that time the principal business had to do with mapping and breaking down into zones the various types of surveillance by Russia and the United States. Those things were more upsetting to Dulles than they were to the President. The President could deal with them on the basis of his own personal knowledge of the military strategy. I suppose if there was anything in the nature of lack of precision or a common purpose it was the inclination of the President to put to the test a particular line of policy by infusing into the planning process a person of Stassen's and Rockerfeller's capability.

For instance, Dulles came in one day during the course of these planning experiments in a state of impending apoplexy. Rockefeller had seen it as one of his duties to get all the people together who were on his mission. They all met down at Quantico, Virginia for an extended conference. Dulles came in and said to me, "I don't feel very good today. I don't know what all the people are doing or talking about down at Quantico," and so on.

But the validity of any particular line of action had to be staffed and tested by looking at it from various points of view through lenses other than simply the President's. Eisenhower understood that and employed whatever procedure was needed in order to check the validity of his own opinion. But Dulles asked me, "What do they know about the cold war, for example, or the strategy behind it?" To be sure, the Governor of New York (Rockefeller) couldn't have learned very much about the logistic problems that were important matters of concern. So Dulles felt that the strategic military questions and the evaluations of striking power and intelligence should be left to him. Incidentally, Colonel Andrew Goodpaster (later General Goodpaster as Chief of the American Mission to NATO), every morning the first thing when he came in, went over with the President three sources of information very carefully screened. He made up a digest of this information which was reduced to a memorandum and then made an evaluation of it. He then took it into the President and read it to him. Thus he had the opportunity to ask any questions or give any directions that he wished to have carried out.

This intelligence and the evaluation thus made of it formed the basis for evaluating progress of the Korean War, for instance. Later on intelligence about other sensitive international problems were similarly handled. The dispatches collected by Goodpaster came from three principal sources. First intelligence reports from the diplomatic communiques (State Department), second from military intelligence dispatches, and third from agencies such as the FBI and the National Security Agency. In time of conflict there are frequent messages that require Presidential evaluation.

This business of kicking around codes and spying on your adversaries raises tremendously interesting points. We had practically all those codes broken without the knowledge of the sending nation and any whisper of that at that time could have been extremely detrimental in picking up their intentions. A good deal of our policies were based upon what we learned from those sources.

MR. THOMPSON: Why did this business of having countervailing viewpoints work for Eisenhower, even though there was some criticism that got out into the press, whereas for Carter it caused great trouble? Carter said during the campaign when asked who his advisors were that his principal foreign policy advisors were Paul Warneke and Paul Nitze and later on Brzezinski and Vance. The Carter administration was undermined when it appeared in the outside world that there were opposite and irreconcilable viewpoints at the heart of the administration. That didn't happen to the Eisenhower administration.

GOVERNOR ADAMS: It was Eisenhower's purpose to require the State Department and his special duty staff people to evolve a program reflecting not only unity of purpose, but a well considered concensus on how to resolve the conflicts and differences with the Soviets with which we were confronted. This approach required that differences in the Executive Department had to be resolved and policies evolved that would reflect American unity of purpose and determination.

The speech that Eisenhower made to the Society of Newspaper editors in the spring of 1953 was as near a classic example of carrying out that purpose as I can recall. What Eisenhower was saying to the Soviets was simply that so far as we're concerned we will keep no secrets from your country provided that you will abide by the same agreement. You will be aware of our motives and our proposals for maintaining peace in the world. We ask that you do likewise.

Returning to Stassen, you asked what prompted the President to put him to work on this very subject. Actually Stassen prompted it himself. He had this idea (others would call it an obsession) that a mutual program of surveillance by the United States and the Soviets could be made to work. At that time Stassen had about finished up with his assignments and the President was puzzled about what he could usefully do. He was as well aware as I was of the difficulty of convincing other people who had the responsibility of working out foreign policy problems and overcoming his credibility gap. Eisenhower spoke to me about the dilemma. I knew that it would be very difficult for him to have offered Stassen any such responsibility without having on our hands a distressed and very likely obstinate secretary of state. I did not go into details of this question with Eisenhower at that particular time. In answer to his question I simply said that the success of any such venture, as he well knew, would be problematical. Provided a confrontation with Dulles could be avoided there was a bare possibility that Stassen could open up policy opportunities that had not at that time been put to the task.

As could have been predicted, it wasn't long before Dulles came in and said to me, "I simply can't stand this any longer. I can't work with a situation where tentative decisions in policy are bandied about and then speculations keep popping up as to what we are up to. To spread these experiments all over the newspapers creates an impossible situation. I just can't live that way." As expected, Dulles had his way and Stassen was temporarily transferred to other work.

Nelson Rockefeller ran up against his own stone wall. He lacked the diplomatic dexterity and the comprehensive knowledge anyone would need to put a puzzle like the Overflight and Surveillance Plan to work. Rockefeller was a man of aggressive and introspective ideas that were new and sometimes startling. But in practice he kept his theories within his own staff and was therefore never quite the threat that Stassen was.

MR. THOMPSON: You said the President didn't ask you about the appointment of Stassen. Was that characteristic? Did he consult you about other key foreign policy decisions?

GOVERNOR ADAMS: On foreign policy the only key diplomatic post that I can recall that I had effectively to deal with was Ambassador to West Germany. You remember the publisher of the *Washington Post*, Katherine Graham of New York; she married Phil Graham. Phil Graham came to me one day and said, "You've got one of the best diplomats in the country. David Bruce isn't doing anything. Why don't you put him to work?" I said, "Well, I don't know why we don't." I said, "What makes you think we can get him?" Then he says, "Well, he's got to be asked." I said, "Well, all right." This man was on the tip of everybody's tongue at the time in the Truman administration, one of the most outstanding diplomats in the foreign service. I said to Graham, "I won't agree that he's going to be asked to do anything but at least I'll find out." And he said, "Well, that suits me. Go ahead." So I called up Dulles and said, "If you knew he was available for that job would you consider him?" He said, "You don't think he would take it, do you?" I said, "I really don't know. I don't mess around with these things." He said, "I'll find out."

The next thing in this chain of events was that Dulles recommended to the President that the President send his name to the Congress for confirmation.

MR. THOMPSON: The literature says that President Eisenhower never defined your job. I wonder if you could define it.

GOVERNOR ADAMS: The Congress did that. You mentioned Steelman. John Steelman was assistant to the President. That post and the salary was a matter of statute and what mixed this thing up was Eisenhower's reference to me as Chief of Staff. I never used that expression. But Bedell Smith did. He was Eisenhower's Chief of Staff in Europe. Eisenhower gave him credit for being the best staff person he ever had to deal with. He came into the office one day when I was at the Commodore with an aide and an armful of top secret papers and said, "I want an office." He had steely black eyes and only a little bit of a fellow. He was about 5′ 7″ or 5′ 8″ or something like that. I said, "What do you want that for?" Everybody called him Beetle. His name was Bedell but it was always Beetle. He said, "I've got these documents. Don't you know that I have to report to the candidate? The President-elect has as much right to my knowledge of these matters as anybody in the country. That's my job." And I said, "I appreciate that but what do you need a room for?" Well, he looked at me as though I was a small size mouse and said, "To lock them up, of course." And I said, "Well, we've got this hotel pretty well occupied now." I mentioned the money that it took and the prohibition I had not to spend any more money than was essential. All of that I could see was falling on deaf ears. So I said, "All right. You've asked for something. I'll have to ask General Eisenhower about it." So I went to his office and I said, "Beetle's in there; he wants a room." He said, "What does he want that for?" "He wants to lock up his papers." Then he said, "Take them over to a vault at the bank and put them away. I'm not going to spend any more money to run this place." So I went back and said, "Now Beetle, what do you think we can do? We have about all the money we can raise for this. There is a tremendous expense in running a campaign. What could you do?"

"Oh, well, if it comes to that I'll find a way." And that was it. We always got along fine. I had a lot of fun with him.

MR. THOMPSON: I suppose the question that we've asked everyone or that I may have mentioned in my letter was whether you've changed your mind about the capacities of Eisenhower, his strengths and maybe his weaknesses because everyone has mentioned some weakness that they thought President Eisenhower had. Did you change your mind as the administration proceeded and did you feel that you had discovered some strengths and weaknesses you hadn't known at the outset?

GOVERNOR ADAMS: No. He had a truly agile mind and a per-sonality that was captivating. On questions concisely put there were quick answers, sometimes a little too quick perhaps, but you knew precisely where you stood. There was never the slightest doubt about his ability to control any situation involving the policies of the Federal establishment. One of the untouchable independent agencies was the Federal Reserve Board. The Secretary of the Treasury asked me to talk with McChesney Martin, a long-time and highly respected public ser-vant, who had managed the monetary policies of the country with a deft and capable hand. Treasury had an idea that an incipient downturn was not caused by any one particular reason, but was due to money policy. On the telephone I said to Mr. Martin, "This is Sherman Adams. I suppose I'm liable for early court martial for calling you on a matter relating to official duties." He laughed and said, "What's the trouble?" and I said, "Well, Secretary of the Treasury Humphrey feels very strongly that the Board ought to look ahead to forces other than the money supply that portend an economic downturn." He said, "You can tell Mr. Humphrey that in three to four weeks that the ad-justment he has in mind is going to be made." What he was giving me was privileged information to assist the administration in its attempt to administer an even-handed fiscal policy. I was thinking of this ex-perience in the light of your question.

MR. THOMPSON: I suppose the question to me that is more important than any other concerns Cabinet government and you fit into it
someplace and the President obviously does too, and maybe the individual cabinet members do as well. Why did cabinet government
work for Eisenhower and why is it that with almost every other President they begin by saying we're going to have cabinet government and
then they stop?

GOVERNOR ADAMS: Well, they actually don't. A Cabinet government savors too much of government by committee, which is not
responsive to our system. We have a Chief Executive who, by popular
mandate, is the person on whom people rely. Even though this is an
oversimplification of the system, it nevertheless works better than any
other system of representative government so far devised. This is the
way it works. The individual voter bases his judgment on what he
learns from the media, now to a greater extent than ever, and what he
sees on television and the judgment he makes of the capabilities of the
administration by what its officials say and look like.

The Cabinet is not elected, nor are its members constitutional officers. The Constitution makes no mention of them. The secretary of
the treasury, for example, is the Chief Administrative Officer of the
department to which he is duly appointed and confirmed by the Senate
of the United States. While administrative authority does not run from
the Congress to the secretary, he nevertheless looks to Congress for
fiscal support. He appears before the appropriate committees and
defends his need for appropriation of public funds. The committee
defines the public need by line item appropriations and every particular department and activity of Federal Government. Every Cabinet
officer is liable to see that money goes for items which are laid out in
the budget, adopted and approved by the Congress. The cost of effi-
ciency of the expenditure is not controlled as a matter of law, but is
supported by human judgment. It rests on the confidence that people
impose by their choice when they elect a public officer.

Presidents are not immune to vicious attack and public castigation
for their acts, public or private.

During my second term as Governor, I was Chairman of the New
England Governors' Conference, and I went in to see President Truman
with four of my associates. Among them was Governor Lausche of
Ohio and Governor Carvel of Delaware. We went there for Federal
guidance on a subject that seemed at that time on the mind of almost
every citizen in America. The subject was self-protection and the
security that an individual, community or state could and should provide in case of attack. The results in human destruction at Hiroshima
and Nagasaki were so enormous as to give a feeling of insecurity to

most Americans wherever they lived. So Congress rushed headlong into programs for civil defense. Many people were digging holes and reinforcing their cellars and that sort of thing. While these activities could not be said to be the result of a panic, yet they reflected the frustration, or even frenzy, that people felt during the early post war years. The Congress had made the States responsible for the particular framework of civilian defense and the details were left to the States to work out in their own legislatures and local government. We were ushered into President Truman's office and after a few amenities Truman spoke of vicious attacks that were being made upon him, whereupon the Governor of Delaware said, "You know, Mr. President, it is a terrible punishment the occupant of the office of President has to undergo."

Truman didn't seem to have a friend in the country. The complaints reached clear across the country. Nothing was right. Truman was imperturbable and said, "Carvel, do you know who the most maligned President in the United States ever was?" Carvel said, "Well, I guess George Washington didn't get along too well, did he?" He said, "No, he's the first. The second most maligned President was Abe Lincoln. You're looking at the third."

MR. THOMPSON: Would you want to say anything on the way the White House related to the Cabinet?

GOVERNOR ADAMS: Anything I could find out about Roosevelt's Cabinet I got from those people who had worked for him and there were a few of them around. Some described a Cabinet meeting as a good sewing circle. The members would sit around and talk about any questions that happened to occur to them. There was a good feeling, but little attention to the problems of the people.

Truman relied a good deal on certain individuals in whom he had particular faith at that time. Eisenhower had given a charge to each member of the Cabinet that gave each officer a sense of deep responsibility in carrying out the affairs of his office and of maintaining a steadfast loyalty to the President.

The appointment of Martin Durkin was a mistake and largely due to Eisenhower's suggestion to Harold Stassen that he come up with some suggestions for consideration as Secretary of Labor. Stassen had generally a good rapport with labor, particularly in Indianapolis where he had come in close contact with the politics of unions. Pursuant to Eisenhower's suggestion, he would inquire of those having general knowledge and influence among the union membership for the names of individuals who would give the President an opportunity of seeing things from the union's point of view. Stassen suggested that Eisenhower appoint Durkin and although there was no support for Durkin among other Cabinet appointees, the President went ahead on the basis that the minority was entitled to representation. When he asked me about Durkin, I said, "I don't know anything about him." Durkin was thoroughly uncomfortable in the position and, unless questioned by the President, seldom had a word to say. Finally, he quit.

The President called me and asked, "Who are we going to get to be Secretary of Labor?" I said, "I don't know. I'll find somebody to suggest." I did just exactly that. I went to the agency which had to do with that particular Cabinet office and with more labor management problems than any other agency of government. I found that in the Department of Defense, James Mitchell had demonstrated great capability in keeping quiet the altercations and differences that occurred between the purchasing agent and the Department of Defense on all the thousands of government contracts. At my invitation James Mitchell from New Jersey came up to my office and I said, "Jim, I don't very often have this kind of job, but in this case I've been invited by the President to do it. Actually I have rather a liking for this one." When I was first elected to the New Hampshire Legislature I was Chairman of the House Labor Committee and later on in Congress a member of the Committee on Labor. I said to Mitchell, "You came up here because it was suggested that perhaps you would take over this job and do what the President wants done as Secretary of Labor." Mitchell said, "I know if I could I'd like to." I took him in to see Eisenhower and while I wasn't there during the interview, I was told that it went very well. The President sent his name up to Congress and he was speedily confirmed.

MR. THOMPSON: Someone said that one reason the Cabinet operation worked better for Ike was that Brad Patterson and Max Rabb went around to Cabinet people and talked to you and talked to others and prepared the agenda for Cabinet meetings. They said neither you nor the President ever struck an item from the agenda that they prepared. In other words, the ways you had organized the White House assured maximum benefit from discussions in the Cabinet. But they also said the President conducted those Cabinet meetings in a different way. He was an active participant who summarized the discussion very often and then a record of action was taken and there was follow-up immediately in a way that there sometimes hasn't been. So the interaction between the Cabinet secretariat and the staff and the Cabinet members and the President was somewhat different, it is said, and that's why it was more successful. I don't know if you share that view or think that is an exaggeration or there is more to it.

GOVERNOR ADAMS: Substantially that is correct. However, it a rather difficult question that you pose. Your question as I recall it was essentially this—how did the President get along with the Cabinet as well as he did, and how did he make it effective? Well, let's answer both questions. I discovered early on that there were people at the Cabinet meetings popping up questions of policy and administration that had not been properly staffed and that without preparation constituted an imposition upon the time of the President. That feeling was shared, although I think now that it was somewhat of an exaggeration, for it wasn't that bad. So it was agreed fairly early in the administration that we set up a secretariat which, among other things, had position papers prepared which required the personal approval of the secretary of the originating department. This was usually the secretary himself. The paper wouldn't be presented as manuscript but as an argument having applicability to the solution of the certain question that was of sufficient importance to have been supported by the secretary.

This practice was immediately commenced. The secretary was Max Rabb. He had enough experience with Congressional affairs, having been Secretary to the Governor of Massachusetts and also to Senator Cabot Lodge, to understand the weight of the questions and how to see that they were properly presented. The argument would have been gone over by me or with the Staff Secretary, Andrew Goodpaster, to make as sure as we could that the item was properly prepared and essentially digested so that irrelevant material was eliminated.

Now there were a lot of questions that obviously wouldn't have come up that way which the President had to deal with. There were questions on the military, questions of appointments, differences between a congressman's opinion about who should be appointed to some particular job and other candidates suggested by the staff. The economy often came up in proposals from the Council of Economic Advisors. This subject excited more discussion than any other single matter.

This brings up the subject of Presidential appointments with which, as a staff responsibility, I had to do. Most of the appointees of the previous administration were automatically out. With the change of political party of the President, appointees usually sent in their resignation as a matter of courtesy which created the vacancies which the new President must fill. One of these which was disposed of quite early was that of Chairman of the Council of Economic Advisors to the President. This was a matter within the scope of Gabriel Hauge's responsibility. We discussed the several possibilities that Hauge had in mind and he finally suggested that the President should consider Arthur Burns, then a professor at Columbia University. I asked Hauge to bring him in for a discussion preliminary to his conference with the President. When Hauge brought him in, I said to myself, "This is exactly the kind of candidate whose image is anathema to a good many Republicans." Burns had overabundant hair, thick glasses, and a typical professorial Ph.D. But I found Burns had some characteristics that were exceptional. He answered questions in succinct and knowledgeable language that immediately impressed his interviewer. In short, he knew what he was talking about. After he left, I turned to Hauge and we had a discussion, and I asked, "Who's going to support him?" Phenomenally, Burns was interviewed by George Humphrey, Joseph Dodge in the Bureau of Budget, and others concerned with hard fiscal matters with whom Burns had no difficulty at all. He appealed to his interviewers as a person whose great knowledge enabled him to deal realistically with the important questions that underscore fiscal responsibilities in government. Whatever doubt there may have been concerning Arthur Burns' qualifications was soon dissipated by his adept manner in dealing with various committees of the Congress and, just as important to us, with conservative Republicans.

Turning to other appointments, Douglas McKay, the Secretary of the Interior, was persuaded with the President's approval, to resign his office to run for Senator from Oregon, a seat then vacant. At the convention in '52 I made a bad mistake. As Floor Leader for Eisenhower, I happened to be assigned a seat directly in front of the podium. Across the aisle from me was Wayne Morse and the Oregon delegation. I had never met Morse and made the mistake of not giving him a strong feeling of the Eisenhower interest in winning Morse to the Eisenhower cause. I had some reluctance in appearing to curry the favor from a particular delegate as that primarily was the responsibility of the National Committee. I never spoke to Morse during the whole convention and when he came out against the candidacy of Eisenhower, that was one of our chief political problems in the United States Senate. When we made the mistake of encouraging Douglas McKay to give up his Cabinet post to run for the Senate, I could well imagine the satisfaction that his defeat at the polls gave Morse. In many ways he was a good senator and when he died, I felt the loss as many of his friends did in the White House.

Looking again at the management of the business of operating the White House, the secretariat became a device to deal with derailments or unexpected situations that needed judgment and close surveillance. This staff arrangement had almost exclusively to do with special cases.

Obviously it had nothing to do with military strategic questions. It did not often have to do battle with the budget or other matters of overriding importance. It was of principal interest because it put the meetings of the Cabinet on a systematic basis. It began a system in an area where there was virtually no system at all.

MR. THOMPSON: In addition to the military was there a tendency for other big issues not to be discussed in Cabinet meetings or among its members or is that going too far?

GOVERNOR ADAMS: Let's take the Salk matter as an example. Jonas Salk had discovered a serum which had given indications of being reliable in the control of infantile paralysis, a disease that had occasionally ravaged the country. The administration of the Government's role in the distribution and administration of this drug belonged to the Department of Health, Education and Welfare of which Oveta Culp Hobby was the Secretary. Before she appeared at the White House to consult with the President's staff preparatory to bringing the matter up with the Cabinet she had already accomplished considerably by researching and planning for the discharge of the responsibility of the Federal Government. That was a subject that necessarily concerned everybody in the White House. This was bound to be one of the questions that would come up at the next ensuing Cabinet meeting for it was recognized as a tremendous discovery. It was about to revolutionize one of the aspects of the administration of all federal officials that had to do with public health. When this subject went to the Cabinet it was well organized and handled in such a way that the President could come to a decision about the steps that his Administration should take in order to make the use of the vaccine completely effective.

MR. THOMPSON: And everybody would have had a chance to express their opinion if they wanted to.
    The thing that surprised us a little bit was when Brad Patterson said that he couldn't remember a case where the President struck an item from the agenda that the staff had brought forward either from a Cabinet member or their own "radar system".

GOVERNOR ADAMS: The request for the review and Cabinet consideration of a subject came primarily from the administrative official having the principal responsibility, in this case Secretary Hobby. Where any Cabinet member attached sufficient importance to any question to request that it be brought up for full discussion, that request immediately concerned the secretariat. But in the subject case Chairman Rabb and his associates would have been chiefly, if not exclusively, concerned that subjects had adequate preparation with specific recommendations to the Cabinet and a public statement by the President or such other action as, in its opinion, the importance of the subject warranted.

MR. THOMPSON: I suppose the biggest question I want to ask is what will history, if that's not too cosmic a way to put it, say about the Eisenhower presidency? On the one hand, you had an early disparagement of the Eisenhower presidency. Now we've got revisionism.

GOVERNOR ADAMS: Fred I. Greenstein was a Henry Luce Professor of Politics, Law and Society at Princeton. Greenstein wrote an article that I had little to do with except that he came to see me looking for source information on the operation of the White House. I gave him considerable information with particular regard to the notes that were made of the President's work, a good deal of which necessarily took place behind the scenes. Among other things we talked about the role of Eisenhower's private secretary (Ann Whitman) and the notes that she made after each Presidential appointment. Many of these notes were the result of the President telling her what the subject of the discussion was and the particular points of any decision or directive that the President made. Greenstein sought access to these papers and came to the conclusion that the record of the activities that took place in the office of President disproved the notion that he was a "do nothing" person, a President who played good golf but not much else. Perusal of those papers indicated to him that the evaluation of Eisenhower as an administrator and as a president needed revision and he proceeded to write an article for the *Princetonian* which had quite an impact upon academia.

I sent this article over to a professor of government at Dartmouth by several students who came to see me who wanted to discuss some details in connection with their courses in government. This had the result of initiating an invitation to me to come and give a series of lectures at the college, for the professors who read Greenstein's articles came to the conclusion that the country had been misled by the stories, many of which were fraught more with fiction than with fact.

This, I think, as much as any single instance relating to the dissemination of information to the public, modified public opinion about the Eisenhower years. This transformed the critic to a revisionist. There was sufficient solid material in the Whitman papers to give the researcher a base for further research and a reevaluation of the Eisenhower presidency. From the questions that were put to me about the merits of the articles that came out of Princeton and other institutions, I could see that reassessment was finding its way into institutions of learning all over the country.

MR. THOMPSON: The one issue where there seems to be some difference of opinion I can illustrate from Milton Eisenhower's views. He says that the notion that Eisenhower was operating behind the scenes with a hidden hand trying to affect actions and quite conscious of the politics of decisions as they came along is overstated. He claims that the reason that Eisenhower stayed behind the scenes—and Andy Goodpaster to some extent says the same thing—is because he felt more could be accomplished if each person got credit for what he did. So he turned over the White House to you, turned over something else to somebody else, especially where his own competence was limited, and let that person be out front, make the decisions and take the credit or blame. That was the reason, according to Milton Eisenhower, that Eisenhower appeared to be operating with a hidden hand but it wasn't so much in a conniving or manipulating political sense but it was more this moral sense of feeling that people really did best if they were able to take responsibility for what they did. Besides he couldn't get into all these things. That's a little different emphasis than the hidden hand theory and I don't know which you think comes closer to the truth or whether both have elements of truth about them.

GOVERNOR ADAMS: Taking any series of questions or issues and putting that question to the test would have prompted any scholar to come to the conclusion that the merits of the issue depended to what extent Eisenhower got into it.

Let's take an extreme case, the McCarthy case. The President, in a positive way, encouraged the elimination of this man from public life. Political history contains somewhat similar cases. Neither Senator Watkins, the author of the McCarthy censure resolution, nor Senator Flanders of Vermont, nor anybody else had been coerced or importuned by the President to bring about the political demise of Senator McCarthy. What Eisenhower did do was to encourage the dissemination of information concerning the dishonorable and shabby tactics that the senator used in bringing certain cases before the public.

Whenever it came to the President's attention that a United States Senator, or anyone having a position of influence in the Government, wanted to participate in a critical discussion in the quiet sanctity of the Oval Office he occasionally made such a discussion convenient.

Eisenhower had a very sincere but persistent and penetrating way of getting people to understand what the weight of the question was and how the tactics of certain public personages upset the Government and sometimes even the decision-making process. He also referred to the questionable and cloudy effect it had on other nations of the world.

Expressing these sentiments to senators had its effect. Not only did they have respect for his opinion but they understood the rectitude of his motives. To some considerable extent this was the genesis of the downfall of Senator McCarthy, culminating in the resolution of censure.

This is, of course, an unusual instance of the use of presidential power made effective by the force of Eisenhower's personality.

The incidents just related reflect Eisenhower's good judgment and decency. Another instance which reflected Eisenhower's great human concern for people in trouble came with an invitation supported by all the governors in the Southwest to come to Amarillo to talk about the distressful situation accompanying the extreme and prolonged drought that held the ranges in tight grip.

Eisenhower asked me to accompany him which gave me the opportunity to witness and understand his way of facing a calamatous situation with understanding and effective action. The President reflected on a visit that he had had early in the campaign from the representatives of the Cattlemen's Association, pleading with Eisenhower to "Let us alone. Keep Government off our backs. We want no price supports. We want no federal programs. We just don't want anything. We are perfectly capable of taking care of ourselves."

Within three or four months after the election in 1952 the drought in the Southwest got so bad that the cattlemen were calling for a federal purchase program.

We found Amarillo covered with grime and dust blown in from the parched fields. The Governors of most of the Southwest states were waiting. There followed a long and graphic description of the plight in which the cattlemen found themselves and the need for salvaging as early as possible the cattle that were close to destruction. Eisenhower was born in Texas and lived his early life in rural Kansas. Eisenhower impressed his listeners with his knowledge and understanding of what they were going through and agreed that he would work with Secretary Benson in devising some means of assistance.

Coming out to the plane, we were in Air Force One, ready to go back to Washington, the President said, "You know, this looks a good deal like the situation that we faced in the drought of the 1920's and '30's." Then, "Farmers had to have faith because the law didn't provide any relief for them. The only way they could save their stock was to get it to market for whatever they could get for it." Then, reminiscing about those days Eisenhower said, "My father went bankrupt in a situation similar to this. He ran a grain store and the cattlemen would come in and ask for credit and, knowing their distress, he would allow them to build up a bill which, in the trouble they were in, they never could pay." So Eisenhower had his heart in their predicament.

Arriving back in Washington he and Secretary Benson worked out a cattlemen's relief program and got it going. But over at Amarillo one of the cattlemen brought in as a witness to their distress looked familiar to the President. He said to him, "Weren't you one of the ones that came into Denver last summer? Do you remember what you told me? You told me to leave you alone and here you are back within six months asking for a support program."

Their chagrin did not change their mood nor diminish their hope for a federal purchase program, which went through and once more furnished the temporary relief that this situation warranted.

To some extent questions as to certification of airline routes came up to bother him from time to time. He accepted as his personal duty as President the decisions that went with his office, but had to turn to the staff for recommendations and sufficient preparation in order to have at his disposal all of the needed evidence on which to base a decision. Such information came up from State agencies and segments of the user-public who were concerned with the decision. Some of these questions had political considerations and many had to do with the maladjustments that were the product of the freedom built into the whole economic system.

Then there were questions that ran all the way from those that affected a large segment of regions and the operation of the economic system. Occasionally the President was requested to discuss certain decisions and appointments by individual members of Congress. Eisenhower had a way of dealing with these matters by reminding the questioner that anyone in his office could not take questions of that nature. In this category lie all of the matters that he could not turn over to others for a decision. There was no disposition on the part of Eisenhower to duck a Constitutional responsibility.

MR. THOMPSON: I have a colleague, a very interesting fellow, who won the Bancroft Prize earlier for a book called *The Washington Community*. His name is James Sterling Young. He used to teach at Columbia. He has a theory of the presidency and I wonder if it fits Eisenhower's conception and yours. He says that presidentialism comes into effect on those great issues where either an emergency has occurred or the survival of the Republic is at stake or something very fundamental is involved.

Constitutionalism is the way our system works all the rest of the time, or should, on all the ordinary routine, day-by-day things. There the balance of power, equilibrium between Congress and the executive all of that process is in effect on those things. But he says that what really has happened with special interest groups, for instance represented on White House staff, is that those issues that would normally have been dealt with as part of the constitutional process and involve the interplay of executive and legislature now have been exported into the White House and that what we have done is to require the President to be not only presidential on a few great things to which he can devote his time and attention but presidential on everything and that's one reason we're in trouble today. Did Eisenhower have any sympathy for that view, or do you?

GOVERNOR ADAMS: We must be careful that we do not confuse the responsibilities that belong to Congress and those that are assigned to the Executive. As long as we continue to believe in representative government, the representatives that are sent to Washington will continue to bring discrete questions to the White House staff and, to some extent, directly to the President. It is the routine duty of the President's staff to compress, research and to resolve these questions to the extent that they are assigned the authority to do so. Your witness, James Sterling Young, should have kept in mind that the President has Constitutional duties as well as mandates that originate in Congress and are incorporated into law. On the other hand, there is a vast body of other duties which cut across both state and national lines and which have to do with the administration of diplomatic policy. Purposely I make no reference to the ceremonial duties of the office, nor to the fact that he is head of his political party and is looked to by this constituency to give force and direction to the political questions that surround and immerse him from day to day. In any discussion of the ability of a person to discharge the duties of his office, the discharge of every one of these responsibilities has to be subject to a careful evaluation of the adequacies of the staff and sufficient funds appropriated to be disbursed at the pleasure of the President in order to accomplish the duties assigned to him in every one of these categories.

MR. THOMPSON: But in that sense maybe history will say that this was a distinguishing characteristic of the Eisenhower presidency that differed from some of the more recent presidencies.

GOVERNOR ADAMS: Well, this President dealt very little with special interests. Occasionally he was persuaded to listen to representatives of special interests provided that the subject of any particular interest was related to the health, welfare, or economic well being of a large segment of the population. I mentioned two instances. There are others. You cannot divide the President from the fact that he's a human being, and being a human being persuades him to do certain things that are characteristic of a human being. They comprise the exercise of mercy, understanding and delving into questions for the purpose of finding what the social pressures are. When it comes to the trivia, he must delegate. When he delegates he charges that individual or agency with the duty of making decisions that correlate with his own policies and positions. The independent agencies present difficult problems. Whether or not you could take all of these regulating boards and commissions and put them into a single department or agency for administrative purposes is a moot question. Politically that is a very difficult thing to attempt because both political and personality questions interfere. The opposition of Congress is likely because it is reluctant to lose their hold on the President.

Thus, it is very difficult to get a clear cut delegation of responsibility that will lighten the President's load. He has to be ambidextrous to be able to put those problems in the hands of those he knows are capable and to be assured that the decisions will be as valid as his own would have been. They must have the imprimatur of the President and be as soundly reasoned as though the decision was his alone.

MR. THOMPSON: Thank you, Governor Adams.

IV.
EISENHOWER AND THE BUDGET

THE EISENHOWER PRESIDENCY AND BEYOND

Maurice Stans

NARRATOR: We are pleased to welcome the Honorable Maurice Stans, Secretary of Commerce in the Nixon administration.

After study at Northwestern University and at Columbia, Secretary Stans entered the field of business and became a leader among certified public accountants. He was associated with Alexander Grant and Company in Chicago, with The Moore Corporation in Juliet, Illinois and with other companies, and then moved in the 1950s into public service as financial consultant to the Postmaster General, Deputy Postmaster General, Deputy Director of the Bureau of the Budget, and Director of the Bureau of the Budget. Then he went back to business, and among other things was director of ten listed corporations, director, senior partner and then president of William R. Staats and Co., securities brokers; and vice-chairman of a large California bank. Then he moved back into government, and was active in the campaign for President Nixon in 1968 and again in the campaign to re-elect President Nixon and received a Cabinet appointment thereafter.

We feel that, in addition to scholarship, it's absolutely vital that somehow or another the Miller Center be in touch with those people who in their life and work have concerned themselves with the presidency. We also feel that the questions and the searching concerns of private citizens can do every bit as much, as it were, to debrief these men and women in order to help the rest of us understand how American government actually works and thereby perhaps to think of ways that it might be further strengthened and made to serve more effectively the needs of the American people. That's too long an introduction, but it is our privilege to have Secretary Stans with us to discuss "The Eisenhower Presidency and Beyond."

SECRETARY STANS: Thank you, Ken, and thanks to the Miller Center and to all of you for making it possible for me to talk today about one of my favorite, and one of the greatest, Presidents.

If you will permit me, I'm going to reserve the usual order and give my conclusions at the beginning. If I do that it will lay the groundwork for the subsequent remarks and fit them in to the total picture. Now, ten points about Dwight Eisenhower:

First, he was a person born with traditional, mid-Western conservatism, whose career was formed less by a driving ambition than by force of circumstance and the recognition of his abilities.

Second, he was a polished man, confident, charming in manner, with a good sense of humor, comfortable in social settings but somewhat uneasy in political or very wealthy groups.

Third, he was an extroverted personality with a genuine feel for people—good or bad.

Fourth, he was a military man recognized, by his peers for high technical skill and persuasion, fully current about military technology and the practicalities of warfare.

Fifth, he was a person of prodigious recollection, seldom confused by any variety of factual situations; a decisive person but insisting on carefully developed position papers as a ground for his decisions; and was courageous in the ensuring actions; relaxed about political responsibility and willing to lean on others of greater experience.

Sixth, he was often intolerant of political opposition to his proposals, contentions over turf, disorder in government organization, leaks, and the delays of bureaucracy. And he could be profane under continued frustration.

Seventh, he was excessively tolerant of actions by subordinates, disliking having to discipline them or dismiss them; not frequent with direct compliments to people but praiseful to third parties.

Eighth, he was an orderly and self-disciplined executive diligent and hardworking, accustomed to delegating responsibility and avoiding detail; a compromiser rather than a militant; an administrator rather than an initiator, but positive in attitude toward moderate change.

Ninth, he was unsophisticated in political tactics, but adjustable to the realities of vote counting in legislative matters; highly respectful of precedent in the presidency.

Tenth, and perhaps in summary, he was a man with an overall record of outstanding performance as President, whose most notable accomplishment, based on his dedication to conservative economic policies, was his control of the major economic trends in the country during his administration, through management of fiscal policy.

Now let me go back for a moment to qualify myself. Some people get into Washington in strange ways. In 1953 I was one of seventy-five certified public accountants who volunteered six weeks' time to help the incoming Eisenhower administration review the federal budget left by President Truman. I stayed ten years. Given the assignment to study the Post Office Department I concluded with several hundred recommendations to modernize the Department's accounting and finances and operations, and to institute the first research program in its history. Postmaster General Summerfield then hired me on the spot as a consultant to give half my time to putting those recommendations into effect. That was my start in government. Two years later, I was named to be Deputy Postmaster General; two years later to be Director of the Budget of the United States. When Richard Nixon became President in 1969 he named me to the position of Secretary of Commerce. These are in essence my qualifications to express my opinions on the talents and the working characteristics of President Eisenhower in handling the immensely complex duties of the presidency.

As Director of the Budget from 1958 to 1961, a post which carried membership in the Cabinet and in the National Security Council, I saw Dwight Eisenhower almost every day for the last three years he was in office. It's not unusual therefore that I think of him and his administration first in connection with fiscal policy.

Now I want to tell you a fairly long story about 1960. It was one of the most difficult budgetary times that the country had ever faced up to that time. The Russian feat of orbiting the Sputnik not many months earlier had thrown a panic into American educational, scientific, and military circles. The Congress was confronted with a myriad of proposed programs alleged to be absolutely necessary to reestablish our national superiority over the Soviets. Some of them were enacted in haste; more were under consideration. Eisenhower knew he had to think about an increase in the defense budget. A new civilian space agency was being promoted. The spectre of Soviet strength was being used by many interests and lobbyists to support all kinds of new spending ideas. In addition, a recession had set in threatening federal revenues and engendering another vast array of proposals to stimulate the economy. There were demands for a tax cut; for billions of dollars in new public works; for enhancing the unemployment insurance benefits; and a host of other welfare and other programs to "get things going again."

The immediate fiscal situation was building to a crisis. The 1958 budget which was supposed to be in surplus had evaporated into a certain deficit. Fiscal 1959 was in worse shape. Months before the year was to begin it was clear that my predecessor's planned surplus of a half billion dollars was going to become a massive deficit.

I went to Eisenhower the very first day for guidance as to his policies. I knew him to be conservative insofar as government finances were concerned but I wanted a confirmation of his attitude in the present circumstances of alternative choices in direction so I'd be sure to know how he wanted me to proceed. He left no doubt where he stood. "I came into office believing that our budget should be balanced," he said. "I was determined to hold spending down by using necessity rather than desirability as a test for what we would do and thereby reduce the share of the national income that is spent by the government. We'll be better off as a nation if we leave a greater share for the people to act as they will. There have been some setbacks but by and large we've done pretty well. I want to continue the same policy even though Congress will always give us trouble. I don't like people using this recession to clamor for tax cuts or spending. It just seems that we can't get the public to see how dangerous such things can be," he said rather plaintively. "They ought to have more confidence that this economy will turn itself around."

I took Eisenhower's desires to be to ride out the immediate situation with confidence while resisting raids on the treasury that would only make things worse in the long run. That focused our mutual attention on the 1960 budget which was already in preparation.

In good times and bad there is always constant pressure for the government to do more things, far beyond its ability to pay for them. Eisenhower said it to me this way: "I've been trying to hold down the cost of government but these things keep coming to me in separate pieces and they all look good at the time but invariably they cost a lot more money than anybody ever guessed or said and it's only when you see the real aggregate that you understand what's happening."

Well, the first run of the spending requests of the government agencies for 1960 had them up to eighty-five billion dollars and, with the best revenue estimate from treasury at seventy-five, we were headed for a deficit of ten billion dollars. That was not acceptable under his policies. I went back to the President; he told me that he would be very disappointed to leave office without bringing the budget back into balance. The 1960 fiscal year was the only one left that would begin and end in his term. I told him it was not impossible to bring out a balance for 1960 but to do so would require rather unusual austerity. He told me to work along that line and said I would have his backing. From this point on we were both determined to present a picture with all the expenditures met and a surplus, however small it was.

That job was tough for all the usual reasons: some of the department heads cooperated willingly, others resisted with objections they thought valid: some programs had to be expanded; there was built-in growth; benefit programs had to be entangled; many new needs had to be met; and there was no way to reduce present programs without unfair loss to their momentum and their objectives. Pressures to ease up began to grow from some of the Cabinet liberals.

When I told Eisenhower about these events on November 6, he called a special executive meeting of the Cabinet and laid down the law: "All budget allowances including those already tentatively approved are going to be given another hard look," he said. He wanted a balanced budget and I had assured him that I could produce it. He called for drastic reductions and said, "We're going to take hold of the bush, thorns and all. I'm tired of being liberal with other people's money." He followed up that lecture with a memo to the heads of all the departments and agencies with even stronger language. He asked each one to live within the amount that would be allocated by the Budget Bureau, "appealing to me only when you feel that to keep within that amount will endanger the security or welfare of the country." No director of the federal budget ever had a mandate that strong.

Well, finally the figures came together at seventy-seven billion dollars with a paper-thin surplus of seventy million. It was austere and severe but it wasn't heartless. We had proved that even with so many uncontrollable commitments there were ways to cut and save or generate revenues to make ends meet. Eisenhower was so delighted that he announced the balancing of the budget the minute we had a final figure on December 22, which was a month before it would normally have been made public.

Of course sending a budget in balance to Congress was only the first step. The second was to make it stick and that was bound to be tougher. What followed was 1960s "Battle of the Budget" which the press dignified with capital Bs. The details of that campaign are not very important here except for one thing:

Since Eisenhower believed that excessive government spending and deficits led to inevitable inflation, inflation became our enemy. The keynote is expressed in one paragraph of mine and a sentence of Eisenhower. I said:

The idea that a little inflation is good for us is a dangerous delusion. America dare not become so intoxicated by the tasty stimulant of inflationary expansion that it loses sight of the essential importance of financial integrity. A bit of inflation works out to be an installment on a lot of inflation.

Eisenhower chimed in to emphasize that point with this prediction:

If we let expenditures go up, and never pay our government bills, the day will come when the housewife will take a market basket full of money to the grocery store and bring back a pocketbook filled with groceries.

On another occasion he said:

Thrift is one of the characteristics that have made this nation great. Why should we abandon it now?

It was a team effort. Full of conviction, Eisenhower fought constantly at Cabinet meetings, in press conferences, and in speeches for conservatism and for a budget on the theme; "No doubt there are many ways to fight inflation, but there is only one way uniquely within our power to do and that is for us to put our fiscal house in order."

With this encouragement, I dropped the customary anonymity of past budget directors and traveled the country, lecturing to audience after audience on the terrible consequences of fiscal irresponsibility. Others in the administration joined the battle. The press took note of this as a concentrated effort, recognizing that it was an abnormal and determined fight. The result was more than gratifying. The audiences at my talks, the press reports, and hundreds of endorsing editorials had an impact that confirmed that we had aroused public opinion. An avalanche of letters followed; thousands of them came to members of the Congress, more thousands came to the White House and the Bureau of the Budget, asking what they could do to help. The results began to appear. Legislation for spending was postponed or reduced in the Congress to save money, and appropriations were even reduced below the President's request. When Congress did overstep, Eisenhower vetoed its bills and the vetoes stuck. All in all, his vetoes saved billions of dollars for future years as well as large amounts for that year.

Well, when the books were closed in 1960, on June 30, the end of the fiscal year, we had made the balance stick with a surplus of one and a quarter billion dollars. Eisenhower was so tickled again when he made the announcement that he boasted: "This reaffirms to the world that the United States intends to run its fiscal affairs on a sound basis." That "impossible" battle of the budget had been won. There had never been a sharper and more significant improvement in the government's finances in the space of one year, from the highest peacetime deficit in history (twelve and one-half billion in 1959) to a surplus in 1960. It was one of the few occasions that expenditures had been reduced from the previous year except immediately after a war.

This is the remarkable record of the Eisenhower economic policy, still not recognized as it should be: First, the budget was balanced in three years out of eight despite that sizable recession in 1958 and the spending frenzy that followed the Sputnik shock. Second, two more budgets in balance, one of them half fulfilled when he left office in January 1961, were left for the next administration. Third, in his eight years (and please note this) inflation averaged 1.4 percent and unemployment ran less than five percent.

Eisenhower's policies were vindicated by the course of events in the next five years. None of the disasters predicted by his skeptics and adversaries came to pass. To the contrary, as his economic adviser Saulnier said in retrospect, "Looking back ten years later, it's highly likely that without his policies it would have been impossible to achieve the favorable record of growth and improvement recorded in the first half of the sixties." It carried over; wage and price inflation was minimal; a balance between labor costs and productivity was achieved; interest rates were stabilized; the budget was in balance and a trade surplus was rebuilt. Prices increased less than one and one-half percent through 1965. Then the new forces of high spending came forward and pushed budgets upward and skyrocketing deficits began.

There is a very sad lesson for history in what followed. As subsequent Presidents and Congresses allowed the dike Eisenhower had built to be broken, first by a trickle and then by an uncontrollable flood, the nation moved toward unmanageable deficits of now close to two hundred billion dollars with predictable consequences of economic turmoil. As it turned out, the budget has been balanced only once in the twenty-five years since 1960. And budgetary commitments and entitlements are so overburdening that no surplus is in sight as far ahead as anyone can calculate.

Government spending grew from seventy-seven billion in 1960 to nine hundred and twenty-five billion in 1985. The national debt grew from two hundred and eighty-six billion in 1960 to 1.8 trillion in 1985. And interest on the national debt, which is a price we pay for overspending, exploded from nine billion in 1960 to one hundred and one billion right now. The cost of living index, I believe, approximately tripled in that period of time.

It didn't have to be that way. I have no doubt that had Eisenhower remained in office or been succeeded by Presidents with his fiscal determination the country could have balanced its budgets right along except for the few years of cyclical recessions. The powerful American economy would have brought them back to health and they would have survived as Eisenhower's 1958 budget survived, and we would not have had to pay the intervening price of double-digit inflation followed by a surcharge of double-digit unemployment in forcing down the inflation.

That's a long story and it is enough about his fiscal policy, but it certainly is one of the distinctive features of the Eisenhower presidency. He believed in solvency and he stuck to his word.

There were many other aspects to this great man and his character. One of my earliest experiences as budget director taught me how earth-shaking small problems can be to people in high places. I had been in office only two days when I got my first phone call directly from the President on the red phone. "Stans, I've got a big problem over here," he started out, "and if I don't get it straightened out quick all hell will break loose." Well, I shuddered at the obviously monumental size of the first assignment he was going to give me, but I spoke up bravely, "All right, Mr. President, what can I do to help?" "Well," he said, "I've got this fine secretary here, Ann Whitman, and she's a Grade 15. I just found out Fred Seaton's secretary over in Interior is a 16. Now if I don't get that fixed right away I'll lose all the little hair that I've got." I saw to it that Ann Whitman got her advance to Grade 16 and resolved that national emergency. After it was done I sat back amused that with all his worldwide responsibilities he had been sensitive enough to anticipate and deal with a human matter like that.

Eisenhower didn't like the idea of dealing with those tough budget questions. He had an obvious dislike for the pressures and the time-tables of that whole budget process, one part of which is that he had to give up most of New Year's Day every year to review the budget message so it could get to the printer to be ready for Congress right after the twentieth of January. He seemed to tense up when those tables of figures were put before him but he never tried to shortcut the pro-cedure, always listened intently to the presentation of pros and cons when I pointed out important differences on issues between the Budget Bureau and the departments of the government. I know he didn't like that part of his job and considered it one of his unpleasant duties.

I had another interesting experience I want to tell you about: his dis-like of financial decisions was confirmed to me after he retired by Mrs. Eisenhower on an occasion when we visited his farm in Gettysburg. He was out playing golf when I arrived and I had a chat with her. I asked her how he was feeling and how things were going on at the ranch. Her answer was, "Everything's well with him but he sure needs a budget director up here."

There is a footnote on the Bay of Pigs invasion that I've never seen recorded. One day in the summer of 1960 Allen Dulles, the head of the CIA, came to me with a request for fifteen million dollars. "It is needed," he said, "to supply and train somewhere in Central America a group of exiled Cubans who are preparing for a guerrilla invasion to overthrow Castro." He refused to give me any details or documentation saying he had cleared everything with the President and there would be no accounting. Well, I rebelled. Dulles was high-handed and contemptuous and he said, "It's none of your damn business. If you question my authority go to the President and ask him." I went to Eisenhower in considerable dudgeon but he told me to calm down. He said, "I authorized Dulles to spend that money but I did not authorize any specific military action by the anti-Castro Cubans. That will have to come later, and I won't give it an O.K. unless I'm convinced it is essential and I'm convinced that it won't fail." What happened after Eisenhower left office is painful history. The action did fail because the authorization that was given by the next President was not backed up with strength.

As if to concede that he had given inadequate attention to politics while in the White House, he was very active in supporting the Republican Party after he left office. In the summer of 1961 he invited several hundred of its leaders to a big lawn affair at his home in Gettysburg for a full day to discuss the Republican future. Out of that meeting was created the Republican Coordinating Committee, which was an active group of top-level party people organized into subcommittees and task forces to study and express positions on public issues that would be uniform across the country. That work carried on for several years with a series of meetings, in which Eisenhower always participated, that included intensive reviews of position papers clarifying and defining party aims. The preparation and dissemination of those papers provided an effective means of reviving Republican enthusiasm after the Nixon defeat in 1960.

Another personal experience: One time I sought his advice on how to fashion a college commencement speech that I had been asked to give. I thought that his experience as President of Columbia University might give him some insight as to what approach would be most likely to appeal to the graduates on that day. He thought for a moment and then he replied with a rather impish smile, "Maury, the only virtue that can be sold in a commencement speech is brevity."

He was criticized sometimes for not being enough of a politician, particularly for not building a Republican Party when he was President, and for not being more positive in his support of Nixon in 1960. I think I know the reason for both: perhaps naively, he felt that good government like virtue brought its own reward. If he did an honest job as President he expected the credit to rub off on the party. It didn't. He would not make decisions solely on political grounds. In 1958 the Democratic-controlled Congress put a bill on his desk forcing him to sign or veto an economic development proposal within the week before a special election in Maine. There were communities in Maine that would have benefited from the bill and the pleas for him to sign it were many, maintaining it would ensure a Republican victory in Maine. But he felt it was a bad law and the only course of honor was for him to veto it. He did and he took the criticisms for losing a Senate seat for his party. That was his code and he stuck with it.

In 1960 he wanted Nixon elected to succeed him and I have no doubt that he would have done anything physically possible to help him bring that about, but he didn't want to force himself on Nixon, especially believing that Nixon should run on his own and be free to agree or disagree with the Eisenhower record. So he waited until he was asked. Most people think that came too late and a bigger effort by Ike would have put Nixon across. There was obviously some misunderstanding between the two as to his intentions. Eisenhower's doctors wanted his activity limited but I know that he was all out for Nixon and was terribly disappointed when he lost.

Again, in 1968 his enthusiasm for Nixon was extremely strong. He was anxious to avoid the kind of criticism that had come after 1960. In March 1968 he told me that he was telling his friends quietly that he was all for Dick. He went on to say, "People ask me if I'll do more this year than I did in 1960. I guess I should have made more political speeches at that time. But Dick and I agreed on what I should do. I don't know what I can do in 1968 but I'll make my position strong after the convention."

Eisenhower could be profane at times under the conflicting currents of the presidency, as has been almost every President confronted with the daily mass of matters requiring hairline decisions and the knowledge that there is no one else to resolve them. He was often torn between his own essentially conservative views and the more liberal beliefs of some of his own appointees. But I never heard him engage in any vulgarity or obscenity. He did not often praise his subordinates for good performance but he would frequently speak favorably to someone else about a man's performance.

He was by all measures that I can apply to people a splendid and beloved man. I never found occasion to doubt his character or integrity; his sole aim was to do the right thing for the country; he was uniquely forthright and direct, never devious; his mind was sharp and his questions were precise, sometimes cutting. He insisted on a tight organization of the presidency and an orderly way of resolving problems. If he had to listen to one side of an issue he wanted the other side present at the same time something almost strange, as most Presidents don't do it. One of his innovations was to require that all policy papers that went before the National Security Council be accompanied by financial appendixes in order to show what the current and future cost implications of any policy change would be. He would not make spending commitments to any agency without having consulted the Budget Bureau (a principle also violated by many Presidents).

Whereas budget officials of prior and succeeding administrations sometimes learned about new programs in the newspapers, he wanted his budget director in on the discussion and the decisions. His Cabinet meetings were on a regular schedule, and so were his press conferences. Agendas for his Cabinet meetings were prepared in advance; position papers were circulated to the Cabinet members beforehand; those who attended were able to organize their responses ahead of time instead of by surprise. The meetings were fast moving and effective, with very little random talk. The same procedure obtained in the National Security Council: again, position papers were written, considered, and adopted regularly covering every foreign country individually and every conceivable aspect of foreign affairs, anticipating every likely eventuality. And these were brought up to date every time a new development occurred somewhere in the world.

It was a uniquely profound experience to work that closely with Dwight Eisenhower. He was a great human being and a much better President than he has been credited with being, although lately he has been moving up in opinion polls. A most recent tally of professional historians puts him eighth among the Presidents. Unfortunately his two serious bouts with illness broke his stride a bit, and the unplanned U-2 incident with the Soviet Union prevented him from being the peacemaker that he seriously wanted to be. But, all in all, he was the right President for that particular time in history, which seemed to call more for stability than for innovation.

His years as President were good years, almost the very best in our history. We had peace and order with a sense of security at home and abroad. There was a high degree of unity in the nation. Though not an economist, he was nevertheless interested in fostering the principles of a sound economy. Though not a businessman, he respected the contributions of competitive business to the nation's progress. Though not a legislator, he knew that the key to legislation was compromise. Though not a dogooder, he felt that government had a responsibility to help the underprivileged. Though not a crusading states rightser, he believed that the best place for government was close to the people back home.

He often quoted Lincoln's precept that government should do for people only those things which they couldn't do as well for themselves. He decried the belief that money could solve all problems. To emphasize that one day he looked out of his office and pointed to a big elm tree. "Money won't make that tree grow faster and throwing dollars at every difficulty will not automatically bring solutions." He had two other interesting aphorisms which he sometimes used to slow down people whose language was too forceful for the realities of Washington. "Never say never" was one he repeated. "You may save the embarrassment of having to accommodate another viewpoint sometimes in the future." The other one which he credited to some earlier sage whose name I don't remember was this: "All generalizations are false including this one." I heard him say each of these half a dozen times and I didn't catch him violating either one. He always tried to keep a way out.

As President of the United States, Dwight Eisenhower was the right man in the right place at the right time.

NARRATOR: Secretary Stans has kindly agreed, in addition to this very thoughtful and careful presentation, to answer any questions that are stimulated by what he said or by your reading or thoughts you have about the Eisenhower presidency. Who would like to ask the first question?

QUESTION: A very difficult decision was made during the Eisenhower administration and that was to leave our troops in Europe but bring back their dependents, one decision which President Kennedy, when he became President, overruled. Would you care to comment on that?

SECRETARY STANS: Yes. After the war we stationed quite a few divisions in Europe and Eisenhower had the opinion that most of that was a temporary move. The idea was that if we got into any trouble over there, or there was an invasion of Europe we should have enough troops on the ground to trigger our participation in the war but not enough to risk the destruction of a lot of our forces. As President he tried a number of times to reduce the number of troops. I don't remember the figures precisely but I think it was something like seven hundred thousand men and dependents that we were keeping in Europe.

The Congress would not go along with a major reduction nor would the military in the Department of Defense. So they stayed over there. The next best move to try to reduce the cost of doing all of that was to suggest that the dependents be brought back from Europe. I forget what the saving in money was but it didn't have a chance. The military wouldn't stand for it; the men over there would probably have become both restless and reckless, and he had to withdraw the idea awfully fast.

QUESTION: I would be interested in your comments about the personal relationship between President Eisenhower and Secretary Dulles.

SECRETARY STANS: The relationship between Eisenhower and Dulles was always very close. Eisenhower respected Dulles as the brightest mind in foreign policy in that era. I saw him overrule opposition to Dulles on a number of occasions. I remember one time when Harold Stassen was chairman of a committee on disarmament. He spent a long time working hard on it, brought his proposals to a Cabinet meeting and presented them to the Cabinet. Immediately after he finished, Dulles was on his feet and absolutely sliced to bits the Stassen proposal. I wasn't sufficiently familiar with all the aspects of it to know whether Dulles was right on every point but he certainly commanded that meeting. And when it was over Eisenhower merely said, "Well, Harold, I guess you'll have to go back to the drawing board again and see what you can come up with." That was the best example, but Eisenhower really, in all of the experiences I had (and this was toward the end of his term so I am sure it prevailed earlier), showed extreme confidence in Dulles and backed him up all the way.

QUESTION: I wonder if you would comment on President Eisenhower's relationship with and his thinking about Senator McCarthy, particularly as it related to General Marshall and the President's attack on Marshall?

SECRETARY STANS: I can't do well on that because in those days I was over in the Post Office Department looking after the stamps and the mail, so I wasn't very close to it. All I had was secondary gossip which was to the effect that Eisenhower was unhappy with McCarthy from the beginning. Ike thought he was an extremist and that he was going to falter and stumble along the way and that his own best course was to let him proceed for a time until he got himself in that position where he couldn't extricate himself any longer. And McCarthy did just that.

I know that many people have criticized Eisenhower for not moving faster on McCarthy but his feeling was that the man would destroy himself by the extreme positions he was taking and by the unprovable statements he was making. Also, you've got to remember that that was a time when the country was pretty well scared of communists in the closets and under the bed. There were special provisions in law (I remember some of them that we had to deal with when we got into government) requiring a review of the employment of everyone in an agency to see whether there were any communist activities or communist leaning statements in their backgrounds. McCarthy was, to a considerable extent, carrying along a public concern about communism in this country, and Eisenhower undoubtedly was playing the smart hand in waiting for McCarthy to fail rather than pushing him.

QUESTION: Would you care to compare the performances of the United States Postal Service in your era and the performance today in relative costs of the operation as it stands now?

SECRETARY STANS: I would love to do that. I'll make some comments on it, but I could give you a three hour address on that subject alone. When Arthur Summerfield went in as Postmaster General in 1953, he was the first businessman ever appointed to that post, unless you consider Benjamin Franklin's early business as a publisher. The Post Office was still running exactly the same as Benjamin Franklin had set it up, with the letter sorting cases and the scratchy pens and the clumsy money order form applications and all that. So it was no stroke of genius that I came up with two hundred recommendations to improve it.

The Department was not spending anything, and had no people in the department doing any research, on improving the service. If somebody wanted to buy an office device there was no standard of performance expected, and nothing new being looked at. So the incredible fact was that the mail was being carried then by brute force and manpower. We had a tremendous number of people working in the service. The postage was three cents.

Today if you go into a modern post office you will be astounded at what's being done: addresses are being read by a machine; letters are being sorted by machines; parcels are being sorted by machines; everything is operated in modern style and they're making every effort to keep up with the state of the art.

I know there is a tendency on the part of people today, as there was then, to criticize the mail service. I do myself once in a while. But when you consider that even now a very large part of the operation of the department is manpower and when you consider the frailties of human nature, it's very easy to understand why a letter might get misdirected or something might not be delivered on the day you expect it.

Our service in the United States carries more mail than all the rest of the world combined. As of today it is the best in the world, even better than the highly vaunted British mail service in the time I was in the department. The French service gimmick of mail boxes on the back of streetcars were utterly immaterial but they made people think they were great in carrying the mail.

If you ever make an statistics, sit down and keep a record of the mail you get and when it was mailed, and you will find out that the service isn't bad, it's pretty good.

QUESTION: Would you care to compare the power influence of the Office of Management and Budget today with its equivalent at the time you were there?

SECRETARY STANS: Yes. At the time I was director of the budget, we did have an Office of Management. It was relatively small; I think it had fifteen people that issued promulgations on various subjects to the government agencies and departments but it had no enforcement power whatever. The only thing we could do if an order went out to adopt a certain type of procedure that would save money, and an agency didn't like it, didn't do it, was to tackle its next budget and cut some money out of it to force it to go back and take another look.

Today the management responsibility has been greatly upgraded in the Bureau; even in its title it has the word management. The staff is much larger and it has authority. As a result of that it is much more effective but still not adequate by far. The government of the United States needs an overall business manager somehow or other to coordinate everything.

Do you read the recent statistics about how many different kinds of computers the government has and how many are twenty years old and archaic, and all of those things? The report of the Grace Commission is fascinating reading for anybody who has anywhere from twenty to one hundred hours of time to spend. Look it over and see how badly our government is still run simply because the agencies, the bureaucrats, and the heads of the departments are all independent individuals. They like the way they do things better than having someone giving them an order telling them exactly what equipment they should use and what procedure they should follow.

QUESTION: Mr. Secretary, do you favor a constitutional amendment to have a balanced budget? Would it be effective if it were passed? Would it be implemented?

SECRETARY STANS: I will tell you unequivocally that I don't think there is any other possible solution for our deficits, and that without it we won't have a balanced budget by the year 2000. The demands are so great for spending; they are so rifled in by the special interest groups; there is so much in the way of commitments already in the budget that have to be paid to classes of people whose numbers grow and grow and grow, that there is no way short of a mandate in the Constitution that will cause the Congress to hold back from the special interest groups and retreat on the spending programs to bring things in balance. The constitutional requirement for a balanced budget exists in something like twenty-seven states right now. State governments can balance their budgets; the federal government can balance its budgets, too, if it is required to do so, and it will be a tremendous contribution to stability in terms of inflation, unemployment, and all those economic factors that are so critical to us now. I'm one hundred percent of the opinion that that's the only way out.

V.
EISENHOWER'S MORAL AND POLITICAL VALUES

PERSPECTIVE ON EISENHOWER'S VALUES

Arthur S. Flemming

NARRATOR: I'd like to welcome you to the Forum of the Honorable Arthur S. Flemming, formerly secretary of health, education, and welfare and director of the Office of Defense Mobilization in the Eisenhower administration. His experience spans the period from Franklin Delano Roosevelt to the present. He has continued to serve in positions of highest responsibility both in the government and in the field of higher education. As many of you know, he served as president of three of our great universities—Ohio Wesleyan, Oregon, and Macalester in the Midwest. He served as chairman of the Civil Service Commission and in numerous capacities in other areas of our government.

Arthur Flemming received his A.B. from Ohio Wesleyan, his M.A. from American University, his LL.B. from George Washington University. He returned to American University to be director of the School of Public Affairs at that institution. He was a member of both the first and second Hoover commission on the organization of the executive branch of government. He was a member of the Civil Service Advisory Board and then the Civil Service Board. He is the recipient of the United States Medal of Freedom and of the Alexander Meikle-john Award for Academic Freedom accorded by the American Associ-ation of University Professors. One could go on in that vein reciting honorary degrees and other awards which he has had. It is a great pleasure because of Arthur Flemming's long interest in the theory and practice of the presidency to have him talk with us this afternoon about the Eisenhower presidency.

MR. FLEMMING: Thank you very much. I'm very happy to have the opportunity of being here and talking with you about one of my favorite subjects.

It was suggested that I might start by telling you about an experience I had with former President Truman which does provide a relationship with former President Eisenhower. As indicated, I served as a member of the Civil Service Commission from 1939 to 1948. When President Roosevelt died the question came up as to whether or not the three of us who were serving as members of the Civil Service Commission should submit our resignations. At that time members of the Civil Service Commission did not have a term of office. We served at the pleasure of the President of the United States as the commission agreed for the time being. The civil service community urged us not to submit our resignations because they felt that to do so would weaken the status of the commission as an independent bipartisan commis-sion. So we did not submit our resignations.

But after a few weeks word came to me second hand from the White House that they were disappointed that the Republican member of the Commission had not submitted his resignation. Well, at that time I was about to turn down an offer to serve as president of a college up in the state of Pennsylvania. I thought to myself I'd better be careful here or I'll find myself without anything to do. So I went up to talk with congressman Robert Ramspeck, some of you may recall that name. He was the author of a considerable amount of significant legislation in the civil service field and also at that time he was majority whip of the House of Representatives. He had chaired the Speakers Committee for Mr. Truman when Mr. Truman had been a candidate for vice presi-dent. So I told him what my problem was and he said, "Well, I really don't think that they do want your resignation but you should hear that from the President not from me." So in a couple of days I got a call asking me to come down to see the President and I went in to see him and he opened up the conversation by saying, "Bob Ramspeck tells me that somebody around here has been telling you that I would like to have your resignation." I said, "Yes, that's been my under-standing." He said, "There's not a damn bit of truth to it." He said,

"I don't know anything about civil service, that hasn't been my background. I need somebody around that does know something about it. Bob Ramspeck tells me you do know something about it and I want you to stay." And I said, "Okay, Mr. President, I'll stay."

A little later on in 1948 I received an invitation to go back to my alma mater Ohio Wesleyan as president. I thought as a courtesy I should go and tell the President what I decided so I did go in to see him and told him what I was about to do. He thought that was a good idea but because I was going to take on the presidency of an educational institution and because Dwight Eisenhower was then president of Columbia University he began to talk about General Eisenhower. If you recall, this was in February of 1948, and General Eisenhower had just announced that he would not run for President on either ticket and President Truman said to me, "I knew that Ike wouldn't run against me." He didn't say it in any egotistical sense at all but he just said it from the point of view that we're good friends and I felt sure that General Eisenhower or Ike would not run against me. Then he told me about the fact that he had asked General Eisenhower to go to China to talk with General Marshall about coming back to serve as secretary of state. So really I heard President Truman talk about General Eisenhower before I had ever had the opportunity of meeting General Eisenhower. I had known his brother Milton very well over the years because we had served together in the executive branch of the federal government and our paths had crossed a good many times.

As I talk about the Eisenhower presidency, I'll talk about it from the standpoint of three types of experiences that I had. One was as a member of what was referred to as the President's Advisory Committee on Government Organization. That was my first contact with the President-elect and later the President. Around Thanksgiving of 1952 I received a call from the Commodore Hotel saying that they would like to have me come up and would like to talk with me. I really didn't have any clear indication as to who it was that wanted to talk with me but I was just asked to come up and be there at a certain time the next day. I discovered that the person who wanted to talk to me was Sherman Adams. Sherman Adams in his characteristic way said, "The President has decided to have an advisory committee on government organization. He has asked Nelson Rockefeller to chair it, his brother Milton is going to serve on it. Mr. Hoover has told him that he ought to ask you to serve on it, will you do it?" I said, "Yes, I'll do it." And then he said, "Now, you would expect at this point to have the opportunity of talking with him, but you are not going to have that opportunity. You are a part of a cover and he's on his way to Korea." And he said, "You and the other two members of the committee are going to meet up at Morningside Heights but you are not going to meet with him and you are really under instructions not to let on that you are not going to meet with him." But soon after that, in about ten days we did meet with him at Morningside Heights. And that was the beginning of a relationship that extended throughout both of his terms. Nelson Rockefeller continued to chair that committee until he was elected governor of New York and then I took over as chairman and Don Price of Harvard became the third member of the committee.

My second major contact with President Eisenhower was as director of Defense Mobilization. When the Korean War broke out I was back at Ohio Wesleyan and I was asked by Charlie Wilson to come back to head up his work in the manpower field. He became director of the Office of Defense Mobilization, the first director of that office. During World War II in addition to serving as a member of the Civil Service Commission I also represented the government in its capacity as an employer on the War Manpower Commission and I was the government chairman of the Labor Management Agriculture Committee of the War Manpower Commission and that's why I was invited to come back and get back into that particular area when hostilities broke out in Korea.

So when President Eisenhower was elected I was there. By that time Henry Fowler was the director of the Office of Defense Mobilization and as you know he later became secretary of the treasury. But I was the only Republican around so they named me acting director of the Office of Defense Mobilization in order to keep things moving during the transition period and I fully expected I would be acting for just a very short period of time. And one day President Eisenhower asked to see me and he said, "I'd like to submit your name to the Senate for confirmation as director of the Office of Defense Mobilization." My response was, "Mr. President, I felt sure that you would want to bring a leader from the field of business or industry into your administration to serve in this particular capacity." He said, "No, I've thought it through and I want someone in the job who understands government and the way in which government operates. If we need help from people from the field of business and industry I know how to get that help and I'm sure the people that we want will respond but I'd like you to take it over." Well, I was very pleased to have him say that and I was confirmed and during his first term served as director of the Office of Defense Mobilization.

The understanding was that I would be on leave from Ohio Wesleyan during that period of time and would return at the end of the first term, which I did. But I had only been back about six or seven months when Marion Folsom became ill. He was the secretary of health, education and welfare, the second secretary, you'll recall the first was Ovetta Culp Hobby and the President asked me to come back as secretary which I agreed to do and then resigned, of course, as president of Ohio Wesleyan. So for between two and a half to three years I had the opportunity of serving as secretary of health, education and welfare.

Let me make a few overall comments relative to my reactions to the relationships that I had with President Eisenhower before I identify maybe two or three specific examples of those relationships. First of all I think the one aspect of his presidency that stood out in my mind and continues to stand out in my mind was the manner in which he related to the Cabinet as a collegial group and to the National Security Council as a collegial group. I've sometimes summed it up in this way. I have said that in my judgment he was the best practitioner of consultative management that I have ever seen in operation in the public sector or in the private sector.

In the discussion that we had at Morningside Heights we brought up the question of the relationship between the President and his Cabinet. Milton and I had had breakfast together that morning and we had decided we were going to bring that up as an agenda item. We had heard about the way in which Cabinet meetings were conducted under President Roosevelt. Both of us had been around long enough to have picked up fairly authentic information relative to the way in which those Cabinet meetings were conducted. And we had concluded that they were pretty non-productive. They were what people call "show and tell" sessions and we had learned that Cabinet members really didn't bring up anything of a substance because the last thing that Harold Ickes wanted to do is to bring up a substantive issue and expose it to a discussion where Harry Hopkins would be one of the participants and vice versa. Consequently the Cabinet meetings themselves were not productive and the members of the Cabinet would simply arrange to see the President alone and take up the important items with the President alone.

Milton and I both thought that although you couldn't duplicate the way Cabinets function under a parliamentary form of government that Presidents could make better use of the Cabinet that has a collegial body. So we brought that up in our discussion with President Eisenhower at Morningside Heights and he said, "Well, I've been thinking along that line, too. But everybody tells me you can't do it under our form of government." He was very emphatic about it and neither Milton or I pursued the matter at all. I then became a member of the Cabinet because when he invited me to become director of the

Office of Defense Mobilization he said, "I'm going to put that job at the Cabinet level and I expect you to attend and participate in Cabinet meetings just like any other Cabinet officer," and of course by law the director of the Office of Defense Mobilization was a member of the National Security Council.

So at the very first meeting of the Cabinet I was impressed by his saying to us, "Now look, when you come and participate in Cabinet meetings I don't want you to feel that you are coming here just to represent your own departments. I want you to feel that you are coming here as general advisers to me." I remember his using this illustration. He said, "If I put an item on the agenda in the area of foreign policy I don't want just to hear Foster Dulles talk." He said, "If I just wanted to hear Foster Dulles talk I would invite him to come to my office and listen to him. But when I put it on the Cabinet agenda, I expect to hear from all of you. I expect that all of you will read the papers that are distributed to back up that particular item." That really impressed me. I doubt that any other President had approached his Cabinet in that particular way.

I noted right away that we did have a formal agenda and that was unheard of and that very quickly he asked to have a staff paper or papers to back up each item on the agenda. And within a few weeks he appointed a secretary to the Cabinet who was Max Rabb, now the ambassador to Italy, and then a young lawyer from the city of Boston. And after the secretary had been appointed we began to get minutes. Not discussion minutes at all. He didn't want any discussion minutes, but minutes which would simply indicate that this item was discussed and the President decided so and so and then directed the following departments to implement his decision.

Normally at Cabinet meetings the President would indicate his decision but not always. Sometimes he would say, "I'm going to shoot from the hip on this one" or "I'm going to sleep on it and you'll get my decision in the minutes." But those minutes of course were invaluable to us because we knew he'd initialed those minutes and consequently we didn't have to guess as to what his decision was. We didn't have to worry about whether we had heard what we might want to hear and hadn't heard what we didn't want to hear and so on but we had it in front of us.

But, the thing that I noticed more than anything else was his style in conducting the meetings of the Cabinet. He participated very actively in the discussion himself but never in such a way as to convey to a member of the Cabinet the feeling that he had made a decision and therefore there wasn't any point to a member of the Cabinet expressing himself or expressing his views on a particular issue. Quite the contrary. He participated in such a way as to encourage the persons sitting around the Cabinet table to become involved in the discussion. He listened, he participated and then after he thought the discussion had gone long enough he would usually indicate what his decision was. And sometimes he would postpone that decision for twenty-four hours.

Now I know there is a great deal that has been written as to the effectiveness of that particular approach and I appreciate the fact that some have felt that a President conceivably is wasting his time putting in that much time on giving the Cabinet the opportunity to discuss these issues. I remember during his administration when I would go to various parts of the country and try to describe what was going on I would often get this question—they would say, "What kind of a contribution can Arthur Summerfield make to a discussion of foreign policy?" Arthur Summerfield as some of you will recall was the postmaster general and he was also the chairman of the Republican National Committee. And my response to that was this—"Well, Arthur Summerfield probably keeps closer to the grassroots of this country than any other member of the Cabinet and I have listened to discussions relative to foreign policy where Arthur has become involved in the discussion and said, well look, you seem to think that people out in the country have perceived this situation to be the way you're describing it but in reality they don't look at it that way." And then he would try to represent the grassroots in indicating where people were on that particular issue. Actually some of those discussions were very lively and I felt very constructive.

I'll give you my favorite case history in terms of my own experience. Actually it's written up in Fred Greenstein's book but it's written up because of the fact that the assistant secretary of the Cabinet could take shorthand. He didn't always take shorthand when the discussions were going on but in this particular instance he sensed that this was going to be a rather lively discussion and he decided he would take it down in shorthand. He apparently made his notes available to Dr. Greenstein. I won't attempt to go into detail as far as the substantive issue was concerned. Elliot Richardson was then assistant secretary of HEW. He was my assistant secretary in charge of planning and congressional liaison. He held down both jobs. These days you have an assistant secretary for planning and an assistant secretary for congressional liaison but he held down both of the jobs. He and I had developed a plan for what we thought would be a more significant involvement on the part of the federal government in the field of education. I had tried to sell the plan to the Bureau of the Budget and I hadn't gotten very far and I had also tried to sell it to some of the people on the White House staff and I hadn't gotten very far. So, one Thursday afternoon I was in talking to General Persons who had by that time succeeded Sherman Adams as chief of staff. I said to him, "Look, I've been trying to sell this to the Bureau of the Budget and staff around here at the White House and I think it's time to give the President an opportunity to make up his mind because if we're going to get moving on this time is running out." This was in 1959. And General Persons said, "Well, I agree with you. I think you are entitled to a decision." He said, "The President is in there right now, let's go in and chat with him."

This was a little bit different than the style of Sherman Adams. There was a difference in the style of Sherman Adams and Gerry Persons. Sherman Adams wouldn't cut you off from the President ever. The fact of the matter is that if you indicated that you wanted to go in and see him he would facilitate it. He wouldn't attempt to try to interpret the President's views to you either. He would always insist on your hearing the President's views directly from him. But I couldn't imagine him doing what General Persons did in that particular instance, saying let's go in and talk with the President.

Well, we did. I laid it out and the President wasn't very enthusiastic about it. He began to talk about some of his experiences at Columbia University. That is one of the things I had to contend with as secretary of HEW, the fact that he had been President of Columbia University. He had some plus experiences and some minus experiences as President of Columbia University and I always had to keep that in mind. Well, I felt that we should make a decision on it and I kept pressing on it. We used to say informally when you're talking with the President and when you're pressing for a decision if you see the blood moving up the back of his neck and see his neck getting a little red you'd better lay off. I observed that going on at this particular time, but I thought well, I still need a decision. Finally he said, "Well, let's take it up at Cabinet meeting tomorrow." And General Persons said, "You don't mean tomorrow, you mean a week from tomorrow." Because normally we gave the Cabinet a week's notice on these staff papers. He said, "No, Arthur's right, if we're going to get something up to the Hill we ought to get it up fairly soon. Let's take it up tomorrow."

We had our Cabinet paper all ready, "we" meaning primarily Elliot Richardson and so the next morning it was the first item on the agenda. The President introduced it in a rather unenthusiastic manner and then turned it over to me to present. I had some fairly conservative colleagues on that Cabinet when it came to federal participation in the field of education. Ezra Taft Benson was one of my colleagues and he didn't think anything of federal participation in the field of education. Neil McElroy wasn't very enthusiastic about it, Fred Seaton wasn't very enthusiastic about it. But Jim Mitchell was. Jim was secretary of labor and we used to team up on matters of this kind. He got into the discussion on the positive side and finally when it was obvious that we probably had exhausted the time that would be devoted to a discussion of this manner, the vice president got into it, Richard Nixon. He got into it from a strictly pragmatic point of view, politically speaking. But he came down on our side of it.

Finally, after about two hours of discussion the President in effect said, "Well, I guess we better send something up." Then he said to me, "You come over next Tuesday and talk with the legislative leaders about it and see if you can persuade Joe Martin and Charlie Halleck (he put those two together) that they ought to get back of that." He had a twinkle in his eye when he said that because he realized that that was a rather difficult assignment. But let me say this—if I had obtained a decision Thursday afternoon it would have been a negative decision in my judgment and that proposal would never have gone to Capitol Hill. But as a result of his listening to and participating in the discussion, and he participated in a very vigorous manner, he finally came around to the point where he decided that the best thing to do was to send it to the Hill. President Eisenhower was not enthusiastic about too heavy involvement on the part of the federal government in education, I mean in terms of financing education. But he decided that this was the best thing to do.

I saw that process happen or take place quite often in connection with Cabinet meetings. His work with the Cabinet as a collegial group did have an effect on the evolution of policy in the Eisenhower administration. Nothing was ever put to a vote and it was clear we were there talking about these matters as general advisers to him. He is the only person that voted. He is the only person that made a decision and also, contrary to the impression that people had at that time, he didn't have any difficulty making up his mind either, usually. He gave us a decision and gave us a prompt decision. Once in a while, as I say, he asked to think about it for a period of time.

Let me shift to my experiences with him as a member of the National Security Council. Cabinet meetings took place in the eight years of the Eisenhower administration on an average of thirty-four times during the course of the year. Meetings of the National Security Council took place on an average of forty-four times during the course of the year. The National Security Council meetings were structured in somewhat the same way as the Cabinet meetings although I'd say that from a staffing point of view there was more emphasis on the preparatory staff work. And as you know the National Security Council exists by law. It came into existence during the Truman administration and the law provided that the members of the Security Council would be the secretary of defense, secretary of state, vice president and the director of the Office of Defense Mobilization. Those were the only statutory members. But the President invited others to become members of the council and participate in the work of the council; the attorney general always participated, the secretary of the treasury always participated, the director of CIA always participated and so on.

But soon after President Eisenhower came into office he provided for the establishment of a planning board for the National Security Council to be chaired by his National Security advisor who was General Robert Cutler, a banker from Boston but a person with whom President Eisenhower had had contact and association over the years. Each one of us who had membership on the National Security Council had a member on the planning board. And we were directed to put a senior member of our staff on the planning board. My representative on the planning board was Professor William Yandell Elliott of Harvard. He was a person with very decided views on some of these issues and he didn't hesitate. In other words he wasn't a yes man as far as I was concerned or as far as his colleagues on the planning board were concerned. But this planning board met twice a week and they hammered out the basic papers that backed up the items on the agenda of the National Security Council. Then once an item had been discussed at the National Security Council meeting the President would make a decision, minutes would be made of those decisions just as in the case of the Cabinet meeting. Then there was an Operations Coordinating Board which had the responsibility for implementing the decision made by the National Security Council. And here again that had on it representatives of the agencies that were members of the National Security Council.

Obviously, President Eisenhower felt very much at home in dealing with the issues that came before the National Security Council. Here again, I thought that he was an ideal presiding officer. Even though at times, as his memoirs and other letters indicate, he was listening to something for maybe the second or third time, he would sit there and listen to it so that the members of the council were at the same point that he was at before the discussion took place. And then he would invite the members of the council to get into the discussion and he would participate very vigorously in some.

Dr. Greenstein in his book dealing with certain issues talks about the issue of whether or not we should have gone into Indochina to bail out the French in 1954. He says that the minutes of the National Security

Council for that particular period have not yet been declassified and consequently he doesn't know what went on in the National Security Council. I guess I shoudn't discuss it either if they haven't been declassified. But he does indicate some of the reasons why the President decided not to become involved. I listened to a very, very vigorous discussion, what I'm sure historians will regard as a very historic type of discussion, where the Council was split—I won't say down the middle necessarily but it was certainly split. I listened to him participate and so on and then listened to him decide very quietly that no, we were not going to get involved in helping to bail out the French.

The Security Council under President Eisenhower played a tremendously important role in the evolution of our security policy. And one of the things that I noted and would comment on from time to time as I sat and listened to those discussions was the fact that I was listening to a President who knew and understood the world leaders no matter where they might be located. I used to find myself commenting to my colleagues on the council what a tremendous asset it was for our nation to have a President who knew these people, who knew their strengths and weaknesses and could evaluate their strengths and their weaknesses. Dr. Greenstein points out that one of the things that President Eisenhower paid a lot of attention to was evaluating people with whom it was necessary to have relationships whether on the domestic front or the foreign front. I was not as conscious of that as I am now having read Dr. Greenstein's book but I can think of instance after instance where I saw him go through that particular process.

I remember when we were dealing with the Korean situation before the truce had been arranged and when Syngman Rhee was giving us some real difficulty. This was fascinating to me because for fifty years I had been a member of the Foundary Methodist Church in Washington, D.C. During World War II one of the regular attendants of the Foundary Methodist Church was Syngman Rhee. I used to usher on the side of the church where he sat and I used to usher him to his pew and I used to chat with him afterward and I thought of him as a very quiet and reserved type of person. Then I sat around the Security Council table and heard the people talk about him. I didn't think I was hearing them talk about the same man. They were really upset about him. I remember a couple of times President Eisenhower said, "Now, wait a minute. Syngman Rhee isn't the enemy—he's our friend!" He said, "You're talking as though he is the enemy! Keep in mind the fact that he is a patriot. He would give his life tomorrow morning for his nation if he thought that by doing that he could help to accomplish what he wants to see accomplished." Then he would go through this analysis of what was going through Syngman Rhee's mind. I remember his doing that a couple of times.

I'll just give you one illustration of my contact with him, not in connection with a National Security Council meeting, but on a person to person basis while I was director of the Office of Defense Mobilization. During that period of time hostilities broke out on the Suez Canal. The day they broke out I happened to be on his schedule for a late afternoon appointment because the director of the Office of Defense Mobilization had responsibility for developing plans for an oil method to be used if necessary to help the French and the British in case things went in a particular direction and my date was to report to him on where we stood on working out those particular plans.

I walked in there and he was alone and I didn't have anybody with me, and I told him what I wanted to do and he said, "I'm the worst person in the world to talk with about this at the present time." And then he began to talk to me about his experiences that morning and he had said he had done his best to persuade the British in particular not to commit their forces. He said, "I don't understand why they've done it. Certainly they know I'm their friend. To my knowledge this is the first time that a nation resting on a democratic foundation has committed its forces without the support of its people." He said, "It won't work." The support of people was at the center of his thinking, the center of his administration whether dealing with foreign policy or dealing with domestic policy. He recognized that under a democracy you had to work to get the support of a bill. I don't mean by that that he was just sitting around waiting to see whether or not a particular policy had the support of the people but he had the feeling that if he was going to get any place with a policy in which he believed that one of the things he had to do was to work on getting the support of the people. That particular comment stood out in my mind and I had the opportunity of chatting with him about that again just about a year before he died.

Let me just say on the President's Advisory Committee on Government Organization—this is a fascinating technique that he used there. No other President has used it in that way. It is an example of his kind of reaching out for informal as contrasted with formal relations. Now we were formally constituted. There was an executive order constituting us as the President's Advisory Committee on Government Organization but we worked very informally. We didn't have regularly scheduled meetings. If he had an idea in the field of organization or reorganization, he'd ask to have breakfast with us and he would try the idea out on us and if we rejected it on the ground that we didn't think it was worth pursuing he would probably go along with us. Not always, he would sometimes say, "Well, I'd like you to have some staff worked in on it." We got our staff work from the Bureau of the Budget. We didn't have a staff of our own at all. We had gone to the Bureau of the Budget for our staff work on it. But if we had an idea before we had a lot of staff work done on it we would sit down with him and chat with him about it and get his reactions, too. It was this committee that took the lead and putting together the pieces that led to the creation of the Department of Health, Education, and Welfare. We took the lead in major reorganization in connection with the Defense Department and we were involved in a lot of different things over a period of eight years. The informal relationship, I recognized, grew out to a considerable extent from the fact that his brother was a member of our committee. And as you all know he had a very close relationship with Milton and a very high regard and respect for him. So that contributed to the informal nature of the relationship. But he felt very much at home dealing in that particular way.

The second Hoover commission came along in his administration. I served on that. He appointed me as a member of it, constituting one of the two representatives from government. Herb Brownell was the other one. But it was this committee of three that kind of picked up the recommendations of this second Hoover commission and then recommended to him what he should do about it. So this is a good illustration of his kind of informal approach to administration as contrasted with a formal structured approach to administration.

I'll stop and give people an opportunity to ask questions and I'll do my best to respond.

QUESTION: You mentioned that Mr. Eisenhower was not terribly enthusiastic about government expenditures for education. I wonder how you interacted with him in the other two areas, specifically of health and also welfare.

MR. FLEMMING: I had no real problem at all there and really I should qualify what I said about his feeling as far as education is concerned. Keep in mind the fact that he took the lead in recommending the adoption of the National Defense Education Act which was the first piece of legislation at the federal level involving post-secondary education since the passage of the Land Grant Act. He did that with a considerable degree of enthusiasm. There were parts of it that he questioned and so on. But it was through the Senate when I took office and it passed the House after I had taken office and then I had the responsibility, again working with Elliot Richardson, to implement that particular act. I think he took great pride in the fact that that act had been passed during his administration.

He didn't come down and say, no, the federal government should not be involved in a financial way—he was just kind of reluctant to keep moving forward in that particular area. I sometimes put it this way. I think that in the thirties that first as a reporter and then later as a member of the Civil Service Commission I had the opportunity of seeing the beginning of what I would call a people-oriented type of federalism and it is my thesis that this nation has continued to evolve in that direction consistently right down to 1981 and I think that was the case during the Eisenhower administration. You can point not to any what I would call quantum leap forward but rather consistent moving in that particular direction.

For example, while I was director of Defense Mobilization with his blessing I appointed an ad hoc committee to take a look at the legislation in the field of vocational rehabilitation which was in very bad shape at that time. And that led to the enactment of the 1954 amendments in vocational rehabilitation. He was very supportive of those amendments. As secretary of HEW I'd get into arguments with the Bureau of the Budget as to the amount of money that ought to go into that program. I remember one very vigorous argument with one of the budget analysts and I finally said to him, "Look, I'm not going to argue any further. Your boss and I work for the same man. If you are going to insist on this, I'm going to ask to see the President and I'll tell your boss (that was Maurice Stans in those days) when I'm going to see him so he can be there so he can argue your side of the case but I'm not going to take a defeat on this." I went back to my office and about three or four hours later I got a call from this fellow. He said, "Look, it won't be necessary for you to see the President, we've decided to go along with you." They understood where he stood on that.

We got through some very significant amendments in the area of social security. At that particular time, right after I went into office, he talked with me about the disability aspects of social security. Then it applied only to people age 55 and above. He said that didn't make any sense to him. He said, "People 55 and above have problems because they become disabled so they can't work and so do people 45 have the same problems. Why should there be any age requirement?" So we went to Congress and asked Congress to remove the age requirement which they did.

We were able to keep moving forward. Some people would say "inching forward." I'd say that I think we did even better than that. He had no problem at all with accepting the fact that the federal government had an obligation and a responsibility in the areas of health, welfare, and education. I think he'd probably put them in that order—health, welfare, and education—but he had no philosophical problem with that at all. In fact, I'll never forget one experience that I had with him on what is now Medicare. We didn't have Medicare in those days but there was a great deal of agitation to move in that direction. There was what was called the Poran Bill. Congressman Poran of Rhode Island was pressing for action in that area. One day his secretary called me and Ann Whitman, and said that he had just been talking with an insurance executive friend of his from up in New England and he indicated he would like this person to talk with me. Well, this fellow came in and started to try to sell me on the idea that we ought to use the social security mechanism for a medicare program. I said, "Is this what the President asked you to come over and talk with me about?" And he said, "Yes." So I listened and then I called Ann Whitman and I knew he would every now and then dictate a memorandum and I said, "Did he dictate a memorandum on this?" She indicated he had. I said, "Is this the subject matter?" She said, "Yes." And I said, "Then you better get me in to see him." So I went over to see him and I said, "I listened to your friend and of course your friend's arguments are arguments that I also would advance. Do you want me to move in that direction?" And he said, "Yes, I do." Then he said, "I'd like you to develop a plan to get a good size deductible, you know, like these automobile insurance policies." Then he began to tell me about Mrs. Eisenhower's mother had just gone through a two-year illness where they had to have care around the clock and so on and what that had done to their finances and so on. He said, "See what you can do in developing a plan of that kind." And I went back and I got our people in and put them to work on it and they thought I'd been hearing things because they didn't expect to get an assignment of that kind from him. But in about two weeks he had a press conference. Somebody asked him a question about that issue and he responded to them exactly in the same way he had talked to me and I felt much relieved then. But then everything broke loose. The American Medical Association went to work on it and others.

Back in October of 1952 he had made a speech in San Francisco where he said that he would not utilize the social security mechanism for dealing with health care problems. So he sent for me again and he said, "I'm sorry I've got to change signals on you." But he said, "I still want to get a program up there. Let's give up financing it out of general revenues and get a federal/state type of program. Make it a liberal program. Prescription drugs, care of eyes, care of teeth and so on." We did and I submitted that to the Ways and Means Committee and over the objections of the director of the Bureau of the Budget—he was fit to be tied about it. I remember Wilbur Mills when I finished my testimony saying to me, "Does this have the support of the director of the Bureau of the Budget?" I said, "Mr. Chairman, I said at the beginning it had the support of the President." He said, "That isn't the question I asked you." I said, "He and I both work for the same person." Well, that did not get through but it was the most liberal package that ever went to the hill in that particular area. And he himself had no problem at all with utilizing the social security mechanism. Of course, when people talked to him about that being a threat of socialized medicine and so on he wasn't concerned about that. After all he had lived under a federal health insurance program all his life and consequently he didn't think that it really represented a danger.

So philosophically I did not have any problem at all as secretary of health, education, and welfare in working with him. If I proposed making the kind of a jump that was represented by a number of the programs in the sixties I probably would have had a pretty vigorous argument.

QUESTION: When Eisenhower's wife's mother had gone through that period of illness do you have any indication at all that that experience might have influenced his thinking?

MR. FLEMMING: I think it did. This is so often the case. I'm sure he had been thinking along those lines prior to that but he was using it as an illustration and he used it in a very forceful way. It had made quite an impression on him. I suspect when his friend, the insurance executive, was in talking with him that the insurance executive had been telling him how important it was to introduce the concept of insurance into the area of health care that he had probably said, "Well, I know what you are talking about" and he probably laid this on top of the table just as he did when talking with me.

QUESTION: Did President Eisenhower play any role or use any influence in defeat of the Bricker Amendment?

MR. FLEEMING: Oh, yes he was very much involved in that. When you talk with Mr. Brownell that's where you'll get the firsthand information on that. I wasn't close to him at that particular time but I listened to discussions on it and he was very upset over the Bricker

Amendment. Mr. Brownell lived through that and he was the President's leader on it. They worked together on it and the President spent a great deal of time on it with Mr. Brownell. I might say I followed it with a good deal of interest because after all I was then in legal residence in the state of Ohio. There was some tension between Mr. Bricker and the administration at that point.

QUESTION: Would you interpret for us President Eisenhower's farewell address and particularly the famous phrase of the military industrial complex?

MR. FLEMMING: Well, I left as director of Defense Mobilization in 1956 or beginning of 1957 so I wasn't in that particular position at the end of the second term but I had seen enough of him during the first term and listened to him enough during that term and had listened to discussions in Cabinet meetings during the second term to know that this came from way down deep as far as he was concerned. He saw this as a real menace, as a very fundamental issue. His relationships with the Defense Department, I think, would make a kind of fascinating case history all by itself in light of its background and so on. As Mr. Greenstein points out, he spent a lot of time on his relations with the Defense Department on developments in that whole area. I suppose some people would say more time than a President should but I don't have that feeling as a result of what I observed. He felt very comfortable with the way in which Tom Gates handled the position of secretary of defense. He was his last secretary of defense. Keep in mind the fact that he had been assistant secretary of navy, secretary of the navy, deputy secretary of defense. In other words he had come up through the ranks. He was driving hard all the time on this issue which he finally identified as the military industrial complex. We would discuss Defense Department budgets in the National Security Council in that first term and I assume they did the same thing in the second term.

I remember at one point he was bound and determined to cut back those budgets and he felt he knew where they could be cut back and the rest of us felt he probably does know where they can be cut back. But normally only the chairman of the Joint Chiefs of Staff participated in the meetings of the Security Council. On this particular occasion he invited all of the Chiefs to come and make their presentation. I happened to go into his office afterwards on another matter and he said to me, "What did you think of that meeting?" I said, "It certainly got a lot of information on top of the table" or something like that. And he said, "Well, in view of what I'm going to do, I was determined to give each one of the Chiefs their day in court before me. I wasn't going to get in a position where they could say the chairman did not reflect our views in the right way or in an active way or anything of that kind.'' In other words he did cut and he was determined to cut and he worked at it and he gave the other side the opportunity of putting their case before him.

As I have seen what has evolved, particularly in the last few years, my mind has come back to those experiences time and again. He was on the right track. There isn't any doubt of it. In connection with some of the issues that had been before us, some journalists were willing to dig in and find out and identify all of the contractors that were involved in connection with certain issues and what they were up to in terms of trying to get favorable results out of the Congress on those issues. That's what he was talking about. On that he felt very keenly.

His one overriding desire was some kind of a breakthrough with Russia. This story came to me from Ann Whitman but it's been confirmed. I was on the Security Council when that was worked on from a staff point of view. I wasn't a part of any delegation over in Geneva or anything of that kind but that was presented, of course it didn't get very far in the formal meetings. Ann Whitman told me this story after they came back. The meetings were all over and President Eisenhower was in his office walking up and down and suddenly came out and said to her, ''I'm going down to see Khruschev and make one last effort to get a breakthrough with that fellow.'' Down the corridor he went. Khruschev had left one minute ahead of him. One can speculate as what might have happened because I was in the Cabinet when Khruschev came to this country. I didn't have any conversations with him but I observed him and he gave you the feeling that maybe you could get a breakthrough. Of course his greatest disappointment was when his last scheduled meeting with Khruschev was upset because of the U2 incident. That probably was the greatest single disappointment in the whole eight years in office. But he was a great believer in dialogue and keeping the dialogue going. There isn't any question about that at all.

QUESTION: People have commented frequently that President Eisenhower was acutely conscious of the problems of NATO defense and that he therefore understood the consequences of the decisions to move our reliance so heavily toward nuclear weapons and all of the consequences that we've had since then. In other words that if you are going to get the arms race under control you really as a first step had to have a credible conventional defense in Europe and yet he backed away from that question and went along with the massive retaliation strategy which did emphasize the nuclear response to their conventional edge in Europe.

The other question is if his apprehensions about the military industrial complex were so severe in the face of the European defense problem, did he ever think seriously about trying to break out of this situation in which the upward pressure of the budget is so directly connected with the separate service structure we have now reflected in the Joint Chiefs of Staff? We don't really have a Joint Chiefs of Staff. We have chiefs of staff that sit there together and bring their demands of the services up and add them up in a bunch instead of trying to look at them in terms of overall defense. Did he ever contemplate trying to do something about that military staff organization that has such an enormous inflationary aspect?

MR. FLEMMING: Let me take your last observation. As I indicated to you fairly early in his first term, Nelson Rockefeller, Milton Eisenhower and I along with quite a number of other persons that were added to our activities at that time took a look at the whole defense setup from an organizational point of view. As I recall the best I can at this point, his involvement and his comments, the pressures as far as he was concerned were always in the direction of strengthening the central control, that is, the office of the secretary of defense. I don't recall ever hearing him make the kind of suggestion that you've just made. Furthermore I got involved in a very interesting discussion on this point in the first Hoover commission. Dean Acheson was one of the members of the commission. Mr. Hoover, of course, was chairman. One of the issues that was presented to the commission was the issue of recommending a chief of staff for the armed services. Dean Acheson pressed very, very hard for that. Mr. Hoover was vigorously opposed to it. Most of us felt that Mr. Hoover's opposition stemmed in no small part from his experiences with General MacArthur. He visualized General MacArthur as chief of staff for the armed services and he thought that that would be rather disastrous. I say that advisedly because I don't know how much he got involved in, not in personalities but in trying to visualize the kind of person that would go into the job. We wound up by recommending a stronger chairman back in 1948–49 of the joint chiefs. That's when the chairman first came into the picture. I was on the commission again representing the executive branch and Jim Forrestal was the other representative. I talked with him about this issue at that particular time and I remember his saying he thought that whatever needed to be accomplished could be accomplished through a chairman of the joint chiefs. I remember him saying, "I'm going to ask Ike to come down from Columbia and set it up." Which he did. Eisenhower became the first chairman of the Joint Chiefs of Staff. I really don't recall any discusion along that line.

On your first point, I do recall a good many very vigorous discussions and this was not easy for him for the reasons that you identify and I guess I have to let his own writings give his reasons for coming out at the point that he did on it but it was a real struggle because this whole nuclear issue was an issue that was very, very troublesome to him and of course was one of reasons for pressing very hard for some kind of a breakthrough in terms of arms control and the negotiations with the Russians. I think that is where his drive was.

QUESTION: There is one school of thought that says a military career of considerable duration ill prepares one to be a political leader in a democratic society. In your discussions of Eisenhower's incumbency you had stressed a skill with which he utilized, the collegial approach which seems to be at least in philosophy somewhat in contrast to the dictatorial assumptions in military organizations. Do you feel that he was a bit of an anomaly in this or did he have enough exposures in between time at Columbia and in NATO to give him a broader prospective and enabled him to adopt a more reasonable approach?

MR. FLEMMING: Sometimes people talk about generals who have had primarily field experience and then generals who have had primarily political experience, in its broad sense, not in a narrow sense. It is very clear that President Eisenhower's opportunities were more in the latter category; that is, throughout his career even his experiences as commander of the allied forces were political experiences. He had to develop some kind of collegial climate over there with a group of people who some of them had highly developed ego that this created some very real problems for him. I notice that Dr. Greenstein in analyzing what went on with President Eisenhower while he was President drops back to how he handled his relationships with General Montgomery, for example, quite often. I would say almost from the beginning of his career at the top level he was in a position where if he was going to succeed he really had to develop some real expertise in what I call consultative management.

I believe that others have that experience. For example, I got to know General Bradley very well, not as a general but when he was head of the Veteran's Administration. I was still a member of the Civil Service Commission then and he had some very real personnel problems as he went in there to the Veteran's Administration. I worked very closely with him and it seemed to me that he had some of those same qualities.

So I think that if we indulge in generalizations either way we make a mistake as far as people who have had a rich experience in the armed services is concerned. But I really believe that the secret of President Eisenhower's ability to make a constructive contribution to the life of the country was his willingness to work hard at consultative management. You take the staff papers that backed up items on either the National Security Council or the Cabinet agenda. He always read them. We knew that he had read them. In fact, if you started to get into the discussion without having read them you were going to be embarrassed and you soon learned that. He expected everybody else to have read them. He disciplined himself and the result was that people working with him thought it was necessary to discipline themselves. The time that he was willing to spend on it because he believed that by doing that he was getting constructive results was something that impressed me tremendously.

I think personally when you analize something like that you do have to think in terms of his roots back in Kansas and the whole family atmosphere and so on. I may say that I'm delighted that Dr. Greenstein has put the emphasis that he has on this in his book. He is the first person to have done it and after all he was not a contemporary. He wasn't around at all. He had just gone at it as a scholar to look at it as a scholar. Of course naturally I'm delighted because he confirms some of my feelings and convictions growing out of my contact with President Eisenhower.

QUESTION: Wouldn't you say that the qualities of military people's capacities were a lot more important than experience? One has in mind Alexander Haig who had much the same experience. He was also a commander, he sat in the White House for six years where everything was political and yet when he got into the position of authority, political authority, his capacity to work with other people was, to say the least, suspect.

MR. FLEMMING: I would not regard him as an expert in consultative management. I will give you another one on the positive side though, Al Gruenther, for example, or General Marshall very definitely. I had the opportunity of serving on the Defense Mobilization Board for a while with General Marshall when he chaired that and it was just tremendous from that point of view. You are absolutely right you can't say that because people have gone through a given set of experiences that they will emerge with the capacity of functioning as in this area of consultative management. It *does* depend a lot on what they bring to the experiences that they are going to have.

QUESTION: After hearing you describe the techniques he used, the thoroughness with which he approached the issues and problems, could you see any physical stress that this kind of approach produced on him? Of course I'm thinking later of the heart attack but you made it sound as if he approached all of this so thoroughly that I couldn't help but wonder whether those of you who associated with him daily could see any of this stress.

MR. FLEMMING: This worried, for example, his brother Milton and people who had known him very well over the years, particularly after he had his first heart attack and then his ileitis operation. I of course was involved in some of the discussions dealing with the possibility of his running for a second term and there was certainly a point when I thought that there wasn't a chance in the world of his running for a second term. But he did and in many respects his health was better during his second term that it was during the first term.

He lived with his job. There is no question about that and it used to disturb me a great deal how people tried to make a major issue out of his wanting to break away from it enough to go out and do a little putting out the White House lawn, for example. After watching Presidents from Roosevelt down to the present time, those are the kinds of things that really disturbed me. When I was director of the Defense Mobilization I happened to have a corner office in the old State, War, and Navy building on the first floor so I could overlook the White House garden. I knew when he was out there putting and why not? Some of us walk around a desk. Some of us walk around the block or something of that kind. If the President of the United States, after he has been dealing with some of the things that he was dealing with, wanted to go out there and knock a golf ball around a little bit, why not? He had the ability to do that. He could break away and knock a golf ball around and do other things. He could play bridge. Some people discovered he was an expert at it in every sense of the word. But he did live with his job. There isn't any question about that, morning, noon and night. I do get disturbed about people who talk about him as a President who didn't pay very much attention to his job. That I know is not the case. Here again Dr. Greenstein brings that out very, very well from the records. The records make it clear that that wasn't the case and I *know* it wasn't the case in terms of my own experiences.

He was the kind of person who kept turning over in his mind new ideas and trying out ideas. One idea that for example he tried out a number of times on Milton, Don Price and myself near the end of his term was an idea that expressed his feeling that we needed what he would sometimes refer to as a first secretary. What he was feeling for there was this. He had the feeling that in this kind of a complex world that we ought to have a position in our government which would have the kind of standing and prestige which would make it possible for the incumbent of that position to go out and deal with heads of state as an alter ego for the president. Of course that immediately brings into play the relationship with the secretary of state. He recognized that problem. But he was feeling for something there, growing out of his experience. He recognized that there were situations for heads of state where he would find it difficult to persuade a head of state to sit down and negotiate with the secretary of state. Where he thought that wasn't always possible for the president to do that, was it possible to have what he called a first secretary who could perform that kind of function? He never arrived at a final conclusion on that.

This was the kind of thing he would do though. He would turn things like this over in his mind. He would think about them. He would turn them over in his mind and explore them with other people. He had a very, very active mind and often would come up with something that was really excellent that did get implemented as a result of his willingness to live with the job. He didn't resent spending time on organizational matters or organizational problems. He liked to do that. It was not something that he resisted at all. In other words he was on top of the job constantly.

NARRATOR: Thank you for such a warm and and illuminating discussion. We are delighted to have you here with us today.

A CONCLUDING NOTE

One would hope that a great World War would not be needed to produce a leader of the dimensions of Dwight D. Eisenhower. Yet it is impossible to measure his stature as President without remembering his standing as wartime leader. In World War II, General Eisenhower caught a glimpse of the worldwide responsibilities of the United States. He came to know and be known by the great and near great world leaders. He mastered management and organizational skills which he carried over into the presidency. It would be hard to envisage the Eisenhower presidency without paying heed to his role as Supreme Commander of Allied Forces.

Yet while Eisenhower became a world leader in the school of the soldier, he was also, as his brother explains, a person of rich and varied talents evident early in his career. Like Harry S Truman though, he had the capacity of growth. His famous grin was matched by the fiery furnace of anger that Bryce Harlow describes in an unforgettable vignette. His character was early formed in the plains and cornfields of Kansas and its strengths served him well. He had the wisdom to see that much more was gained when others received full credit and recognition for carrying out their responsibilities than when one leader preempted the stage.

Above all, and perhaps the contributors do not stress this enough, Eisenhower brought about the normalization of political relations at home and abroad. He chose not to lend dignity to cruel and evil men by publicly attacking them. Having fashioned an alliance of diverse nations and proud leaders, Eisenhower succeeded in bringing men together and lowering political tensions. He did not accomplish everything he and his critics thought he should. He did transform the political climate of his times.

253